THE PATH OF THE HUMAN BEING

THE PATH OF THE HUMAN BEING

Zen Teachings on the Bodhisattva Way

DENNIS GENPO MERZEL

Edited by
Wynn Seishin Wright

Foreword by
Bernie Glassman

SHAMBHALA
BOSTON & LONDON
2003

Shambhala Publications, Inc.
Horticultural Hall
300 Massachusetts Avenue
Boston, Massachusetts 02115
www.shambhala.com

9 8 7 6 5 4 3 2 1

First Edition
Printed in the United States of America

♾ This edition is printed on acid-free paper that meets the American National Standards Institute z39.48 Standard.
Distributed in the United States by Random House, Inc., and in Canada by Random House of Canada Ltd

Interior design and composition: Greta D. Sibley & Associates

Library of Congress Cataloging-in-Publication Data
Merzel, Dennis Genpo, 1944–
The path of the human being: Zen teachings on the Bodhisattva way/
Dennis Gempo Merzel; edited by Wynn Seishin Wright.
p. cm.
ISBN 1-57062-948-x
1. Spiritual life—Zen Buddhism. 2. Zen Buddhism—Doctrines.
I. Wright, Wynn Seishin. II. Title.
BQ9288 .M49 2003
294.3'444—DC21
2002014198

This book is dedicated in deepest gratitude to
my late teacher Taizan Maezumi Roshi for his
profound teaching and guidance;
to my wife, Stephanie,
for her continuous love and inspiration;
and to my children,
Tai and Nicole,
for just being who they are.

CONTENTS

FOREWORD

IN THE EARLY 1970s, Dennis Genpo Merzel and I used to like to go to the dump together. We were both practicing in the Zen Center of Los Angeles under our teacher, Taizan Maezumi Roshi. The center was expanding in those years. Buildings were bought and renovated, the block landscaped, walls put up, taken down, then up again, things upturned and upheaved. Genpo and I both liked to get our hands dirty and be in the very middle of the building, the growth, and the change. We liked the grit. So at the end of the work periods, when a dump run had to be made, he and I were often the ones to make it. We'd light up our cigars, drive out to the dump, toss out what the center no longer needed and bring back an empty truck for the next period of disruption and rebuilding.

The Path of the Human Being comes at an important moment in the development not just of Soto Zen in America but of spiritual teachings and practices that respond to a defining moment in our history. After the deep darkness of September 11, there has been much searching and groping, not just for the sense in life, not even for the non-sense of life, but for basic teachings on how to live, on how to be. Wherever I am—in *zendo*s, mosques, churches, or synagogues, whether my company consists of meditators, social activists, businesspeople, or street people—I bear witness to this deep thirst. This casts a special obligation on teachers. Regardless of our spiritual tradition, we have had to look hard at the tools, the *upaya*s, we have grown up with, the teachings, practices, and methods we have used till now; address how useful they are in responding to the needs of this very moment; and be prepared to start from scratch.

The Path of the Human Being is Genpo Roshi's response to this challenge, his living answer to the koan of how to be a human being in these days. *The Path of the Human Being* teaches Zen not as religion and certainly not as dogma, but as it is and always has been in essence, the

Path to awaken. Awaken to what? We say, to our Buddha nature, our true nature—not just ours but the true nature of everyone and everything in the universe. As Genpo Roshi writes, Zen gives us the tools to look inward, to study ourselves, to awaken to and truly appreciate the moments of joy and the moments of grief, the dark and the light. Close friend and Dharma-brother, Genpo has been in the sand and grit of the unfolding of Zen practice in the United States and in Western and Eastern Europe. He founded Zen centers in Maine, Salt Lake City, Paris, Amsterdam, London, Dusseldorf, and Warsaw. And in the spirit of not-knowing, and with the blessings of our teacher, Maezumi Roshi, who explicitly gave his successors permission to explore and adapt, Genpo Roshi explores and adapts. So while continuing to attract flocks of students to his more traditional *sesshin*s in Europe and the United States, he also provides trainings in *Big Mind* around the world and helps give even people who have never meditated before a chance to see their true face and experience the oneness of life.

In *The Path of the Human Being*, Genpo writes, "The self that we begin to recognize as our true Self is forever changing, ultimately unknowable." A great teacher knows that there is no end in sight. Zen needs to unfold, uncover, evolve, and change because life does the same thing. No one tool works all the time, for all human beings. Helping people to awaken is the obligation and commitment of the Zen teacher. In fulfillment of that mitzvah, he or she builds things up, breaks them apart, pares things down to their essence, and makes occasional trips to the dump. Toward what end? Toward helping us all awaken. Toward helping us become mensches, human beings. Toward the end that has no end but only takes us deeper and deeper into not-knowing.

Another great master—of baseball, not Zen—while driving a group of people home, phoned his wife from the car and told her, "We're lost, but we're making good time." Genpo cheerfully continues to meander down unfamiliar trails and paths, farther and farther away from the knowing and the known, endlessly getting lost, always making good time. May all who join him on *The Path of the Human Being* appreciate this practice.

—Bernie Glassman
Santa Barbara, California

EDITOR'S PREFACE

WHEN WE ACCOMPLISH the Buddha Way, we come home to our true nature, the unborn and undying Self that goes far beyond what we usually think of as ourselves and yet is inseparable from our ordinary mind and life. In fact, the maturation to full flowering of Buddha nature takes place in the midst of daily life. This collection of talks given by Dennis Genpo Merzel Roshi over a three-year period from 1999 to 2001 presents that path with all the depth, insight, and heart of one who has walked it himself and can now lend a helping hand to others so that they, too, can realize their full human potential.

These talks were given primarily at Kanzeon Zen Center in Salt Lake City, Utah, in the form of *teisho*, spontaneous and extemporaneous teaching coming from a Zen master's realization and shared with the intent of sparking openings in the hearts and minds of the listeners. It has been my privilege and challenge to compile and edit Genpo Roshi's teisho so that the Buddha-dharma flows as freshly and clearly in these pages as the day the words were spoken. This task has been undertaken with great care to preserve his intent and meaning. I apologize for any shortcomings.

Readers will find that in most cases, a short definition is included in the text whenever Buddhist terms are introduced. Readers may also turn to the glossary at the back of the book for additional information. Several koans are presented herein and interested readers can find the formal texts of these koans in published collections. Genpo Roshi's interpretation of the koans from the *Mumonkan* most closely follows that found in Zenkei Shibayama's translation, *The Gateless Barrier: Zen Comments on the Mumonkan* (Shambhala, 2000). For *Hekiganroku* koans, Genpo Roshi has utilized an unpublished manuscript, "Hekigan Roku," translated by Yamada Koun and Robert Aitken (1974).

A small, enthusiastic group of people has helped make this book possible, and I would like to express my gratitude to them. Foremost, I am deeply grateful to Genpo Roshi for his compassionate teaching and for entrusting me with the task of rendering it for publication. Stephanie Young Merzel, Genpo Roshi's wife, has been a source of patient support from behind the scenes. Anton Tenkei Coppens Sensei and Stephen Muho Proskauer have given generously of their inspiration and expertise, especially during the formative stages of this project. Tenkei Sensei, Dharma-successor to Genpo Roshi, has also served as adviser regarding some of the finer distinctions in interpreting and presenting the teaching. George Jisho Robertson cheerfully transcribed many hours of recorded talks, and David Dohi Scott lent his professional editing advice to an early draft of the manuscript. Shambhala editors Emily Bower and Beth Frankl have patiently led me through the details of publication, and this work has benefited from their guidance. My heartfelt appreciation also goes to my husband, Michael Daijo Wright, who has supported this project in countless ways, from serving as technical reader to grocery shopper and dinner cook.

Genpo Roshi teaches from the understanding that the Dharma is meant to be lived in our ordinary lives as the free and joyous expression of our Buddha nature. It is in this spirit that these teisho are presented here. May we accomplish the Buddha Way together.

—Wynn Seishin Wright

AUTHOR'S PREFACE

THE PATH of the human being is a journey that begins the moment we begin to wonder if there isn't something more to life. Often the catalyst for such questioning is a major challenge or trauma that compels us to search for a deeper dimension to life. The search itself has been called the raising of Bodhi-mind, the "awakened mind," which is the mind that seeks the Way.

What is it we are seeking? At first, we search for a way to relieve our own suffering. We look everywhere for something that will quell our hunger and bring lasting peace. We may try many different approaches, only to abandon them when they fail to satisfy our basic craving. Sometimes we have to become quite desperate before we finally turn the search inward through the practice of meditation. Meditation is the torch that illuminates our true nature—our complete and whole Buddha nature—and we finally taste the relief we have been searching for. Some spiritual paths teach that finding this place of peace is the end of the journey. With Zen, it is just the beginning.

Early glimpses of Buddha nature, Big Mind, are fleeting, and we all fall back into the seeking mind. We want to experience Big Mind again and we want the experience to be deeper and longer lasting, so we may again become quite driven in our practice. But the seeking mind will never be satisfied. Although we can learn how to return to our Buddha nature through meditation, we can never hold on to the experience. We need to *be* the experience—we need to learn how to manifest Big Mind in everything we do, and that takes practice.

One of the first steps is to become familiar with our nonconceptual, nondualistic mind. We do that in meditation. Only then can we see that our seeking is absurd, that it is really part of the problem and another source of suffering. *Shikantaza* ("just sitting") is a pure form of meditation because it is sitting without an aim or a goal. Shikantaza is nonseeking mind itself. As we continue to practice, we learn how to put desire to work by directing it toward realization and mastery over our cravings. Eventually, we let go of trying to satisfy the insatiable ego and learn instead to rest in Big Mind, which craves nothing because it sees that nothing is lacking to begin with. Big Mind is the mind of nirvana, the Truth that we've been looking for.

It's tempting to cling to the transcendent state, to try to remain distant from the world and its suffering. As our realization deepens, however, we see that we really can't separate ourselves from the pain and suffering of others. We are all interconnected, and the suffering of the world is our own suffering. So we are faced with making a conscious choice to return to the world if we want to help relieve the suffering of all beings.

Of course, when we first step onto the spiritual path, none of us feels ready or able to serve the world so selflessly. It takes time and practice to see through the self we've been identified with—the small self made up of the illusions of ego—and to develop confidence in our ungraspable and boundless Buddha nature. Meditation brings us again and again to the experience of Big Mind, where because nothing is lacking, there is nothing to seek. As we become more identified with Big Mind, we come to know beyond any doubt that this very Mind is Buddha! No longer identified with only the limited self, we see that we are one with all things. And because there is no self, there is no one to suffer.

This profound liberation enables us to really choose to live in the world as it is. Our experience of life changes. We become freer, at peace with the world. When we are able to live in the world without resistance, we can take up the work of the bodhisattva, one who helps others find the same liberation.

The life of Zen practice is like a spiral. Meditation is the tool we use to connect with our limitless and whole Buddha nature. But because the experience is completely ungraspable, sooner or later we find ourselves back where we started, in our limited, ego-centered mind. Nevertheless, things will never again be the same for us because something remarkable has happened: we have seen through the illusion of the small self, we *know* that this self is not solid and substantial. We may travel this circle many times over the years, each time becoming less attached to ourselves and our experiences. Neither nirvana nor samsara can trap us as easily as they once did, and we become more resilient and buoyant. Life may knock us down, but we can pop right back up, like a beach ball in a swimming pool. Of course, we still go through human experiences, including pain, anger, and frustration, but we don't seem to stay there very long. Negative experiences don't leave the same old residue. Our mind becomes like a mirror: the reflections that appear don't stick. When the object is gone, so is the reflection; there is just clear awareness. So although we experience pain or emotional disturbances, the effects don't linger and our mind returns more easily to its natural clarity.

By becoming familiar with our true nature, we can learn how to shift our view at will, moving from the limited point of view of the small self to the unlimited view of Big Mind and back again. We begin to embody our unfixed and fluid Buddha nature, and gradually the apparent separation between our ordinary life and our practice dissolves. Practice disappears and there is just life, or one's life disappears and there is just practice. Either way, it is the same realization: life is practice and practice is life. From this vista, everything is the living Dharma. Life itself becomes our teacher: whatever is happening is simply what we need to be going through at the moment. Of course, a teacher can help us maintain this perspective, but it's the teacher's job to always point back to the true master—the Master within. At this advanced stage, there is no more question of motivation to practice: we know that from morning till night, life is nothing but practice! The Path suddenly becomes much broader. The Buddha Way opens up with each step, right under our feet.

Being the master of our life means not only that we see things from the view of Big Mind but that we take responsibility for our life. Although our ego-centered mind would like to be master, we know that it will never measure up to the job because it can't identify with the big picture. Ego always comes from a point of view, a perspective with itself as the center. The *Master*, on the other hand, is one with all things;

it embraces all beings, all perspectives, all phenomena, all dharmas. When we shift control of our life from the ego to the Master, we can genuinely work for the sake of all beings. Our choice to be in the world is a conscious one. We can see with the eyes of Buddha the oneness of all things, and we can hear with the ears of Kanzeon Bodhisattva the cries of the world. True compassion comes only from identification with all beings and their suffering. When we leave the mountaintop and return to the world, we fulfill our life and become a true human being.

—Dennis Genpo Merzel
Salt Lake City, Utah

PART ONE

SEARCHING FOR THE WAY

RAISING THE BODHI-MIND

What leads us to begin spiritual practice? For many of us, a personal crisis brings us face-to-face with human suffering. Perhaps our life feels hollow or meaningless somehow and we wonder if there isn't more to it. Maybe we have encountered a serious illness or calamity, or maybe a loved one has died. Feelings of loss or emptiness will cause us to experience deep suffering. The inescapable truth of suffering was what drove the Buddha to seek and attain his enlightenment twenty-five hundred years ago, and it motivates many of us to begin the spiritual search today. The mind that seeks the Truth is called Bodhi-mind. When life awakens Bodhi-mind within us, we embark on a journey to find Truth. After searching far and wide without quenching our thirst, and perhaps after receiving guidance from a teacher, we finally understand that we must shift our focus 180 degrees and turn the light of inquiry inward.

1

Buddha's Path

Buddha's Path has been tried and tested for more than twenty-five hundred years. It was Buddha's Path—it is our Path.

TWENTY-FIVE HUNDRED years ago, Shakyamuni Buddha did something crazy: he left his wife and child, his palace and kingdom, to start a long search. He must have been insane, or desperate—desperate to find something. No one could begin such a search, leaving everything behind, without believing that something was terribly wrong, that something essential was lost or missing.

But was anything really missing? After all, he was the Buddha—Shakyamuni in the flesh! How could anything have been lacking? Apparently he didn't yet know who he really was. He thought he was the prince Siddhartha Gautama, but he was driven to find something more. For him, there was really no choice—he had to leave on the search that would change his life.

You and I have a lot in common with Siddhartha Gautama and his predicament, but at first glance we may not see it. Today we seem to be less open about this search than people who lived in ancient India, where it was fairly common to embark on a spiritual journey at some point in one's life. In our society, we're considered misfits if after adolescence we still don't know who we are. So most of us won't openly admit that really we have no clue. If we admitted having doubts and questions, we might even be labeled insane. Modern society has conditioned many of us to believe that such questioning is senseless and potentially harmful, and that we should be satisfied with simple answers: you are you, of course! We may not pay any attention to our doubts or questions until something shakes us up. Maybe we hear some bad news, maybe someone close to us dies, but some critical life event forces us to look at our deepest questions: Who am I? What is this life? Is there more to this life than I've already discovered? We begin a search for something we can count on, something genuine; what some of us call Truth or Buddha.

Where can you find this Buddha or Truth? Well, you might find a teacher to hang out with for a while, and a little teaching might even rub off on you. But if you believe that you've found someone or something to lean on besides yourself, in the end it won't do you any good. You've got to find the Buddha for yourself. No one can do it for you.

Once we accept that we won't find Buddha outside of ourselves, we usually get stuck in thinking that we will find it inside. "If Buddha is not out there, Buddha must be in here"—as if there might be a little Buddha hidden inside, to be found if we just look hard enough. This is still dualistic thinking; and if we're not paying attention, we can get stuck here for many years.

Along the way in the spiritual journey, it is easy to get sidetracked, and one of the most common dead ends is to spend the first ten years looking outside ourselves for some Buddha. It is easy to hold on to an image of some perfect being, especially if that person has died and can no longer uphold or tear down that image. If we imagine or believe that someone is perfect—even Shakyamuni Buddha—we can devote many years of our lives in striving to become like that person. It's a legitimate path, but it doesn't happen to be the Zen path.

There is a basic problem with striving to become perfect: you *already are* perfect! Now even if this is hard for you to swallow, I'm sure you can see the problem. If you're already perfect but you're striving to become perfect, what's extra? The striving! Striving implies that something is missing; you feel incomplete in some way, discontent with who you are. You want to become someone different from yourself. If you are trying to become a Buddha, or if you are trying to realize that you are already a Buddha, either way, you are still stuck in striving. Those goals are based on deluded, dualistic thinking. Buddha's realization was very clear: desire causes suffering—*any* desire, even the desire for realization. So if you strive for realization, you will create more suffering for yourself.

It's not easy to admit that we create our own suffering, especially when it comes to our spiritual desires. Of course, the desire for enlightenment is only one of many sources of suffering, and maybe it's a small desire compared with others. Still, try to imagine what would happen if you took all your desires and seeking and focused them entirely on the desire to attain realization. That's exactly what Siddhartha Gautama did. He went for it! He spent six years pursuing the major spiritual practices of his time; he tried different kinds of meditation and yoga, fasting and other ascetic practices; he even explored various occult powers. Apparently he was very gifted—intelligent, talented, handsome, and athletic—and when he put his body and mind into practicing these different paths, he mastered each one of them. But in the end, he still had no answer to the basic question that was driving him—driving him insane! After all those years of striving and accomplishing, he came up empty-handed. That's when he became really desperate.

The same question drives you and me, but we can ask it in many different ways. Some of us ask how to end suffering. Some of us wonder about the true purpose or meaning of life. Despite all his struggles with this question, Buddha had not found an answer. In despair, he just sat down. He gave up striving and decided to sit there as long as it took to find the answer. He vowed to sit in *zazen* until he had realized the cause and the end of suffering.

What a joke! Just look at that guy. First of all, he gives up everything—his family, his wealth, and his power; then he spends a bunch of years wandering around as a beggar, pursuing a question that he can never answer. Finally, he sits down under a tree and he refuses to get up. People probably thought he was nuts. And in a way, he must have been. Siddhartha must have been a little crazy to vow to the universe that he would resolve the unresolvable question of suffering.

He just sat there. On the dawn of the eighth day, he glanced up and saw the planet Venus. He must have been in some altered state, not what we would think of as a rational state of mind. But which irrational state of mind was it? Do you have it? Would you and I be in the same irrational state of mind if we sat for days and days? Although we have the potential to enter the same state of mind as the Buddha, it is something that most of us never experience. Instead, we lock it away, deep inside. We are afraid to let go of our rational state of mind and experience the Mind of Shakyamuni Buddha, the Mind that goes beyond sanity and madness.

Society has taught us that we should never let go of our rational mind—that all kinds of terrible things could happen if we do. We might lose control. Of course, it would be stupid to sit down on some street corner and go out of control; there are definitely better places to try this. There's a rumor going around that there are places where people think losing control is actually quite sane. These places let you sit down for thirty minutes, a week, or as long as you want and give up control. At a Zen center, nobody will think you are weird if you sit down and let your mind go. It's the Zen thing to do. In fact, you're encouraged to confront and break through your fear of letting go of the rational mind so that the irrational Mind of the Buddha can reveal itself.

Only after we let go do we discover how deluded we have been. What we thought of as "me" doesn't really exist! To the ego, that discovery feels like death, so of course, it resists. If we want to find the courage to continue the search anyway, the desire to know has to become more important than the fear of death. Who am I? To resolve that question, once and for all, is to realize your true nature, your true Mind. This Mind that we seek has neither limits nor boundaries. This Mind has always been and it will always be, from the beginningless beginning to the endless end. Obviously it is more than just *my* mind or *your* mind. Realizing this Mind is liberation itself: we are liberated from the fear of losing control, from losing our identity, and from losing our ordinary mind. We are liberated from the fear of losing anything, including the self. When we are everything and everyone, how could we possibly fear any loss? But don't believe me. Discover this Mind for yourself. To simply believe the teaching is like counting another person's treasure; what good does it do you if it's not your own?

Siddhartha Gautama became the Buddha when he realized this Mind. He was liberated instantaneously; and at the same time, he saw how all beings could be liberated from suffering. He discovered the Path to liberation. This was a profound discovery, yet how the Buddha achieved it is not really a mystery. He knew the Path because he had walked it himself and he had realized it. Buddha knew the Path intimately. Out of compassion he devoted the rest of his life to sharing the map with all of us.

Siddhartha started out just like you and me: he was confused. He didn't know that he was whole and complete, perfect to begin with, so he started searching for something. He had the same basic question that each and every one of us has, but maybe we don't yet dare to look at it. We can see where that question will lead us—to a realization that society won't accept. Maybe we wish the Path could be made more appealing somehow, or even marketable, like a quick fix. Nevertheless, we can't deny what is true: the path to liberation, freedom, and enlightenment is the same for everyone. Buddha's Path has been tried and tested for more than twenty-five hundred years. It was Buddha's Path—it is our Path.

We have good reason to feel encouraged and hopeful about the journey. It *is* possible to sit in zazen like Siddhartha and to attain the same realization. How can we know this is true? It would be nice to have some sort of guarantee that once we start on this path we are certain to end up at the same place as Siddhartha; but if we want to know beyond a shadow of a doubt that *my* path is the same as Buddha's, we have to walk it. Only then can we move beyond hoping and guessing to true knowing, much deeper than any understanding. You will know because the Buddha's experience has become your own.

Enlightenment means that you have directly experienced your true nature, your intrinsic perfection and wholeness. But that doesn't mean you have somehow gotten rid of your imperfections and become a perfect being. Realization lets you see perfection and imperfection simultaneously. When you can view your imperfections from the place of knowing your intrinsic perfection, your life is forever changed. Then, as you continue along the Path and experience that view more clearly and directly, you become more and more confirmed in your perfection. You will see that your perfection is always present, whether you're striving for it or not.

Every person has the potential to realize for himself or herself the same Heart-Mind as the Buddha, but not everyone will choose to embark on the search. For some, the desire is not strong enough. But let's say that you have decided to step onto the Path. There's a little problem, a paradox you will have to confront: if you strive for realization, you'll cause more suffering for yourself. On the other hand, an important shift will occur: you will be able to place the cause of your suffering where it belongs—on yourself. There really is no one else to blame. You can choose to suffer in order to accomplish the Way. It's OK if you harbor some hope that there will be a way out of your suffering or tell yourself, "If I *choose* my suffering and stop resisting it, then maybe I won't suffer anymore." Unfortunately it doesn't work that way. If you decide to take up the search, you will suffer.

Well, then, what about the liberation from suffering that we've heard about? Didn't the Buddha say that there was a way to end all suffering? If you say "yes," you leave out "no." And if you say "no," you leave out "yes." Either way, you have only half of the truth. To have the whole truth, you need to hold both answers simultaneously. Yet only an irrational mind says that "yes" and "no" can be true at the same time. That same irrational mind is *your* mind, the Mind of Buddha. And just like Siddhartha, we have forgotten who we really are. Although Buddha showed us the way, we will never be satisfied until we have discovered the answer for ourselves. Each one of us has to step onto the Path and search until we remember who we are.

2

The Zen Experience

Anyone at any time can have a direct experience of his or her true nature.

WHAT IS ZEN? Many people have tried to answer that question. There have been very brief answers, and there have been thousands of books written on the subject, yet the definition of Zen remains a mystery. Years ago Kapleau Roshi was speaking at a university in New York when a student asked, "What is Zen?" In reply, the roshi simply picked a banana from a nearby bowl of fruit and began to peel it. He didn't say anything. Someone asked again, "What is Zen?" Kapleau Roshi proceeded to eat the banana. When the question came a third time, he threw the banana peel away.

When I first heard this story, I laughed, even though I really didn't think it was funny. Somehow, Kapleau Roshi's answer seemed pretentious to me. But over the years, I have come to appreciate more and more why he chose to answer in that way. Now I realize it is impossible to say with words what Zen is. Words are simply inadequate. When we try to use words, there is a danger that whatever we say will lead only to confusion. Peeling the banana, eating the banana, and throwing away the peel was Kapleau Roshi's way of directly pointing to the answer.

Although the essence of Zen may be impossible to capture in words, that doesn't mean we cannot say anything about Zen. But when we speak about Zen, we need to remember that no matter what we say, it will miss the mark; it will be limited and insufficient, only one view of the whole. Nevertheless, it can be helpful to discuss Zen—what it is and what it is not. For example, Zen is not a religion. But Zen is almost always taught within the tradition of Buddhism, which is often considered to be and practiced as a religion. The Buddha discovered Zen, but he did not invent it. In a way, Zen invented the Buddha. The word *Zen* refers to the direct experience of one's true nature, and that is what Siddhartha Gautama awakened to when he became the Buddha. So *Zen* and the words *realization*, *enlightenment*, and *awakening* refer to the same experience. Yet words can never capture it; they can only point to the direct experience, which goes beyond any words or name.

Siddhartha was the first person to directly experience his true nature. When he awakened to the truth about who he really was, he became the Buddha Shakyamuni. *Buddha* is the Sanskrit word for "awakened one," and anyone who has the experience of awakening is called a *Buddha*. So we can say that a Buddha is a person who has had a Zen experience, an awakening to his or her true nature. What made Buddha's experience so unique was its depth and clarity. All of Buddha's teachings arose directly from his awakening. Buddha's wisdom, and the teachings that grew from it, would have been impossible for the prince Siddhartha to fathom before he completely realized his own true nature. He had to realize beyond the shadow of a doubt that he and all beings share the same Buddha nature.

What was it, really, that Siddhartha Gautama saw? What did he experience? When Siddhartha looked up and saw the morning star, he experienced that there was nothing between himself and the star. Nothing separated the planet Venus and the one who was meditating because the one meditating dropped out of the picture. Siddhartha dropped the self, and only a twinkling star was left. Not only was there no separation between himself and the star, the Buddha realized that there was no separation between himself and *any* being. He realized that all beings are Buddha, including you and me. But because we ourselves don't realize this, we are caught in the world of suffering, samsara. We continue to suffer because we have not realized what the Buddha realized: there is no self. There is no one suffering!

Buddha's teaching may seem strange, especially to those of us who have been raised in a Western culture. But it is important to know that the essence of Buddha's teaching transcends East and West. The direct experience of one's true nature has nothing to do with east or west, north or south. It goes beyond any kind of discrimination at all. It doesn't matter whether we are American or Indian, male or female, young or old—the experience is universal and accessible to everyone. True nature can be experienced by a young child early in life, and it can be experienced by an aged person at the moment of death.

Anyone at any time can have a direct experience of his or her true nature. Somehow, we keep missing it. Siddhartha would have missed it, too, if he hadn't sat down and looked inside. By sitting in zazen, he was able to enter *samadhi*, what we Americans might call "the zone." When we become one with what we are doing, we enter the zone. Accomplished athletes, musicians, and artists have learned how to do this when they are performing. Through samadhi, Siddhartha discovered and became one with the Truth inside. This Truth was always there, but it had been obscured by what Siddhartha had accepted as reality. When the self he thought he was dropped away, all that remained was his boundless true nature, what we call *Big Mind*. In that moment he was liberated.

Zazen was the key to Siddhartha's awakening, but he couldn't really appreciate that fact until it happened. He sat down in zazen because although he had tried everything else, nothing had worked. Sitting was the only thing left to do. Siddhartha was on a quest to answer the question that had been troubling him and turning his life upside down: Why is there so much suffering in the world? And that question is just as real for us today in the twenty-first century as it was for him more than two millennia ago. The need for each of us to pursue that question is one of Buddha's teachings, a skillful means or upaya. The question of our suffering is a seed that, if attended to, can raise the Bodhi-mind and lead the way to discovering who we really are.

When we look at the question of suffering, we immediately come face-to-face with our own suffering. If we continue on and look a little deeper, we can see the many different ways in which we ourselves have tried—and failed—to end our suffering. We can begin to identify with Siddhartha and his despair. Fortunately, because Buddha's teaching has been transmitted across the generations to us, we don't have to pursue the question of suffering blindly. When Siddhartha experienced Big Mind, the intrinsic wholeness and perfection of all things, he was liberated from suffering. He saw that his true nature was none other than Big Mind itself. Buddha went on to teach that by quieting the mind and looking inside in zazen, we, too, can experience our true nature.

If we practice zazen, after some time we will begin to experience brief openings and glimpses of our true nature. But glimpses are not enough to liberate us. We keep falling back into delusion and suffering because our realization is not clear. It takes time and discipline to go deep with zazen. When we hear about what it takes, we may wonder if it really is possible to have a strong zazen practice while we are living our busy modern lives. It seems obvious to me that the traditional way of practicing zazen in Japan will not work for us in the West. In the thirteenth century, when Zen was flourishing in Japan, the majority of people were also too busy with daily life to sit long hours in zazen. Most people worked in the fields from sunrise to sunset. They were probably busier than we are today. So as a society, they decided to support those people who were willing and able to give up everything else to just sit. A relatively small group of people became monks and went to live in monasteries, and the rest of the Buddhist community, the lay *sangha*, supported the monks by donating food and money.

That arrangement worked very well in ancient Japan, but it doesn't work so well in modern Western cultures. Instead, a new kind of sangha is emerging, one that is not particularly based on the practice of giving to others. The new Western sangha is based on the practice of zazen. Westerners want to experience Big Mind for themselves. We want to live our ordinary lives *and* realize our true nature, so we practice zazen when we can. This form of lay practice is very different from traditional monastic practice, but that doesn't mean it is a superior or inferior form of practice. Even in the time of the Buddha, many followers practiced zazen in the midst of ordinary life and attained realization. The Truth that we discover in zazen is always present, regardless of whether we are engaged in lay or monastic practice.

The Buddha taught that zazen is essential for realization, but he also taught that giving, or *dana paramita*, is in fact the most direct path to liberation. He said that we can liberate ourselves by "giving completely." Zazen and giving are not really two different things, and we can see this if we understand what the Buddha meant when he said, "give completely." One way to approach this is to ask ourselves what it is that we *can* give completely. The answer is obvious: the only thing we can give completely is ourself. Buddha discovered that when he gave himself completely to zazen, his entire view of reality shifted. He awakened. And the same thing can happen for you and me. If you give yourself completely to the samadhi of zazen, the self falls away and Big Mind is revealed.

Buddha knew that in the beginning, most of us are not ready to give ourselves completely to zazen. At first, he himself wasn't. It took him many years before he was willing to throw everything into zazen. So he taught that the path to liberation is to give what you can. And that is how the first lay sangha came to be. That sangha was very similar to the lay sangha of Japan: it was made of people who practiced the Buddha Way by giving alms and food to monks who were devoting their lives to sitting in meditation and traveling with the Buddha from place to place.

Modern life doesn't allow most of us to devote our days to zazen, and monastic life is quite rare in Western cultures. Even among those of us who have taken monk's vows, many also live typical lives, with bills to pay and families to raise. So how do we practice Buddha's Way in these circumstances? You and I can make daily life our practice by giving ourselves completely to whatever we are doing. Our practice becomes simply staying focused and concentrated on what we are doing.

As soon as you make awareness your practice, you realize just how unconscious you are most of the time. It takes effort and dedication to learn how to focus your mind. It was no different for Siddhartha. He learned to quiet his mind and put himself entirely into what he was doing through various kinds of meditation and yoga. It is important to remember, however, that he didn't experience awakening until he put himself entirely into zazen. Buddha's awakening took only a moment, but the years he had devoted to other practices laid the groundwork for that moment in zazen. And looking back, he could see which practices had been helpful and which practices had not been helpful in preparing himself for the experience. His teaching about how we can awaken was based on his own experience. He said, for example, that any kind of asceticism or self-mortification will not lead to peace or nirvana. Neither will self-indulgence. Before taking up his ascetic practices, Siddhartha thought that possessions and pleasurable experiences would bring him happiness and peace. Having been born a prince, he was able to indulge in every imaginable form of pleasure. Siddhartha learned from experience that even a life of indulgence leads to more pain, confusion, and suffering.

Not only was Buddha able to look at his life and see what contributed to his moment of realization, he was able to put his insights to work in his teaching. This was no small task because what he discovered contains a paradox: the experience of awakening is universally attainable, but in that moment Buddha experienced that realization is *not* attainable. The only way to go beyond this paradox is to have the direct experience, to awaken to your own true nature.

The school of Zen Buddhism focuses on the Buddha's teachings about direct realization. Buddha used his wisdom to come up with skillful means to help us go about liberating ourselves. Zazen is the most direct path, but because we all have other obligations to fulfill, the Buddha taught how we can maximize each sitting: practice awareness every moment of the day. In a way, it is a waste of time to sit on the cushion if we are not also practicing being attentive, awake, and conscious the rest of the day. By practicing awareness throughout the day, our zazen and our daily life will reap the rewards.

Personally, I believe that most of us who have been raised in a Western culture will not be satisfied with the forms of Zen that developed in China or Japan. Our whole culture is based on the individual. We don't identify as easily with the group, so many of us will not be inspired by a practice that is primarily about giving to others. Of course, the importance we place on the individual can itself become an obstacle. We need to be able to grow beyond our attachment to the self and to our individuality. Nevertheless, there is a positive side to our self-interest: most of us want a personal practice of meditation. We want to learn how to focus and concentrate our minds so that we can get into the zone, the samadhi of zazen. And we don't want to stop there; we also want to learn how to deepen our samadhi so that we, too, can have a Zen experience and wake up. Who am I? What is my true nature? What is the purpose of this life? Why am I here? What is God? What is Truth? We want to resolve these questions for ourselves. There is no need to settle for anything less than direct realization.

To ask such fundamental and deep questions seems to be part of being human. As with Siddhartha's question about the cause of suffering, these questions can also lead us to the realization of our true nature. How could there be anything else to realize? There is only one realization, only one Big Mind. Most of us come to know this Mind through many realization experiences, many different glimpses of the One Mind. Realization is not black-and-white, and you and I are not either realized or deluded. Each one of us has some degree of realization, and we are all somewhere on the Path. The Path does not exist out there—it is inside. We are each our own Path. The boundless and unfathomable Big Mind is revealed only when we look deep into our own minds.

3

The Beggar and the Gem

To accept the truth of who you really are takes nothing short of realization. You have to see the diamond for yourself.

BUDDHA OFTEN TAUGHT through parables, and this story shows us how to appreciate what is most precious. One day, a wealthy official was riding in his carriage on his way to conduct important business when he noticed a beggar lying in the roadside ditch. Feeling pity for the man, the official asked his driver to stop the horses so that he could speak with the beggar. It turned out that the man was so drunk, he couldn't be roused. Even so, the official felt compassion and wanted to help the poor guy out of his poverty. He reached into his purse and pulled out a precious gem, thinking to himself, "Although this gift is relatively easy for me to give because of my good fortune and wealth, it could make all the difference in the world for this poor man. With this gem he will be able to lift himself out of these shabby and miserable conditions and buy a life of comfort and security." To make sure that the gem wouldn't be lost, the official tucked it deep into the corner of a pocket on the inside of the beggar's shirt. Then he went on his way.

As the story goes, years later these two men meet again along the same road. The official is riding in his carriage when he spots the poor man walking along the road, still dressed in the rags of a beggar. The official stops his carriage and calls out, "What happened? When I found you lying in the ditch some years ago, I gave you a gem of such great value, you could have easily bought your way out of your poverty and suffering. Why are you still living the life of a beggar?" The man was startled and confused by these words, and he replied, "What are you talking about? I don't know of any such stone." So the official climbed down from his carriage and reached inside the beggar's shirt. Pulling out the gem, he said, "Here it is. It's been in your pocket all these years!" The beggar was stunned. All he had ever known was a life of such terrible poverty, he couldn't be sure he would live to see the next day. Suddenly he realized that he could have been living a comfortable and secure life all along, if only he had found the gem inside his pocket.

If we take this story as a koan, we can appreciate it from many different perspectives. What is the most precious gem in the world? Certainly this life is precious—the opportunity to be alive is an irreplaceable gift—but can we really appreciate this life for what it is? If we want to find the precious gem in our life, where do we begin? Where do we look? Should we look outside somewhere, or should we look inside? And what does it mean to look inside? Are we really going to find something of value in our body, perhaps in our head or our belly? By pursuing these questions with your whole body and mind, you can discover the truth of the Dharma for yourself. You, too, can realize what the Buddha realized. But no matter how hard you try, you will never find what is truly precious if you look outside of yourself. You have to look within.

Buddha discovered that this very life is Dharma, the manifestation of Buddha Mind. Simply hearing that, though, doesn't help us appreciate our lives any better. So the Buddha taught that each one of us must look into his or her own mind. First, we need to find the Mind that the Buddha was talking about—and the only way to discover this Mind is to turn your own light inward. No one can teach you how to do this. You have to learn by doing it for yourself.

Fortunately, perhaps incredibly, we can rely on some good hints and suggestions passed down to us by people who have taken this journey long before us. When I think about the fact that Shakyamuni Buddha's teaching is still here and available to us in the twenty-first century, I'm amazed! More than two thousand years have passed since the time of the Buddha, and in that time the Dharma could have been lost or distorted in many ways. If you have ever played the party game in which a dozen or so people line up and whisper a message from one person to the next, you know what I'm talking about. No matter how careful you are, there is no guarantee that the message at the end will hold the same meaning as the original. The only reason we have Buddha's teaching today is because thousands of people have given their lives to making sure that the Dharma was taught and passed on faithfully. And remarkably, we can rest assured that what has been passed down to us is in fact the true Dharma because from generation to generation, this precious gem has been carried through mind-to-mind *transmission*. Bodhidharma called it the "mind seal." It's the Buddha's guarantee.

Buddha was the first to discover the Truth about this life, and he did it through zazen. When you look into your own mind in zazen, you can have the same realization: this very mind is *It*! But in the beginning of zazen practice, all we see is the chaos of our mind—the endless parade of thoughts, emotions, sensations, and judgments that the Buddha called "monkey mind." Seeing the chaos within, it's only natural that tremendous doubt comes up: "Maybe Buddha's Mind was *It*, but certainly my mind is not! My mind gives me no peace at all." When we're going through this stage, we need to persevere and look deeper. Where does the doubt come from? You could answer "from my mind," but which mind is that? Is it your Big Mind or small mind? Almost automatically you might think, "It must be my small mind that is creating all of these thoughts and doubts." Now, try to notice the next thought that appears: it will always be some kind of judgment or preference, something like, "A nondualistic mind must be better than a small, dualistic mind, so I want that!" Don't stop there, though. If the Buddha realized it is all one Mind, how could there be a Big Mind or a small mind? That's just more dualistic thinking.

As we become more familiar with looking into the mind, we recognize what seem to be two minds, one dualistic and the other nondualistic. We experience these two realities, but they are actually two realities in one or, we could say, two sides of the same reality. It's not necessary to try to get rid of the dualistic mind. Instead, we can put it to work doing what it does best—trying to figure things out. The little mind wants to understand everything, so it never stops making evaluations and judgments. Why not let it just work away and occupy itself? Your true Mind, what does it care?

For centuries Zen masters have given their students questions to put the little mind to work: Who am I? What is Mind? What is *Mu*? What is Buddha? Although Shakyamuni Buddha knew that such questions cannot be answered with the dualistic mind, he also saw the wisdom of asking them. The Buddha had a deep understanding of human nature. He knew that it is our nature to question, so he encouraged it. He told his followers, "Don't just believe what I say. Go find out for yourself. Test this teaching and see if it's the real thing."

Why not go for it? Ask yourself any of these questions and try to figure out the answers. In the process you may learn how to focus your mind and how to put yourself completely into the question. It doesn't really matter which question you pursue as long as you go into it with all your might. Explore every possibility, every conceivable answer. In the end you still will be empty-handed—and that's the point! By looking deeply into your own mind, you realize beyond any doubt that your Mind is completely ungraspable. It can't be understood and it can't be held. Discover for yourself that Mind is Buddha. Your Mind is *It*! There is no other Mind.

Don't settle for some abstract understanding. *This* body and *this* mind, your physical form and your very mind, all together are nothing but that gem. Your ordinary mind is *It*—and yet it's not *It*. Having a concept of this oneness will never be enough. We have to embrace the absolute, Big Mind, and also the small conventional mind. Buddha's teaching says: not two and not one.

When you look into your mind, you experience for yourself what the Buddha was talking about: Mind does not exclude anything, not even your physical body and little mind. This Mind is your true Self, your original face. Your body is the body of the Buddha—the Buddha just happens to look like you this time around. Of course, the little mind rebels: "That can't be true! There's no way that *my* life and *my* body can be the life and body of the Buddha." To really accept the truth takes nothing short of realization. You have to see the diamond for yourself.

4

Your Life Is the Buddha Bowl

Your life contains just the right amount.

THE OTHER DAY just before going into the meditation hall, I was standing on a busy street corner waiting for my daughter Nicole's puppy to do what she is supposed to do—and I was in full robes. It struck me how strange it can be when East meets West. The robes that many of us wear must look pretty strange to newcomers. Our bows and offerings of incense may even look silly. And our chanting is weird. We often chant in a foreign tongue, usually Japanese, but we also throw in Sanskrit here and there. A person attending one of our Soto Zen services for the first time might well wonder why Westerners today would choose to become involved with such a peculiar practice with such ancient roots. Are we simply trying to act Buddhist, or is the living Dharma still maintained somehow in these ancient rituals? This is a fair and important question to ask.

The Zen that we practice today began fairly recently, when Dogen Zenji brought the teachings of the great Chinese Zen ancestors to Japan eight hundred years ago. But Zen itself has ancient roots that reach across several cultures. Shakyamuni Buddha lived and taught more than twenty-five hundred years ago. Zen developed later, when Bodhidharma brought the Dharma from India to China. Although Zen Buddhism didn't become strongly established in America until the 1960s, the practice has since gone through many changes. In fact, the way we Westerners practice Zen is nearly unrecognizable to a monk from Japan. Something as simple as the way we sit when we listen to a teisho or dharma talk—facing the speaker—would be unheard of in Japan, where they listen while facing the wall in zazen. Practice would never be as informal as it is here. So even though Western Zen is very young, our practice already looks quite different from traditional Zen.

Zen teachers in the West are struggling with the question of how much change can be introduced without risk of losing the living essence of the Dharma. We successors of Maezumi Roshi have been talking about this issue for thirty years, and yet none of us can say anything specific about how much change is acceptable. Each one of us must accept the responsibility of bringing Zen into our culture in a way that seems right. Thus, we are helping to transform Zen to fit in this culture. One of the beauties of Zen always has been its ability to adapt to new situations, to fill any container into which it is poured. Western culture is the new pot that is being filled by Zen—and for everyone, whether we're a teacher or a beginning student, our body is a container for the practice. Zen will fill this container perfectly.

We have a beautiful Zen tradition of eating meals together in meditative silence. Special bowls are used for these meals, and the largest is called *oryoki*. In the time of the Buddha, monks carried one large bowl when they begged for food, and this is the basis of the oryoki bowl used today. *Oryoki* is a Japanese word that means "contains just the right amount." On a deeper level it means that this very body-mind, *your* body-mind, is also oryoki, the Buddha bowl itself.

Your life is the Buddha bowl, and the food of your life is everything that happens, even things of which you're not aware. Our awareness of life is very limited—we really see only the tip of the iceberg—and yet this life always contains just the right amount. Whatever happens in your life is the teaching, is Dharma. When we see our lives in that way, nothing that happens can be taken as accidental.

Each of us has our own path of development, and it sometimes looks like we are each going in different directions. Some people say they are looking for peace or peace of mind; others say freedom or liberation. Some of us want to feel truly sufficient, confirmed, or more empowered. Even though we say different things, what we are looking for or aspiring to is really the same: we want to be free of suffering.

When he talked about the path of spiritual development and how to find lasting peace, the Buddha urged his disciples to focus on the root of the problem and not to be distracted by the leaves and branches. Western culture, on the other hand, tells us we should be interested in many different things, and centuries have passed while we have fussed with all sorts of distractions. Actually the root of the problem isn't so easy to see. It's just too obvious. This doesn't mean that we Westerners are especially stupid or blind; even Shakyamuni Buddha found seeing the cause of suffering difficult. The Buddha spent years in training and went through many ordeals before making his discovery: the root cause of our suffering is *ignorance*—seeing ourselves as separate and incomplete. This is delusion, and it leads to desire—wanting, craving, and clinging. The wanting itself is the cause of our suffering.

We may already have some understanding of how ignorance leads to our discontentedness and neediness. Still, because of our conditioning, we all encounter resistance to waking up. It seems like it should be simple: if my ignorance is caused by staying in the dark, then all I need to do is lift my head, shift my view; just turn around. But what does that mean—to turn around? Buddha taught that we need to change the way we usually see the world—the perspective that I am here and everything else is out there. If I've never seen the world in any other way, then of course, I will believe that I see the world as it really is, that I see reality. To try to shift the way we perceive things simply doesn't occur to us.

Early in practice, it is very helpful to have a glimpse of the other side of reality. Even the tiniest glimpse will put a dent in our armor. Yet in order to have a glimpse, we must first be willing to ask a simple question: "Is there a perspective other than my own?" It is impossible to know what kinds of life experiences a person will need in order to have that question come up. What did it take to get you right here, right now, in this very moment of space and time? Only a few of those forces can ever be known because you are the karmic result of everything that happened in the past. Everything! So it took exactly what it took for you to be where you are at this moment. This very moment is Dharma: perfect and complete as the total karma of each one of us.

When we begin to question whether there is another way to perceive reality, a deep desire and craving for the Truth emerges. We want to understand, to see, hear, and feel the Truth. But as with every desire, the desire for Truth will cause us to suffer. To really put an end to our suffering, we have to heal our basic illness: we have to stop *all* craving, desiring, and wanting.

It can be a shock to look in and see just how many desires we have, and serious doubts may arise about the possibility of ever becoming free of suffering. How can we possibly put an end to our wanting when we want and crave almost every moment of our lives? Buddha discovered the way, and so can we, because his discovery has been transmitted to us through the lineage of realized ancestors.

What is this Buddha treasure that has been so carefully transmitted to our present day? Zazen! Through zazen, we can finally put the seeking mind to rest. Zazen itself contains the answer. When we simply sit, with our spine erect and yet naturally relaxed, we can just be. In the beginning, however, there might not be anything natural or relaxing about it. It's just a lot of hard work. We might even mistake straining for accomplishing. However, the point is not to strain and strive, but to practice until our sitting is really effortless. The goal of our practice is to relax, surrender, and let go into our lives.

It is important to be clear about what is meant by *letting go*. To let go into our lives does not mean just doing whatever we want. To let go and surrender to life is to become free from desire and clinging. Zazen goes to the root of our grasping by revealing to us our true nature—our complete and whole Buddha nature. What could we possibly need or desire when we have realized that nothing is lacking to begin with?

Until we become familiar with our true nature, it can seem unlikely that we ourselves really have Buddha nature. It seems impossible to be nothing but Buddha nature through and through—but that is the truth. There is a beautiful story about this. Nansen was a great Chinese Zen master of the Tang era and the abbot of a monastery. Flax was grown in the fields around the monastery, and the townspeople used the flax to make fabric. Nansen worked with the flax like everybody else. One day while he was weighing some flax, someone asked him, "What is Buddha?" Nansen replied, "Three pounds of flax."

Nansen knew that he embodied Truth—the ordinary and the Buddha. Nansen and great teachers like him are not the only ones who embody these two aspects. We all do. But because no two people are the same, Buddha nature will be manifested uniquely in each individual. You and I embody Buddha and the ordinary, from moment to moment, in our own way.

True nature is Buddha nature, unfixed and able to adapt to any container, so we will all express Buddha nature differently. Every person is a unique container, and what is appropriate in one bowl may not be appropriate in another bowl. Our lives, too, are made up of different containers. Your body-mind is one container, and your family is another. Your work and living situation are containers, and our Earth is a container. For each situation a different manifestation is appropriate. Practice is all about learning how to recognize and manifest our true nature in everything we do. To become confident, free, and joyful in manifesting our true nature takes a lot of attention and practice. Zazen is the way we accomplish this. Through zazen, we learn how to be who we really are.

5

The Root of Our Discontent

It's natural for life to have ups and downs, yet we judge them and form preferences. We create a very narrow path, our own razor's edge of contentment.

WHY ARE WE so dissatisfied? Do you ever ask yourself that question? On the surface we may think our unhappiness stems from some need or desire that hasn't yet been fulfilled. If we look no deeper, we will never stop running, trying to satisfy our endless desires. When we really look at what we think we need in order to be content, we will notice a pattern: we create a very narrow path for ourselves between what we judge as good and acceptable and what we judge as bad and intolerable. We imagine that somewhere between loving and hating the way things are, there is a nice place of satisfaction and contentment. So we aim for that ideal, even though it is a razor-thin line. Every once in a while we can feel satisfied when we manage to touch that ideal, but the experience is rare and it never lasts very long. Most of the time we feel dissatisfied, and we hope and believe that things could be better.

The problem is our perception, the way we look at our discontentment. As long as we think that discontentment exists because something is lacking, then of course, we will keep searching for a way to fill ourselves up. We will keep seeking and acquiring the next thing and the next thing and the next thing that we hope will bring us to that ideal state of contentment. But there is another way to approach our predicament: we don't need to create such a thin line to begin with. Instead of thinking that in order for things to be OK they have to be this way or that, what if we accepted the way things are? What if we embraced it all?

If we could learn to be at peace with whatever is, then every day would be a good day. Yet doesn't something inside rebel when we hear that? The rational mind argues, for every day to be a good day, every day would have to be all good and no bad. That's impossible! It's natural for life to have ups and downs, and we should expect to have good moments and bad moments. If we could simply accept that, we wouldn't end up causing more problems for ourselves. Instead, we judge the moments and form preferences. We create a very narrow path, our own razor's edge of contentment.

Buddha called this insanity. He saw that our basic problem is the way we view life. Somehow we see things inside out. Instead of seeing the big picture, we see things from a self-centered perspective. By putting the ego aside, the Buddha was able to look at life from the perspective of Big Mind, which sees the oneness of all things. Now, that doesn't mean that the Buddha was some sort of god. He was just someone who was able to quiet his mind enough to perceive the nature of the disease and its cure. To be able to see what Buddha saw is not really that difficult. Discipline is all that is required to put the ego aside—even if only for a moment—so that life can be glimpsed from the perspective of Big Mind.

The cure for our problem seems simple enough: If we see things inside out, we need to change the way we see things. We need to make a shift in the way we perceive reality. To admit that we are not perceiving life as it really is, is the first step—and this, in itself, is very difficult. It is not easy to let go of our perspective, the way we view reality, because it is all tied up with the way we view ourselves, our self-identity. When we drop our perspective, we also lose our identity—at least the identity we know—and this is something we're not eager to do. If you've ever gone through an experience that caused you to drop your identity, you already know how frightening it can be. When we drop our identity, it is as if we have to start over again. We have to face the question "Who am I if I am not who I thought I was?"

Buddha taught that we can find peace of mind and contentment by following the *Middle Way*. He was not, however, referring to a middle way according to the rational mind, some strategy for walking a thin line between what we like and dislike. The Way that the Buddha was talking about goes far beyond that.

The Middle Way does not depend on judgment or preferences. It does not depend on the rational mind at all. The Middle Way embraces the whole; it transcends this and that. There is no need to judge what is good or bad and no need to prefer one thing over another. If we try to exclude the parts of life that we don't enjoy, then we won't be able to experience every day as a good day. When we live the Middle Way, we don't exclude anything, even our dissatisfaction and suffering. We learn how to embrace all the experiences of life, including sadness, pain, craving, and neediness. All are aspects of life. Why go about dissecting life, cutting it into pieces and judging only certain parts as good?

We habitually judge what we see when we look at the world. The daily news reminds us that terrible things are happening all around the globe. We bear witness to unimaginable horrors and tragedies, seething hatred and fear. How can all of these be embraced? Is it really possible to find peace and contentment when there is so much suffering in the world? Our rational, judging mind always has an opinion: "The situation of the world is not acceptable! It is terrible and something needs to change!" But how do we really change the situation? Where do we even begin?

In a way, it's beautiful that we react so strongly when we see the suffering of the world. It means that we have dropped our ego-centered view, no matter how briefly, and opened our hearts to the pain of others. If we could just stay with that pain instead of pulling away into our thoughts and judgments, then we would not need to dissect life into tolerable and intolerable pieces. We could embrace the whole, life as it truly is. Instead, most of us feel overwhelmed by the pain and suffering of others.

To put the suffering of others on top of our own seems like too much to bear, so we don't stay there very long. For a moment we may be able to empathize so closely with another that we see a bit of the world through his or her eyes; but we can't stay with the experience—it's just too painful and we withdraw. Because we don't know how to deal with pain and suffering in our own lives, we also don't know how to deal with pain and suffering in another person's life. When we muster the courage to look at ourselves, we can see how this defensive reaction occurs in many of our encounters with beings who are suffering. It can be especially jarring to see that we also withdraw from loved ones when they are suffering. Truly, we may find it just as difficult to open ourselves to the pain of our partners, our children, our parents, and our friends as to be open to the pain of those we hardly know. We simply don't want to experience their pain, so we hide behind our self-centered perceptions and protect our hearts. At the same time, however, we block ourselves from the chance of helping relieve someone's suffering by simply remaining truly present and open.

Being present in our own lives and being present for others require the same openness. When we drop the self, we can look at all the suffering of life with the eyes of a Buddha. We can embrace all the pain and joy that life offers without making judgments and divisions. On the other hand, when we fear pain and suffering, we resist dropping our perspective as a separate self. Buddha was able to cut through the illusion of separateness by sitting in zazen, and so can we.

When we sit in zazen, we have the capacity, the ability, and the potential to face our own fear. Zazen gives us the space and the freedom to do that. By sitting, we create the opportunity to change the world. We can begin to make this world a better place by simply facing ourselves. Imagine the possibilities if we didn't feel the need to put so much effort into pushing the world away, trying to stay separate and safe. We spend tremendous energy trying to maintain the illusion of a separate self. All that energy becomes available to us when we let go of the self.

We can look to the Dalai Lama as an example of someone who puts this into practice. He travels the world, never stopping his effort to spread the Dharma, and yet he never seems to run out of energy. How does he do it? He doesn't divert his energy into struggling with himself and with life. Because he sees the absolute oneness of life, his heart naturally opens to all things. We, too, can accomplish this by walking the Middle Way. By dropping our ideas and preferences about the way things should be, we can open our hearts and minds to what is and give up struggling against life. Freed from the chains of self-preoccupation, our Heart-Mind can expand to its true potential, and our life can be lived for the benefit of the world.

6

One Taste

When we begin to feel truly intimate with Tokusan, it's not so much that we can understand him but that we have shared the same taste—we have touched the same Buddha Mind.

SOMETIMES when I enter the zendo, instead of already having an idea of what to talk about, I just sit and see what comes up. A year or so ago, I was sitting there when I suddenly saw something very clearly. Although I hadn't noticed, it had actually been bugging me for quite a while. I needed to face it squarely, of course, before things could shift and a new perspective could open up. Only then could I move forward. It's so easy to forget this basic lesson about the importance of staying awake and responsive in daily life.

What came up for me was that I didn't enjoy teaching anymore. The drive that had kept me going in Zen practice, and had pushed me to become a teacher, seemed to have dried up. Teaching just wasn't fun anymore. After facing my feelings and just sitting with them, some space opened up and I was able to decide all over again to enjoy this. You see, I had fallen into the trap of thinking too much before each talk. I'd even debate with myself: "If I talk about this, then some people won't understand because they don't have the background; but if I talk about that, then some of the old-timers will be bored to death." With my mind so full of thoughts, how could there be any space to simply enjoy teaching? After I saw the rut I was in, I was able to renew my commitment to just have fun and not worry about trying to teach anyone anything. As long as I am enjoying teaching, everyone else seems to enjoy it more, too.

Maybe you have noticed the same kind of thing in your life. If you enjoy what you're doing, you don't feel stuck and imprisoned by your work or your life. Think back to a time in your life when you felt trapped. Did the thing that led to a change or some sort of liberation really have much to do with the situation itself? In my own experience, the shift has usually taken place within myself, not in the external situation. The feeling of being trapped has often had more to do with an attitude, a stuck way of viewing things. This is very good news: liberation can be found in the way we approach situations.

Now, of course, important shifts also occur when outside circumstances change. Nothing is permanent—change is constant. In response, we need to keep making adjustments in our lives. More than thirty years ago when I first started teaching, I taught in much the same way as my teacher had taught me. My teaching looked very Japanese. But I've gradually moved away from some of the traditional ways. Now most of my classes are very informal. People wear casual clothes instead of robes; sometimes we even wear sweats. I've noticed that most of my Dharma brothers and sisters don't teach in the same way as Maezumi Roshi did, either. Each of us has found ways to adapt the form of the teaching to our Western culture, while remaining loyal to the essence of this great tradition.

Sometimes a particular piece of the Zen tradition doesn't fit very well with our Western culture. When I see that happening, I ask myself whether or not I should introduce some change. What I find myself coming back to again and again is *trust*, a basic faith in the process of change. It's important to let the process of change unfold naturally without hurrying it along or pushing it in a certain direction. One of the best ways to support the natural flow of change is to avoid judging, trying to figure out whether something is good or bad, right or wrong. I could endlessly debate certain changes in the tradition—especially if I allowed myself to think too much. For example, is some talking during sesshins good, or should sesshins be completely silent? Should formal robes always be worn in the zendo? What about casual clothes? To wear black robes at our desert wilderness retreats would be ridiculous, so we decided that people can wear shorts and flip-flops. That change simply made good sense in the desert. But what about the sitting schedule in the desert? At traditional sesshins we sit zazen eight or more hours each day; is it still Zen if we sit together for only a few hours and spend the rest of the day sitting by ourselves, hiking, enjoying nature, or even napping? We can drive ourselves crazy with such questions, stifling the natural process of change and killing our own joy and creativity.

Koan study is a traditional form of Zen training that most successors of Maezumi Roshi have retained. Many koans include short stories about the great Chinese Zen ancestors and their interactions with students. As we study koans, our ideas and beliefs are challenged, including our ideas about how teaching should look and sound. Koans show us that there is no mold for what a Zen teacher should be. The great masters were a creative bunch, and what made them truly great was their ability to adapt to the moment so that their teaching fit the student and the situation perfectly. By studying koans, we can learn how to be more open and flexible with teaching that doesn't necessarily conform to our ideas.

One thing I really enjoy about koan study is the opportunity to learn about the lives of the great ancestors. The more koans we study, the better understanding we develop about who the ancestors really were. We begin to feel that we know them and to identify with them as real people. Nevertheless, our understanding of those famous characters will always be limited, and we will never know exactly what they understood or realized. Even if all the teachings of a particular master had been written down, would they add up to everything he or she had ever taught? Would they tell us who that teacher was? Even though there are many sutras, we don't presume that they account for all of the Buddha's teaching. And we would never assume to know who Shakyamuni Buddha was simply on the basis of having studied the sutras. No matter how much we know about a person, we can never grasp him or her. Still, we often presume that we know someone. When we get stuck in the way we perceive someone, we put them in a box.

There is a koan that teaches how our assumptions can blind us, especially our assumptions about the Dharma and what teaching and realization should look like. Master Tokusan had a reputation for being just about the toughest Zen master who ever walked this planet. Now, some Zen teachers teach by words and some teach by shouts; but in his early years, Tokusan was famous for using his stick. His way of teaching became known as "Tokusan's thirty blows." No matter who it was or how long he had been practicing, when a monk approached Tokusan, he got thirty blows. If the monk said something, he got thirty blows; if he didn't say anything, he still got thirty blows. Tokusan showed no preferences. His stick was his sole teaching for years and years.

The koan I'm thinking of tells one of my favorite stories about Tokusan. It takes place when he was very old, somewhere between the ages of eighty and one hundred, and at this stage of his life, his teaching had become much more subtle. Tokusan was on his way to the dining room, carrying his eating bowls, when Seppo the cook saw him. And since Seppo hadn't yet rung the bell for the meal, he shouted out, "Hey, old man! Where do you think you're going? The bell and the drum have not been sounded." Tough old Tokusan simply turned around and went back to his room.

Seppo was delighted. He had really gotten the old guy! He ran to tell his buddy Ganto all about it. Now, Ganto was a little younger than Seppo, but his understanding was very, very clear. Seppo had not yet had a clear insight. After Seppo told his story, Ganto replied, "The old man has not realized the last word of Zen. If he had, you couldn't have gotten him like that."

"The old man hasn't realized the last word of Zen." Of course, Seppo took the bait. And we're just like Seppo: when we start to work on this koan, we're going to sit there and try to figure out what the first word of Zen is. Once we think we've got the first word, we will try to figure out the last word. It's insane, really, but does it seem insane? That is just our usual way of dealing with things. We automatically assume it is possible to figure out, once and for all, whether we are OK or not; whether or not we have succeeded; and who is really right, us or them. Yet how far will all this trying to figure out things really take us? Trying to find conclusive answers to such questions is just as crazy as trying to figure out the last word of Zen!

In order to pass this koan, we have to go *beyond* dualistic thinking, which means we have to drop all fixed notions of right and wrong, good and bad, first and last, this and that. Why do we find that so difficult to do? Something keeps pulling us back into our old habits of judging our life, ourselves, and others. The same thing always hooks us: our conditioning. In order to be free, we have to cut through our conditioned patterns of thinking.

No matter who you are, or where you are on the globe, when you go to the sea and scoop up a handful of seawater, it will taste the same. The realization experience that the ancestors all talk about is like that. When we begin to feel truly intimate with Tokusan, it's not so much that we can understand him but that we have shared the same taste—we have touched the same Buddha Mind. Every one of us can have that same experience—young or old, male or female, brilliant or not. There are no exceptions. How could there be an exception when what we experience is our own Mind?

I suppose there is one thing that could prevent someone from having that experience: never making the trip to the Sea. One person may need to journey farther than someone else, and on the surface our experiences may look different, but the taste of the Sea is always the same. Some people touch it with their tongues; others take a big gulp. Some don't dare to take a taste and only get their toes wet. The Sea is untamed and not always gentle, so not everyone is ready to drop their guard and open themselves to the experience. Yet every person has the potential to experience this Mind if they really want to.

Each individual has to look inside to see whether he or she truly wants the experience, because it requires a shift in the way we perceive reality—and that's scary. For now, though, let's imagine that we've found the courage to say "Yes!" to the journey. How, then, do we go about shifting our perception? How can we begin to see the world in a new way? It's really quite simple: *move*. A new view always opens up when we change position. Then, looking back, it's easier to see where we were stuck. The tricky thing is to not become attached to every new view. There are two ways we can avoid getting stuck again: we can give up *all* points of view, or we can give up our attachment to *my* point of view and embrace all views.

If we take a moment to consider these possibilities, we may notice something coming up inside: fear. We all feel more safe and secure when we stick to a point of view. We might even harbor the belief that we should have a point of view; that's what we've been taught. Schools, family, and friends reward us for understanding, comprehending, knowing, and proving. But what can we possibly know or understand when we have no point of view and come from no point of view? Buddha Mind has no point of view. The experience of Buddha Mind goes beyond any knowing or understanding; it can't be explained or even spoken about. We can experience Buddha Mind for ourselves, but we can't prove it to anyone. How can the tang of seawater be explained to someone who has never tasted the sea?

Throughout the ages, Zen teachers have relied on different means to bring people to the Sea. Even so, no one can force us to swallow. You know what they say: you can bring a horse to water but you can't make it drink. We can go on doubting, questioning, and trying to figure it out, and still refuse to drink. For years and years, Seppo went on trying to figure out the last word of Zen.

That brings me back to the story, and I want to tell you what happened next. Tokusan learned about what Ganto had said and sent for him. The master was a little upset. When Ganto arrived, Tokusan confronted him: "What's the matter? You don't approve of this old man and his understanding?" Ganto walked over to Tokusan and whispered something in his ear—and the master was satisfied.

So now, what is the problem? Or should I say, *who* is the problem? This is just a cute little story of a few deranged guys playing some weird game with one another a long, long time ago, but what is going through your mind? "What did Ganto whisper to Tokusan? What could it have been?" It's so easy to fall right back into trying to understand and figure it out, trying to second-guess!

Almost everyone who works on this koan steps into the big trap: we sit with it . . . meditate on it . . . and suddenly, *we know!* "I know what Ganto whispered!" Or at least we assume we know. Yet always, the Zen experience is: I *can't* know! Why, then, do we all fall back into assuming we know? Obviously we don't trust the experience. We start to doubt and question: "Maybe, just maybe, there is *something* to be known"—and understood and grasped and figured out. And clung to. And depended on. But each time we look into it, we discover the same thing: It can't be grasped. Buddha Mind goes beyond any point of view. It embraces all points of view—real, unreal, good, bad, right, wrong, known, not known. Any view is partial, never whole.

What would you say if someone asked, "Do you exist?" Most of us would answer immediately, "Of course!" We take this so-called *I* for granted. But do you really exist? It's a good question. The only problem is, we turn the question into a problem. First, we are stuck, deluded: we assume that we are what we think we are and that we exist in the way we think we exist. Then, we begin to question: "Is it so? Is there something more, something to be realized?" Somewhere along the way, we hear or read, "Yes! There is something to be realized, something to be tasted." What does the mind do next? The small mind wants to figure out exactly what was experienced, precisely what was realized. Before we know it, we've started on a journey to the Sea. If we could have just one taste, then we could relax, right? No! The small mind is insatiable: we always want more, a bigger and better taste. One doughnut is never enough, we want the whole doughnut shop! Our grasping mind keeps us in the loop, always seeking more. Nobody is doing this to me, and nobody is doing this to you. We do it to ourselves.

Zen practice puts our grasping mind to work. We have an itch, so we're encouraged to go right ahead and scratch. Don't you really want to know, to finally discover and grasp the Truth? Tempting, isn't it? Paradoxically, we have to try and we have to search, in order to discover that it can't be grasped. Simply hearing about the experience is never enough. We have to go to the Sea, scoop up the water, and taste it for ourselves. So in Zen, we are encouraged to take the journey. We use fire to burn down the fuel and put out the fire.

Zen practice gives us a framework in which to do what is absolutely insane to do in the first place. I'm not talking about becoming even more insane, but admitting our insanity and becoming more sane in the process. All of us ask impossible questions: Am I a good person or a bad person? Is my life a success? Am I on the right path? Zen says: Go for it! Burn it out!

We have a lot of koans because it takes a lot to burn it all out. Still, every koan is really about the same point. If we could see even one koan through and through, that would take care of it. Somehow, we keep missing it. Or we don't trust it. Tokusan resolved the question. When he was young, he questioned just as much as we do. Eventually he realized, "That was it!" He really wanted others to see it, so he beat them. Well, that was it, too. Finally Tokusan grew old and he just didn't care anymore: "OK, I'm early. So what? I'll go back, have some tea and come back a little later."

7

Empty Your Cup

Only our ideas block us from realizing our true Self and fulfilling our potential as human beings.

FOR SOME OF US, it can take years to clarify why we are practicing Zen and what the real issue is. I have been sitting for more than thirty years—just a short time as this practice goes—but it has been long enough for me to see that the problem we encounter at the beginning is still a problem after practicing for more than a quarter century. Always, the problem is our ideas. Our ideas and concepts are endless, and yet we can become very attached to them. We would rather die than let go of some of our favorites.

Maybe you've heard the tale of the American professor who went to Japan to meet with a Zen master. When at last he was received into the teacher's quarters, the professor announced, "I've come to see you because I would really like to practice here and attain enlightenment." The teacher didn't say anything. He simply went on serving tea. He poured the professor's cup full and just kept pouring. The professor cried, "Wait, wait, *stop*! My cup is full!" The master replied, "Then empty your cup." This is the first teaching in Zen. It is also the last.

In the Yiddish, Dutch, and Polish languages, the word for *cup* also means "head." So "empty your cup" can also mean "empty your head"—and this is the point of the story. How can we empty our mind so that it becomes like an empty cup, open and receptive? If we want to accomplish the Way, this is a very important question.

Recently I read a book by a Theravadin master who works with both Asian and Western students. Based on his experience, he believes that attachment to ideas is the most difficult issue for students, regardless of where they come from. Helping students give up their attachment to ideas is probably one of the most challenging tasks we teachers encounter. The most difficult ideas to drop are usually the ones that seem most profound, the ones that we feel righteous about. These ideas might not be working for us anymore, but we cherish them anyway. They might be causing suffering for others or ourselves, but we will find something else to blame. We will do almost anything to avoid letting go of our precious ideas, even though they have become our prison.

My mother was quite ill for several years before she died, and sometimes she struggled with confusion. One night she phoned me in a panic and said, "I've lost myself! I can't find myself!" Against my better judgment, I congratulated her and said, "There is no self, Mom! What did you really lose?" She told me not to be so cute. And she was right, I shouldn't make light of it. The self is our heaviest burden and the burden that we are most afraid to lose.

Some of my juiciest, best, and most tender moments of sitting occur just before I give a talk. I let go of my thoughts and just sit, taking in the presence of the group and seeing what comes up as a topic. When we sit in zazen and really let go of the self, we experience what Dogen Zenji described as "dropped off body and mind"—clear awareness, not filtered or colored by the notions and concerns of the self. Freedom from the tyranny of the small self is something each of us can accomplish through practice. Only our ideas block us from realizing our true Self and fulfilling our potential as human beings.

Everyone resists dropping their ideas, and we can practice for many years without ever realizing our true Self. We fear letting go of the very ideas that limit us. We may see that an idea is confining and restricting and yet still cling to it. We can help ourselves by asking, "What do I really need to give up in order to accomplish the Way?" One thought that might occur to you is something we've all heard: to accomplish the Way, we have to give our life to the Dharma. But what does that mean? Just what is being given up, and to whom? And really, who wants your life? To anyone else, it would be excess baggage.

When we sit with the question "What do I need to lose in order to accomplish the Way?" we can come up with all kinds of interesting answers. We need to watch out, though, because the mind is very cunning. We can be stupid in every other aspect of our life, but when it comes to deceiving ourselves, the mind has no equal. Our mind can generate a laundry list of ideas about what it would take, but if we examine them, we will see that they are only excuses. We don't need to give up our families or our jobs, our lifestyle or our culture, to accomplish the Buddha Way. We only have to let go of the self.

The real question is, what stops us from letting go of the self? If the self is just a bunch of ideas, why do we find it so hard to drop? Again, we can come up with all kinds of reasons and excuses. "I'm too old. I can't sit like the young people." Or maybe, "I can't do it because I'm a man. Women have a better chance. They aren't as stubborn." We may laugh, but a lot of us men think like that. I've heard some women complain that men have it easier because men are more confident. We can think that we're too young, that we haven't practiced long enough, that we don't have the time, or that our lives are just too complicated. We are all experts at finding excuses about why we can't let go of the self. But the truth is, nothing really blocks any of us from dropping off body and mind and letting go of the self.

We create our own barriers to realizing our true Self. Bassui called it halfhearted effort. Rinzai called it lack of faith. It's hard to admit that maybe we don't want it badly enough or that we don't have enough faith to stick with our practice. No one likes to face those possibilities. Still, we need to ask ourselves just how far we want to go with our practice. To really accomplish the Way takes a lot of time and energy, and that means taking time away from other parts of our lives. We're only deceiving ourselves when we put the blame somewhere else. We have to take responsibility for ourselves and our practice. The implications are serious and far-reaching. It boils down to taking responsibility for our lives.

Whether we realize it or not, every moment of every day, we are creating our future, our destiny, our karma. What we have created is waiting for us in the next moment. We come to this practice because we want to become more conscious, and that means waking up—seeing how we are creating our karma every moment and taking responsibility for it. A wonderful and profound shift takes place when we do that: we develop deep appreciation for our lives. Our eyes open up to the amazing truth that everything is the Dharma, and every moment is the teaching. *This is it!* Nirvana is not in the future, and paradise is not somewhere else. Right here, this very moment, *is* the time and place. As my son, Tai, often says, "It doesn't get any better than this!"

If right here and now is it, how can we truly appreciate that? The secret is to travel light: we need to keep dropping our ego, our ideas, and our concepts. We also need to keep facing our fear. We don't need to get rid of fear; we only need to learn how to work with it. The best way to work with fear is to let it be.

When we sit with our fear and really look at it, we can see it for what it is: just another concept. At first, we might worry that our fear will overwhelm us; but if we continue to sit with it, we will see that fear really has no substance. Then, as fear begins to lose its power over us, we can begin to see the irony of it all: the concept of fear is used by the ego to protect another concept—our most valuable concept—the idea of self.

You and I need to empty our own cups; no one can do it for us. It only takes a moment to drop the self, but it must be a moment of complete, wholehearted effort. We have to face our fear and be willing to let go. In order to muster the drive and commitment to do it, we first have to become tired of the burden of self, really hungry for liberation. The key to accomplishing the Way and realizing our true Self rests in our own hands.

PART TWO

STEPPING ONTO THE PATH

PRACTICE

If we are fortunate, we come upon a meditation practice that works for us and a good teacher to help us on the Path to liberation. We may go through many twists and turns in the initial stages of practice. First we learn the form of zazen and the delicate balance between tension and relaxation in which our body can settle and our breathing can assume a natural rhythm. Then we learn the tools that calm the mind. Skills of concentration and focus are gradually honed, and we grow in the ability to sit zazen with attention and clarity. Our efforts are rewarded with the deepening of samadhi and joriki, *the stabilizing power of zazen. The groundwork has been laid to realize our true nature.*

8

Who Binds You?

To be liberated, it is not enough simply to see how we have caused our own suffering through karma. We have to see that we are creating our suffering now, moment by moment, by setting up the delusion of separateness.

THE BUDDHA TAUGHT that suffering is an inevitable aspect of life; this is his first noble truth. But if you stop there and look no further into his teaching, you will miss the whole point. Buddha realized that we need to face the fact of suffering head-on before we can understand its source and discover the Way to liberation. After he himself realized the Way, Buddha couldn't keep the treasure for himself; he was compelled by compassion to tell everyone who would listen: the key to liberation lies within each one of us.

Simply knowing this much about Buddha's teaching can change how you and I experience suffering. If liberation is in our own hands, then we are empowered. We can cut through the conditioning that makes us feel like victims. In contrast, when a problem is perceived as being "out there," we feel powerless to change it. Liberation then depends on overcoming or getting away from whomever or whatever is oppressing us. Given all the problems in the world, we could easily become discouraged, even hopeless, about ever finding true peace of mind. The Buddha's teaching brings hope and confidence in our ability to go to the root cause of suffering.

There is a koan about this, just a short interchange between a student and a teacher. The student already knows the Buddha's basic teaching that liberation from suffering is to be found within oneself, but knowing that hasn't been enough. So he asks the teacher, "Please, could you help me liberate myself?" And the teacher answers, "Who binds you?"

We each need to ask ourselves that question, "Who binds me and causes me to suffer?" Buddha asked himself that question when he decided to sit down under the bodhi tree. He had given up searching for answers outside himself, so he turned his search inward. Yet even then he was confronted by what appeared to be external difficulties. Dangerous beasts appeared and tried to frighten him away from his search, and beautiful women came to distract and seduce him. Buddha knew he had to sit through it all and remain true to his vow. He resolved to stay sitting in meditation until he found the ultimate solution to the problem of suffering. He sat there with great determination, and gradually the distractions faded away. As his samadhi deepened, he found a place of stillness and silence. Still in that state, he glanced up at the planet Venus and experienced a completely new view of reality. Until that moment he had perceived everything dualistically. Suddenly all duality fell away, and he experienced no gap, not the slightest separation between himself and the planet Venus. He realized the absolute side of reality.

Buddha's experience of unity, complete oneness with all things, was the resolution of his search. There was no inside or outside, absolutely nothing to seek. He himself was it! Buddha realized One Mind. The moment his egoistic small mind dropped off, there was only Mind, embracing all things, excluding nothing. Buddha had discovered the natural state of mind, our original nature. Through practice, we, too, can realize our true Self, which is no-self, and come home to our Buddha nature.

When Buddha became enlightened, he could see that Mind creates everything; he experienced this truth directly. The understanding he had been looking for never could be found—he had to experience *being* Mind. He had to experience no outside, no fetters, no beginning, no end. To experience this Mind is to experience no separation;

therefore, there is nothing to fear or desire. Buddha realized that nothing, not even the tiniest particle of dust, exists apart from this Mind. So he could see the cause of suffering: if I create everything, then I also create my suffering.

In order to be liberated, it is not enough simply to see how we have caused our own suffering through *karma*, the law of cause and effect. We have to see that we are creating our suffering *now*, moment by moment, by setting up the delusion of separateness. Our conditioned way of seeing the world, conventional reality, is dualistic. Only the direct experience of conventional reality dropping away can convince us that we have been seeing things in an upside-down, topsy-turvy way. When we see our intrinsic wholeness, we can stop creating the delusion of separateness. Then our ceaselessly seeking mind can rest.

Buddha discovered not only the cause but also the way to end suffering. From the enlightened perspective it was obvious: he was the Way itself. This Path was found by meditating and cultivating samadhi. You could say that through samadhi he was preparing the soil of his mind so the flower could blossom and the ultimate shift could take place. In an instant, his way of perceiving reality shifted from seeing things dualistically to the complete opposite, seeing the reality of One. It was as if he finally looked to the south after spending his entire life looking northward. Until that moment, Buddha simply wasn't aware of the whole landscape. Suddenly the entire view opened up before him.

Buddha's teaching is so simple and obvious: the complete teaching is contained in his life. Yet we tend to forget how essential it is to practice zazen. Modern life seems to get busier all the time. With our cell phones, e-mail, and fax machines, we can carry our busyness around with us twenty-four hours a day, seven days a week. The Buddha spent six years in ascetic and yogic practices, but it wasn't until he dedicated himself to zazen for seven days and nights that he experienced enlightenment. If even the Buddha had to sit, how much more do you and I need to sit?

Nevertheless, we don't need to wait for enlightenment in order to benefit from practice. Glimpses of the other side of reality can help us along the way. Imagine how much better we could cope with the stresses of life if every day we experienced the samadhi that clarifies the true cause of our suffering. In zazen we can step beyond the small mind and reconfirm our true nature—the unborn and undying Buddha Mind. To touch that experience every day, however briefly, is enough to shatter our illusions as victims on the tide of life. We can refresh and empower ourselves with the awareness that we ourselves are the only ones binding us.

Unless we return again and again to our original nature, we tend to forget that the problem lies in the small mind, in the way we perceive reality. We can try to hold on to an experience of Buddha Mind, but it never really works. Reality with a capital *R*, the Absolute, is beyond comprehension. The unchangeable *dharmakaya* cannot be grasped, but it can be experienced. In *jijuyu-zanmai*, "joyful, self-fulfilling samadhi," we can touch it, we can taste it. In jijuyu-zanmai we reaffirm our true Self, Buddha Mind, with no beginning or end, no inside or outside.

Given the pace of modern life, we may question whether it is really possible for us to awaken in the same way as the Buddha did. So we need to remember that even though the Buddha spent years preparing the soil, his realization was instantaneous. We can prepare our own soil in the midst of daily life by not creating a division between periods of practice and everything else we do. This is an important way to cut through our dualistic way of looking at things. Practice is not only the hour or so of zazen each day, but every moment of our day.

Sitting is the best and easiest way to cut through delusion; but the more awake we become, the more we can see that everything we do is practice, and everything that happens is a manifestation of Dharma. Each moment presents an opportunity to do what we learn how to do on the cushion: let go of the self and realize this One. The awareness that we cultivate in zazen enables us to see the whole picture, the relative and absolute realities. When we make zazen part of our day, ordinary life is not separate from the Path to liberation. This life becomes the samadhi of self-fulfilling enlightenment, complete peace and contentment.

9

Our True Self Is No-Self

> We're so full of ideas about who we are, there's no space left to realize our true nature. Zazen is where we begin to empty the cup.

ZEN HAS DEVELOPED a rather strange and glamorous reputation in the West. It is often portrayed in ways that make it seem almost magical, as if Zen could transform the mundane into the sublime. We've all seen book titles that give this suggestion. They begin with *Zen and the Art of* . . . and the blank can be filled in with anything from feeding your cat to sex. The intrigue and glitter aren't always a bad influence; some of us are attracted to an introductory course and carried along through the first year or two of Zen practice before the shine wears off. But sooner or later, we find ourselves facing the plain truth: Zen is about sitting in zazen, hour after hour, year after year.

So what is it about Zen that keeps us going? What could possibly motivate someone to practice zazen for years on end? This is a good question; but it's more interesting to look a little deeper, at what motivates us to ask the question in the first place. It's often easier to spot that motivation in someone else, but all of us are driven by the same thing. We want to know "what's in it for me?" Self-interest can be a great motivator; it helps us accomplish all kinds of goals in life. But the self that underlies self-interest can also cause us all kinds of problems; and that self will never be confirmed in our Zen practice.

The self that wants to achieve goals and attain things is the egoistic self, not our true Self. The egoistic self is what we identify with and think of as "me." In fact, we have become so distracted and intoxicated by the egoistic self that we may never question whether that is who we really are. And tragically, many people live and die without ever coming to know their true Self. In Zen Buddhism, the realization and actualization of one's true nature is the point of practice.

Albert Einstein was a master of rational thought, but he never lost sight of the mysterious and unfathomable. He had great insight into what it means to be human. He said that for us to be fulfilled as human beings, we must first liberate ourselves from the self. In Zen we say that we must break free of the illusion of self in order to wake up to our true Self. How is this done? First, you have to create some space; you have to become like an empty cup. This means letting go of everything you think defines you—all your ideas and conditioning, everything you know and everything you have used to build the self that you think of as "me." It's helpful to remember that this "me" is just an image. We have each created this self; we were not born with it. Over the years, and with a little help from our friends and family, we each build up an image of what constitutes "me." We become so filled with this image that it's all we can see. But since we ourselves constructed it, we can tear it down as well. Before we become like an empty cup, there is simply no space left to realize our true nature. Zazen is where we begin to empty the cup.

Early in our practice, before we have had a few clear glimpses into our true nature, it is difficult to appreciate how important zazen is. It's hard to imagine the tremendous difference that zazen can make in our lives. If we could see that, we would make sitting a priority, something we would do every day. Zazen is just as essential for our health and well-being as are eating and sleeping. Zazen is the way we take care of this great matter of life and death.

Every time we sit in zazen, we empty the mind of some of the ideas that make up the image of self. We have the opportunity to empty the waste bin, bit by bit. By turning our attention inward to the activity of the mind, we gain insight into what all that litter is. We begin to notice how we cling to some things and reject other things. We see the nice stories that we tell ourselves about ourselves—as if somebody were being fooled. By looking into the mind, we begin to notice what is really going on. We begin to see through the illusions we've accepted as the truth about who we are and what life is. We notice our tendency to distort and color reality, how we project our beliefs and judgments onto everything we experience.

Zazen is a tool we can use to clarify and understand how the mind operates. Actually the mind functions very much like a gland. What do glands do? Secrete! What does the mind do? It secretes thoughts! You wouldn't want to stop one of your glands from secreting, so why would you want to stop your mind from producing thoughts? Anyone who has practiced zazen for any length of time realizes that thoughts are simply the natural functioning of the mind. Thoughts are not the problem; the problem is what we do with our thoughts. What do we do with our thoughts? Find out by sitting zazen and paying attention. There is no better way to see what our mind is up to. Walking meditation and meditative martial arts such as taiji and qigong are also very good; but none of them substitutes for simply sitting still and observing. We begin to notice a pattern: as soon as a thought comes up, it spawns a reaction, almost as if thoughts came with little hooks or charges on them. One thought triggers another and another and another, in seemingly endless chatter. Our minds are not just full, they're overflowing!

We become slaves to our thoughts. As soon as a thought arises, we form an opinion or a judgment about it: "I like that one. In fact, I love that one! I think I'll play it out and develop a story." Or we may react with fear or hatred and try hard to think of something else. All we need is a moment of wakefulness to see a thought for what it is—just a thought! But we don't treat thoughts like mere thoughts; we make them into something important and substantial. The thoughts that we like, we hold on to and claim: "I think this, and I don't think that." We build one thought on top of another until we have an entire story called "me." But underneath all that litter is an originally empty Mind, with just an occasional thought being secreted.

Thoughts aren't bad; they help us take action in life. But our suffering is linked to our thoughts through the reactions that we have to them. If we didn't react to thoughts, we wouldn't suffer; we could be at peace, with an occasional thought rising up like a bubble to the surface of a lake. Then, poof. Gone.

Practices of mindfulness, such as simply watching the parade of thoughts in the mind or noticing each movement of walking, are legitimate parts of Zen practice, even though they are not always recognized as such. Mindfulness is the primary practice of *vipashyana*, but it is also an important part of Zen training. In my opinion, mindfulness has been underemphasized in some transmissions of Zen to the West. Instead, sudden or "breakthrough" realization through practices such as koan study has been stressed to such a degree that many people don't realize that Zen also includes other approaches. Sometimes what has been presented as koan study is actually just another way of indulging in thinking. When we focus on deep questions such as "What is the meaning of life?" the small mind wants to find a rational answer that it understands. We can become so caught up in our thoughts, we forget to pay attention to the basic activity of the mind. We're deceiving ourselves if we think that realization has nothing to do with paying attention to what is coming up in the mind.

The confusion about mindfulness as a part of Zen practice seems to have started long ago with variations in how Zen was practiced and taught. From the time of Bodhidharma, Zen has been known as the school of "sudden realization," which refers to awakening to one's true Self. Bodhidharma said that Zen goes beyond words and letters and points directly to one's true nature. In other words, scriptures and teachings can never substitute for the direct experience of realization. The Zen tradition relies on various means to help us wake up to and directly experience our true nature. Working with questions or koans is one way to look into the mind, and paying attention to the activity of the mind is another way. Always, the point is to see beyond questions and thoughts to our true nature.

Being human, we tend to be a little slow. The great Zen ancestors noticed this fact and devised some ways to help. If we want to speed up the process of looking inward, they encourage us to ask ourselves a question: "What is my true Self?" It would be easy to live to old age and never think of asking that question; we are so full of ourselves that the question just doesn't come up. Death can be on our doorstep before we've had a glimpse of who we really are. But if we have been fortunate enough to encounter that question and work with it, we learn right away that the mind produces an endless stream of thoughts. It can be very confusing and unsettling. Am I the happy-go-lucky person that I try to be, or am I the one with these disagreeable thoughts? Which thoughts are the "true" me? What is my true nature?

Zen tells us to look inward and pay attention to all of it, the beautiful *and* the ugly aspects of ourselves. The posture of zazen gives us the strength and grounding we need to face it all. We can look honestly at ourselves and acknowledge everything that comes up. And as we become more familiar with the workings of our mind, our true nature begins to clarify: "My true nature is dynamic and unfixed, every-thing and no-thing. My true Self is no-self!"

In zazen we begin to develop a relationship with who we really are. We learn how to relax and simply observe our thoughts as they bubble up and fade away. Instead of reacting to our thoughts with clinging or rejection, we learn to let them go. Bit by bit we empty our minds of all the litter and noise. The space between the thoughts begins to open up and expand, and we gradually learn how to enter that space and just sit. Our mind becomes an empty cup with boundless space and potential—our true nature.

10

Go beyond Appearances

> This life is not what it appears to be, and we are not who we think we are.

IMAGINE THAT today is your first experience of zazen. What is going to bring you back to the cushion? If you really enjoyed it, maybe you would sit again; but some people don't enjoy their first sitting. In fact, it can be very uncomfortable and unpleasant. Just like when we first pick up a tennis racket or an instrument, our first efforts with zazen can be quite frustrating. So what keeps us going? There are a lot of activities that we choose not to continue; how do we make that kind of choice? When we are young, we base many of our decisions on what feels good. As we gain some experience and maturity, we base our decisions less on what gives us immediate pleasure and more on what seems good for us in the long run. And for many of us, that is how we become motivated to practice.

To become comfortable in meditation, we first must become comfortable in our own skin. This is not as easy as it sounds. We have become habituated to being busy, distracted, and entertained—always doing, watching, listening, or thinking. When we begin a meditation practice, just sitting still can be difficult. In a strange way, I already had ten years of preparation by the time I started practicing zazen. I had been a lifeguard, and sometimes that meant sitting eight hours a day, alone in a little tower on an empty beach. At times I was so uncomfortable and bored, I would do anything and everything to keep my mind occupied. Over and over again, I counted how much money I was making—per second!—purposefully forgetting the answer or adding in a pay raise of ten cents. Just staying awake was tough! For many of us, that's half the battle when we first begin zazen.

Meditation gives us the opportunity to practice simply being with ourselves—with our own body and mind. It's a great chance to confront all the things that make it difficult to just sit. In the beginning we may notice pain in our body. Later on we discover that our mind is also in pain. Just sitting upright and staying attentive can leave us feeling exposed and vulnerable. Over time our discomfort with this lessens, and we begin to feel very alive, awake, and dignified. It becomes easier and easier to sit.

Practice is all that is needed to develop comfort in sitting and in being with ourselves, so we need to decide if achieving some level of comfort is worth the practice it will take. There are so many other things to do, so many things going on in our lives, we may wonder, "Do I really need to add one more thing?" In making our decision, it can be helpful to look at how we usually go about deciding such things. Are our priorities based on what benefits our total well-being, or are they primarily based on avoiding pain and experiencing pleasure? We can also ask our intuition what it says would be good for us. For me it was the feeling of coming home that made me want to continue to meditate. For you, does becoming truly comfortable in your own skin and at peace in your mind seem as if they might be worth some effort? Perhaps the ability to be with ourselves is a good thing for us as individuals and also for the world.

One of the first discoveries of a steady meditation practice is that we hold many conditioned beliefs and ideas. We are not born with beliefs and ideas; we develop and cultivate them over time—and the strongest ideas are usually about ourselves and who we think we are. If I asked you, "Who are you?" how would you answer? When you look into that question, you can begin to see just how attached you are to your ideas of "me." We become attached to all sorts of ideas about ourselves, and it doesn't matter whether they are pleasant or unpleasant. Simply being familiar and comfortable with this "me" is enough.

When you go deeply into the question "Who am I?" you realize that even this so-called me is a concept. That there is a me and that I exist are both concepts—but they are concepts that we definitely want to keep. Still, every concept is just a concept! A concept is not a reality, just as a map is not the territory. A concept never can be the truth, only a fragment of the truth. And because it can never be the whole truth, any concept that we hold about who we are or how we exist is going to be limiting, our personal prison!

Western culture encourages us to try to resolve each uncomfortable feeling, one by one. Since ancient times, the East has taken a different approach: rather than attacking each negative feeling, why not go to the root? Instead of focusing on *my* anxiety, *my* depression, *my* anger, *my* this and that, why not go to the very root of the problem: the "me" who is experiencing this distress? Exactly what is it that feels pain? For pain to exist, there must be one experiencing the pain. Who is this "one"?

For us in the West, this is a radically new way to investigate the source of our suffering. As long as we have a firm belief about who we are, the question simply doesn't come up. In meditation we take time to look into this self so that we can really see who is moving these hands and arms; who is making the decisions, observing what is going on, and thinking all these thoughts. Most of our life can be spent believing that we know who we are—and then suffering because we don't feel complete or at peace with what we believe is true. Something seems to be out of place or missing.

Tremendous courage is needed to begin to question and look in. Yet if we continue to look in, the courage that we need arises, and the desire to get to the root of the question grows. We begin to see that in order to be at peace with ourselves and to appreciate our lives to the fullest, we must be comfortable with who we are. You and I have to make friends with ourselves, our bodies and our minds. But it takes more than just courage to look in: we have to develop the habit and the discipline of looking in. Sitting has to become a priority; otherwise, we can put it off forever, or at least until all the other priorities are taken care of. It really comes down to our attitude about life. Are we merely trying to get through another day or to just achieve the next goal?

What we get out of life depends on how much we put into it. And the kicker is, if we can't appreciate our own lives, we can't appreciate Life—every rock, every plant, every being. This very earth is life!

The only thing more important than learning to appreciate this life is to *live* it. And to do that, we have to put ourselves into life, moment by moment. Most of the time we are not truly present. We live in our thoughts about the future or the past and end up living in our heads, the small, ego-centered mind. Somehow we must penetrate through the thoughts and realize, "I am not my mind!" When we live in the present, no thought divides us from our experience. There is no separation, no subject or object, because there is no *I*. When there is no self, there is just *being*.

We've all experienced moments when we were truly present, when we felt totally alive and aware. Some people are attracted to extreme sports because they may spark that experience. But there is no need to resort to life-threatening activities. We can go to the extreme on our cushions. We only have to take the time to look in and ask, "Who is it that is experiencing this?" Then we begin to see that we are not who we think we are. We begin to notice our ideas about who we are and to realize that we are not any of those ideas. Sure, I am a dad, but that's not the whole of me. I am not just that. I am a man, but I am not just that. We begin to see that we are not "just that"; we are not any constant thing. In fact, our lives are more like movie projections. A movie appears to be a continuous flow of action, but we all know that it is not. Thousands of single frames are passing by every minute. We make ourselves and our lives appear constant in the same way, by keeping our experiences flowing very fast. We tell ourselves "*thisismylife—thisismylife—thisismylife*" to keep the illusion that our life is somehow solid and real. In meditation, however, we can slow things down. Then we can see that each moment contains birth and death: born-dying, born-dying, born-dying. Things only appear solid because they happen so rapidly. This life is not what it appears to be, and we are not who we think we are.

Many of us begin a meditation practice because we want to find out who we *really* are. We want answers. The problem is, every answer is limited, only one view of the whole. After much searching, the realization hits: "I" can never be known. Although we must use the mind to look in, the mind can't turn to see itself. Just as the eye cannot see the eye, the mind can never see the mind. So *what* is doing the looking? We can try to name it by saying "I" am looking, or "my mind" is looking; but that which is doing the looking can never be known. It is ungraspable. What is it that is not graspable? It has been called Mind and true nature, but the simplest answer is "Who I am"—that which cannot be known, that which cannot be conceived.

To be liberated, free, and at peace with ourselves, we need to give up trying to know the true Self. There are two ways to do that. As soon as the question comes up, we can drop it and never want to know again. Still, we are easily hooked; and once hooked, we stay hooked until we take care of it. We have to follow through and take care of the question. The question becomes our top priority because if we do not take care of it, nothing else seems to go quite right. The only way out is forward. We can choose to take the question as a challenge, as we would with learning to play a sport or musical instrument, and dive into practice. By pursuing the unanswerable question, we learn to appreciate life as it truly is.

11

Zazen Posture: Opening to Our Limitless Capacity

> The form of zazen works like a lens: it allows us to focus our body and mind to a point and burn through the layers of our constructed self until only our unborn and undying true nature remains.

HOW WOULD you characterize modern life? If you compare your life to the lives of your grandparents, what differences are most apparent? Perhaps the most notable characteristic of life today is its busyness. Sometimes it seems as if we're being challenged to see how much we can do in a day. Nevertheless, the fast pacc of our lives does have its advantages, including the opportunity to pursue a wide variety of experiences. Our lives can be wonderfully full and rich. On the other hand, our busyness deprives us of something that was once common: the opportunity to focus completely on the task at hand.

Try to remember the last time you were able simply to do what you were doing. It could have been anything, from washing the dishes to figuring the balance in your bank account, but you had the luxury of doing it completely. Part of your attention wasn't split off into planning your next task, watching the clock or the television, or supervising the kids. The freedom to do just one thing at a time is becoming a rare pleasure, and it may take real effort to create enough space to slow down and focus. Weeklong sesshins are one way for us to retreat from our busy lives, but it's important to remember that retreats don't need to last seven days. Every time we sit in zazen, we can enjoy a mini-retreat by simply settling the body and focusing the mind.

Attitude can also make a big difference in how we experience our daily activities, including the practice of zazen. If we approach zazen as we do so many things—with the intention of getting it done quickly so that we can move to the next item on our agenda—then we won't enjoy zazen, and we won't benefit from it. Doing anything well takes focus and intent, whether it is preparing a meal or working out at the gym. When we wholeheartedly put ourselves into what we're doing, no matter what it is, we do a better job and get more out of it.

The practice of zazen works the same way. By approaching each period as a unique opportunity to give ourselves completely to zazen, our zazen itself becomes more complete. But this doesn't mean that we should approach sitting in an intellectual way, trying to figure out exactly how to do it so that we can get more from it. No, we should approach zazen in the same way we approach playing a sport—with our whole body, mind, and spirit, and with the intent to do our best.

Patience is also very important, especially when we are beginners. We need to be willing to take the time to learn the basics of zazen. Before we can play a musical instrument or practice a martial art with freedom, we need to master the forms of those disciplines. With zazen, too, we need to start with the form. That means paying attention to our posture, breathing, and concentration.

In all skilled activities, mastery and freedom are achieved by devoting ourselves to training in the form until it becomes effortless. We train our body and mind to do something *completely*. It is the same process with zazen. Ultimately zazen should be without effort: we go into zazen so completely, there is just sitting. In order to reach that level of practice, however, we have to put in a lot of time and effort. This can be disappointing news. Some people are drawn to Zen practice because they want to experience the samadhi that they've heard about, but they don't understand how much practice it takes. Unless they have the determination and discipline to master the form, they may quit practicing before they've really experienced zazen. Until we've actually experienced for ourselves just how powerful the form is, it's easy to think it doesn't matter that much.

So what is the correct form? We always begin with the posture—the foundation of zazen. When we learn how to assume the correct posture, everything else falls into place. Monks training at Zen monasteries in Japan quickly learn the importance of posture. During zazen, monitors "help" the monks sit with the correct posture. The monitors are very good coaches, and the monks quickly learn that they don't want to be helped very often. Soto Zen monasteries, in particular, are excellent training grounds to learn the importance of form in everything you do, from brushing your teeth to bowing. And when it comes to the form of zazen, posture is most critical.

For most of us Westerners, sitting on the floor with a cushion is quite uncomfortable in the beginning. Certain yoga stretches can be very helpful in developing the flexibility to sit comfortably for long periods. Still, some people are not able to sit on the floor, and for them a chair may work better, even though it lacks the stability of sitting on the floor. It is always best to sit in the traditional posture if you can, but regardless of whether you are sitting in a chair or on a cushion, your back should be straight. In the correct posture, your head is aligned with your navel, your spine is erect but relaxed into its natural curvature, and your hands rest in your lap or in a mudra.

After a couple of deep breaths, you can stop thinking about your breathing. Breathing breathes itself and finds its own rhythm. In the zazen posture, the breath finds its own way, and before long the mind does, too. The body settles into a natural balance, the breath finds a comfortable rhythm, and the mind returns to a place of stillness. Maezumi Roshi used the image of a wooden top to describe what happens when you sit with the correct posture. When the top is upright, perfectly straight, it spins on one point, and it is quite silent and transparent. If the top is not upright, it wobbles about. Zazen is sitting upright and still, doing absolutely nothing. Body and mind drop away, and there is just sitting.

Trying to approach this practice in an intellectual way doesn't work. The rational mind is not able to understand zazen, and it can't really help us master zazen. The mind does its own job very well: it asks questions and tries to gain understanding. When it comes to learning zazen, though, the mind usually just gets in the way. We need to learn zazen in the same way we learn a martial art. If we want to learn how to block in karate, the trick is not to figure out the moves but to let go of the mind and approach it with the body. When the *sensei* shows us how to move in a certain way, we don't need to ask a lot of questions. We can trust that that particular movement has been tested over and over again and that it will work for us. So instead of using our mind, we simply try to follow the form with our body. We mimic the way the teacher moves over and over again until it comes naturally to us.

The movements we go through in assuming the correct zazen posture are not difficult to remember, and unfortunately that makes them very easy to do almost unconsciously. When that happens, our zazen doesn't begin until after we discover ourselves on the cushion. If we instead train ourselves to pay attention to our movements as we prepare for zazen, every session of sitting will hold many opportunities to practice being conscious and present. And if we also pay attention when we finish sitting and stand up, we have suddenly doubled the opportunities to practice awareness. By practicing in this way, it doesn't take long for the correct posture to become second nature. That's when self-consciousness can drop away and we can become *just* movement, *just* posture, *just* breath. We give ourselves away to zazen.

From the perspective of the rational mind, paying attention to posture through the entire period of zazen isn't very wise; there are so many important things to be thinking about. "How am I supposed to be able to relax and hold the form at the same time?" "Am I becoming enlightened?" "I'll never get anywhere just by sitting here!" According to the rational mind, this practice is absurd. There is no rational explanation for why zazen works. But we know from experience that for zazen to work, we have to let go of the rational mind.

Let me tell you a story about what can happen when we surrender the mind and just sit. It's the enlightenment experience of Dogen Zenji, the founder of the Japanese Soto Zen school. At the time,

Dogen Zenji was studying at the monastery of his master, Tendo Nyojo, in China. The monks were practicing shikantaza, "just sitting." Dogen Zenji was sitting there, totally absorbed with just sitting. But the monk sitting next to him was totally absorbed with just sleeping. This is not uncommon. At Soto monasteries the monks begin the day with zazen at four o'clock in the morning. To "help" the monks, the teacher walks through the zendo now and then. As Tendo Nyojo was walking by, he saw this poor fellow, sound asleep. Being a very kind teacher, Tendo Nyojo picked up the monk's slipper and whacked him. Then he shouted, "Zazen is not sleeping. It's dropped-off body and mind!" Hearing those words, Dogen Zenji dropped off body and mind and was enlightened.

Don't think that Tendo Nyojo's words held some special magic. Dogen Zenji was able to let go of body and mind because he was totally involved in just sitting. He was in the samadhi of zazen. Dogen Zenji went on to become one of the greatest Zen teachers of all time, and his teaching is as true today as it was in the thirteenth century. He tells us to approach zazen with the body, not the mind. He stresses the importance of taking the correct posture and then tells us to just sit and be present.

To "just sit" sounds so easy that most of us are surprised to discover we can't do it. We can create a wonderfully quiet and serene place to sit zazen, and yet we must still contend with the restless mind. When we see how much the mind wanders, the most obvious thing to do (according to the rational mind) is to try to take control, to somehow catch and corral the mind. The moment this thought arises, something nasty has happened, and we've created a big problem for ourselves: we've split ourselves in two! Now there is one tending the thoughts, and the thoughts themselves—a shepherd and a flock.

Instead of trying to do something with our thoughts, the best thing to do is to simply refocus on our posture. We don't need to worry about trying to quiet the mind. There's no need to worry about doing anything at all. When we are sitting, we will notice that our mind wanders off again and again. All we need to do is notice, return to our posture, and let the mind be. By working with the mind in this way, it will eventually stop resisting and begin to settle down. We shouldn't be too quick to judge our zazen. If we just sit and do nothing, we will eventually reach the state where nothing is happening. The mind will sit like a well-spun top.

Our first experiences of the mind becoming quiet and still are wonderful. The stillness is a welcome relief from the endless chatter we've grown used to. So, of course, it is surprising when fear suddenly comes up. It seems to come out of nowhere; but if we look into what is going on, the fear becomes more understandable. We were just sitting peacefully when something dropped off—or rather, many things dropped off. No-thing was happening. The things that usually occupy the mind disappeared. But because the small mind had been clinging to those things to create an illusion of solidity, it can be unsettling when Mind begins to show its true transparency.

This experience is not completely new to us. Basically the same thing happens when we do anything completely; we could be swimming laps or playing the piano. So why does it seem like such a big deal when it happens to us in zazen? Simply, when we are completely involved in an activity, we can identify with the activity itself; but when we are completely involved in doing nothing, there is nothing to identify with. The small mind doesn't like that one bit, so it begins to complain. We're completely wasting our time! But isn't it nice to do something completely once in a while? What could be better than learning how to do *nothing* completely? We are so driven to excel, why not excel at doing nothing?

As I said at the beginning, it is important to approach whatever we're doing with the intent to do our best. The practice of zazen is all about form, focus, and doing something completely. Yet in a way, it's good that we react negatively when that "something" is doing nothing. Everything has a positive and a negative side, including doing our best. Even our greatest skills and personal qualities have positive and negative sides. If we want to know where our personal blind spot or Achilles heel is, we only need to look at our best skill or quality. No matter how wonderful it is, in some way it is also our most negative skill or trait, and it causes us the most problems. Some spiritual practices focus on getting rid of negative traits, but not Zen. In Zen practice we work on embracing the whole, and that means *every* aspect of ourselves.

One effect of zazen practice is seeing aspects of ourselves that we haven't noticed before. As we become more familiar with ourselves, we can begin to acknowledge more of our negative qualities. We can stop playing the game of identifying with only our positive qualities while turning a blind eye to our negative ones. It's a cruel game really, because we ignore half of who we truly are. We would never do that to our children; but when it comes to ourselves, most of us find it difficult to embrace our whole being. Why do we find it so difficult? Perhaps we fear that we might get stuck in playing the opposite game, identifying with only our negative side—a scary thought for anyone! But of course, the positive side will always be present, too. Our positive and negative sides are simply two halves of the same whole. We need to embrace both of them if we want to feel complete—and *be* complete. We can never fulfill our true potential if we are denying half of who we are.

The Zen approach of embracing ourselves relies on the same wisdom that forest-fire fighters discovered years ago: fight fire with fire. We tap the drive that brought us to Zen practice and turn it back on itself. That motivation, that hunger, that need, is the very thing that needs to be burned out. Desire is always the cause of suffering, and the best way to burn it out is to encourage it to burn even hotter. We can learn to take all of our passions and desires and focus them into our practice. Incredible energy is generated by gathering and focusing all of our thoughts, emotions, and desires into a point, like a magnifying lens gathering and concentrating the sun's rays. We can burn through anything!

Maybe it seems as if I've contradicted myself. First I said, "Let your mind go," and now I'm saying, "Focus." But we need to learn how to focus the mind in order to let it go. In zazen the form itself works like a lens: it allows us to focus our body and mind to a point. Distractions of thought and sensation drop away, and we begin to see through the illusion of self. The layers of our constructed self are burned away until only our unborn and undying true nature remains.

The stuff that really needs to be burned away is the same stuff that we're most identified with. We need to burn through everything that has been defining and limiting "who I am." This can be a frightening process, and we may wonder why anyone would choose to go through it. Once again, the rational mind can't give us much help with this question. Faith is a better resource here, and boundless faith is intrinsic to our true Self—our Buddha nature. For most of our life, we see only the illusion of self. By burning that constructed self completely away, we discover pure gold.

12

The Three Essentials of Zazen

> The mind of the Great Sage of India was intimately conveyed from west to east.
>
> —Opening verse of *Sandokai*

SHAKYAMUNI BUDDHA'S realization is alive today. Awakened Mind has been transmitted, Buddha to Buddha, for more than twenty-five hundred years through the practice of zazen. To preserve this transmission for future generations, the Zen school of Buddhism maintains zazen as its core practice. Zazen is the heart of Zen. The practice of true zazen is expounded in Dogen Zenji's masterpiece, *Shobogenzo*, literally "Treasury of the True Dharma Eye." In Japanese, *sho* means "the most important" or "true," and *bo* means "Dharma." Dogen Zenji's life of teaching was a proclamation that the true Dharma is transmitted by zazen. The true Dharma *is* zazen.

How can we understand zazen? Traditionally zazen is said to have three aspects: posture, breath, and mind. Maybe that sounds simple, but which one of these aspects is most important, especially if we want to experience awakening? Which aspect of zazen was most essential for the Buddha's realization? Can we turn to the esoteric teachings to find out?

Such questions arise naturally when we first commit to a meditation practice. We don't want to waste our time with a practice that won't get us anywhere. We want the real thing, the teachings that can bring us to the same realization as the Buddha. In some Buddhist traditions you have to work with basic teachings for many years before you can receive the highest and most esoteric teachings. Here's the good news: in the Zen tradition, we give away our secrets the first time you walk in the door. Whether or not you are ready to hear those teachings is another matter. Yet regardless of whether the esoteric teachings are received or not, we put them right out there. Furthermore, every one of the secret teachings can be discovered through zazen.

Some Zen teachers say that *posture* is the most important element of zazen. In a way, they are right. It's all posture! If we don't get the posture right, the door to realization won't open. So it is tempting to think that if we work really hard to master just the posture of zazen, then awakening will happen. We hope that zazen can be approached with the same attitude that works with most skills in life, where it isn't necessary to do something completely or correctly in order to receive the benefits. "If I could learn how to do zazen approximately, just well enough, then I can attain realization." The problem is, awakening doesn't work that way. It would be nice if it did, then everybody would be enlightened. But the truth is, we have to do zazen *completely*, with our whole body and mind. Zazen is like a combination lock with three numbers: posture, breath, and mind. The three numbers have to line up exactly or the lock will not open.

There are other Zen teachers who say that *mind* is the true key. And in a way, they are right. One of the first things we realize when we look into our mind is that it is in constant motion. In fact, the mind moves so fast it appears solid. Unless we find a way to slow down our mind, how can we possibly create enough space, even just a little gap, for a glimpse of our true Mind?

It's absurd, but we would like to believe that by thinking hard enough, long enough, and clearly enough, we will eventually figure out Zen—that all the puzzles will begin to make sense and the secrets will become clear. I know people who are still trying to figure something out even though they've been practicing Zen for many years. They seem to have forgotten the basics, the core teachings that were given the first time they sat down in a Zen meditation hall: the three essentials of zazen—this is the highest and most esoteric teaching!

From day one we are taught the importance of having a quiet and still mind—an empty mind. We are instructed how to quiet the mind in zazen by taking the posture; and to help us assume the correct posture, we are taught to go through certain steps and movements, sort of like warming up before exercising. Nevertheless, most of us eventually stop doing the warm-up exercises. They are so boring! There's nothing more boring than repeating the same steps over and over before we can get on with the "real" practice. Yet where does preparation end and zazen begin?

What if the transmission of Buddha Mind actually comes down to each one of those steps? If we could be completely present for each step and gesture, wouldn't our mind quiet down? And then what would happen if we took the correct posture? The posture of zazen has been handed down across twenty-five hundred years because it works! Approximate posture won't do. If the first number isn't correct, the lock will not open.

Only when we assume the right zazen posture can we take a deep zazen breath. Not just any form of breathing will do. Early in Zen training we are taught to breathe slowly and deeply, so that the in-breaths and out-breaths are smooth and even. We learn to make each breath round and deep. Then we are taught to follow the breath. But that is so boring! Why can't we relax and think about whatever we want? The breath is the second number of the lock; until we master the breath, we can't master the mind.

With practice you can learn to sustain slow and deep breathing, so that you breathe in and out only a few times each minute. And when the breath slows down, the mind slows down. When you align your body with the posture, the mind can align with the breath. The breath becomes you and you become the breath. Space begins to open up between the endless thoughts, and it becomes possible to truly rest in zazen. This is shikantaza, "just sitting." Shikantaza is deeply relaxing for the body and mind, but relaxation is not really the point. The ancestors have transmitted something much more profound.

The point is to open the lock. The secret discovered by the Buddha and the ancestors is the same secret that you and I can discover: zazen is the key to the lock. Through zazen we can experience a deep and profound samadhi; not just any samadhi, but the unique samadhi that Dogen Zenji called jijuyu-zanmai, "joyful, self-fulfilling samadhi." It is this samadhi, jijuyu-zanmai, that has been preserved and maintained for so many generations through the practice of zazen. What's so special about this samadhi? The Mind of the Buddha is transmitted, Buddha to Buddha, through jijuyu-zanmai.

Anyone can experience this samadhi, so absolutely everyone has access to Buddha Mind. If everyone could experience their Buddha nature, their complete, fulfilled, and whole true nature, it would transform our world! Buddha Mind is accessible to anyone and everyone, yet very few people actually awaken to their true nature. Although there are many reasons for this, the most obvious is that so few people ever encounter the Dharma. A chant that is recited in Zen centers and temples around the world puts it very bluntly: "The Dharma, incomparably profound and infinitely subtle, is rarely encountered, even in millions of ages." Even if we have the good fortune to encounter this Dharma and learn the practice of zazen, we still may never realize our Buddha nature. There are so many obstacles to overcome. Besides our lack of discipline, there is our busyness. Just think of all the things you should do before you sit down to practice zazen. Something has to go—but what? Time with your family or friends? Fixing the leaky faucet? Getting ready for the next workday? When we first consider the possibility of our own awakening and imagine what it might take, we may begin to feel discouraged and overwhelmed. Some of us just give up.

Delusion is another obstacle to our awakening. We can delude ourselves into not accepting the Dharma as it is, at face value. For example, look at the way your mind works when you hear the word *deep*. "Oh, deep is good! I want to experience deep meditation and deep samadhi." Now think about the words *narrow* and *broad*. Which one is good? "Broad, of course!" So broad is good, and narrow is bad. But we already decided that deep is good; and to go deep, don't we also need to go narrow? On the other hand, narrow is bad. Who wants to have a narrow view? We've all learned how beneficial it can be to have a broad and open mind. When we narrow our attention, though, we are more likely to notice details. The details of form and ritual are important parts of Zen practice; they have been carefully handed down, ancestor to ancestor, as ways to embody the Dharma. If form and ritual are essential aspects of Zen practice, which one is most important? Which one makes our zazen true zazen?

It should be clear by now: All three aspects—posture, breath, and mind—are essential aspects of zazen. When we take the posture and our breath becomes deep and slow, our mind can enter a space of silence and stillness. In that space we are able to experience our intrinsic wholeness. We can experience being in harmony, at one with our true nature.

The Self that we come to know through zazen is no-self. It is our true nature, our Buddha nature, unfixed and completely ungraspable. Dogen Zenji taught that zazen is the manifestation of Buddha nature, and we can realize this for ourselves by practicing zazen. Our true nature is revealed in the silence of the mind, the space that opens when we sit in harmony with our breath. Thus, through this simple practice, we can realize the most profound teachings. The less we try to know and understand, the more we can see the completeness of the basic teachings.

Zazen practice grows broader and deeper at the same time, and we discover the truth of the Dharma in daily life. Buddha nature can be realized in the simple and mundane acts of daily life when we do them completely. Brushing our teeth and taking out the trash are nothing but manifestations of Buddha nature. But knowing this intellectually is not the same as experiencing it. The key to realizing this truth is simple: be completely present in whatever you are doing. Yet don't we usually go about these daily rituals on automatic pilot? It may look as if we're in the kitchen washing the dishes, but our mind can be in another country.

Am I saying that there is a right way and a wrong way to wash the dishes? Yes, that is exactly what I am saying! We need to be able to let go of the enlightened, nondualistic view and get back to the basics.

There is a right way to take the posture of zazen, a right way to breathe, and a right way for the mind to be. Our aspiration is to come from the state of jijuyu-zanmai no matter what we are doing; then Buddha nature is manifested anywhere and everywhere. But our ego doesn't want any part of that. It's easier to do whatever we want to do while telling ourselves that we are manifesting our true nature. This is a very seductive belief. It's very tempting to cling to our realization, but it is also a dead end. All of the ancestors warn about it. Master Mumon includes a list of warnings—literally, "Zen Warnings"—at the end of the *Mumonkan*. He couldn't have been more explicit.

First, Mumon says: If you adhere to the rules and regulations, you bind yourself without a rope. Then he adds: If you act freely and without restraint, you are practicing the way of the heretics. Harsh words! Warnings to me and you. If we hold too tightly to rules and regulations, we bind ourselves as if we were wrapped in chains. But if we simply do whatever we want, we are worse than heretics. Mumon is alluding to the Middle Way, the path that the Buddha taught as a way to end suffering. The Middle Way doesn't mean walking some fine line between the extremes, and it also doesn't mean swinging from one extreme to the other, following the rules and regulations one day and throwing them out the next. Somehow we must transcend this duality.

If we want to practice the Middle Way, we need to recognize where we are stuck. We can become stuck in not giving a damn about rules, and we can get stuck in caring too much. Society tells us that if we obey all the laws and rules, we are a "good" person. But we are also a stuck person. If, on the other hand, we give in to all of our desires and call that the Way, we may be very free, but we are also creating lots of karma. Mumon is pointing out that half of the picture is just half of the picture—delusion. Half of the picture can never be the whole—the enlightened perspective.

These words of Mumon aren't meant to discourage us. Mumon is simply warning us that the Path has thorns and we had better keep our eyes wide open. Deluded thinking doesn't disappear just because we have seen our true nature. Rather, we exchange one blindness for another, more dangerous blindness. After practicing for some time, it's easy to get stuck in the delusion of enlightenment, trying to cling to whatever realization we have had. That's why Dogen Zenji begs us: After realization, after enlightenment, even after *dai kensho*, "Please do zazen!" Another great Zen master said it this way: At the beginning of practice, the most important element is faith. In the middle of practice, the most important element is faith. And finally, after many years of practice, the most important element is faith. Where do we put our faith? In the true Dharma—zazen.

Now, I could have said that we should put our faith in the Buddha. Yet all of the teachings come down to the same message: Realize who you truly are! This realization is transmitted through zazen. Thus, we return to the posture of the Buddha. When we take the posture of the Buddha, we are the Buddha. When we are the Buddha, we take the Buddha's posture.

13

Put the Mind to Rest

We discover true freedom when we break through the conditioning that fuels our desire to understand.

CHANGE IS everywhere we look. Every day we are bombarded with news about changes in our world, society, and ways of life. It's a struggle to keep up with it all, and sometimes we find ourselves wishing for the "good old days" when things seemed to be more reliable. But in reality there never were any "good old days." Change is the only unchangeable fact of life. Even you and I are continuously changing.

We have problems with change because our conventional mind doesn't like it. The small mind prefers predictability and familiarity. As students of Buddhism, we try to reconcile ourselves with impermanence; but when it comes to things close to our hearts, we still resist change. So it can be unsettling when we notice that our motivation for practice has faded or changed. There is really no need to worry, though; changes in motivation and direction are to be expected when we pursue a spiritual practice for any length of time. Despite time and inevitable change, a subtle undercurrent can persist in our practice—one that we need to rout out eventually. It is the drive to find something to hold on to, something that will make us feel more secure in the midst of so much change.

Perhaps a teacher has told us that seeking is itself the reason we can't find what we're looking for; or maybe we've read that somewhere. Yet it can still take many years of practice before we can see for ourselves that seeking is the problem. This is an essential step, but to give up seeking is still extremely difficult. Continuous seeking is the very nature of our mind. It's just wired in. The small mind is always grasping, wanting, seeking, looking, searching. Always. It's ironic, really. We are looking for answers, but searching is the problem. How can we find peace? The answer is simple, but it's the most difficult thing to do: cease seeking; stop looking for a solution.

We need to give up the hope that there is something to find. As long as we hold even a thread of hope that just maybe, possibly, eventually, we can find something that satisfies our craving, we will stay on the wheel of suffering. Yet to give up hope is one of our biggest fears. Society, religions, friends, and family all teach us to treasure hope above everything else. But the truth is, hope is a trap. It fuels endless seeking. Master Rinzai was famous for telling his students, "All you need to do is put an end to the ceaselessly seeking mind." Then he added, "The only ailment in the world is lack of faith." In order to stop seeking, we have to possess tremendous faith. At first that may seem contradictory, but it's not. When we've given up hope of finding answers "out there," true faith remains—faith that there really isn't anything to find.

To find liberation and freedom, we have to go against our conditioning, our ideas, and everything we've been taught. What imprisons us is never really "out there." We bind ourselves. Until we liberate ourselves from our personal chains, we can have only illusions of freedom. The small mind keeps us imprisoned with endless desires, judgments, and preferences—good, bad, right, wrong, me, you, us, them. How can we silence this noisy mind? When we discover how to do that, we have found the key to lasting peace.

We must look into ourselves to find the source of our discomfort with life, but it takes a lot of quiet time to really do this. In the Zen tradition, we look inward in the meditation hall, the zendo, where the usual rules of courteous interaction are dropped. We can sit silently for as long as we want, and nobody will bother us. Nobody will judge or criticize us. We can just be with ourselves. When we sit in zazen, we enter a very personal space where we can find liberation.

There is a koan that gives insight into the nature of this liberation. Nagarjuna was one of the greatest philosophers from the East. He was known for using logic to defeat every other philosopher. Nagarjuna had a premonition that a great being would visit him soon. So he took a bowl of water, dropped a needle in the bowl, and set it at the front gate. Then he watched to see what would happen. After a short time, a man approached the gate and saw the bowl of water. He didn't hesitate; he just picked up the bowl and carried it to Nagarjuna. This koan presents quite a puzzle: Why did Nagarjuna drop the needle in the water and then put the bowl by the gate? That was strange behavior, especially for the greatest philosopher in the East. He didn't think it over, and he didn't say anything; he just dropped a needle in a bowl of water, set it out by the gate, and watched. We can also wonder, why did the visitor take the bowl back to Nagarjuna? In the end, that man became Nagarjuna's successor.

What does the story mean? Perhaps all sorts of possibilities are going through your mind. No matter how good those possibilities seem, they are all just guesses. We need to go back to the basics: What is the cause of our dissatisfaction? Seeking. Trying to figure it all out. Trying to understand. We fall back into that habit so easily! Koans are like balls thrown at us to see what we are going to grab. The solution to the koan has nothing to do with understanding. Rather than trying to understand, the key is to just *be* the koan.

Many of us are attracted to a spiritual practice because we want to understand life better. To go through life without trying to understand it may seem rather pointless. When we finally admit that we don't have a clue about what life really is, fear and insecurity automatically well up. Our small mind doesn't like mysteries. It wants to figure things out. That's its job. The small mind also believes that it *should* be able to understand life if it tries hard enough. It takes great faith to finally give up the hope of understanding.

One thing that I love about Zen practice is this: the drug that treats the original ailment is also its own antidote. We can't settle for a superficial or temporary cure, so a self-destruct mechanism is built into the cure itself. The Zen way is to try to resolve the unresolvable—to question and really search for the answer. I guess we need to be a little crazy to look for a solution that we know doesn't exist.

The truth is, there is no problem. There never was! So why would a Zen teacher encourage us to look for the answer? That seems like a setup for failure, and maybe it is. Yet knowing we might be headed for failure doesn't resolve the issue. The itch still needs to be scratched. If we are not completely convinced that there is nothing to find, nothing to realize, and nothing to understand, peace and liberation will elude us. We will continue to be enslaved by the craving to understand, looking the world over and grabbing onto whatever ideas and concepts we encounter. No matter what we find, the small mind will never be satisfied. What we eventually realize is, the more we possess and call our own, the more we are possessed and owned.

The only way out of this endless search is to turn around and begin looking inside for the answer. In doing so, we are actually stepping onto another treadmill, but unless we look within and search deeply, we will never realize that there really is nothing to get or to understand. To make this discovery once is not usually enough to put the seeking mind to rest. At some point, doubt comes up again: "Maybe I didn't find anything because I didn't look hard enough." How many times do we need to go through the cycle of seeking and coming up empty-handed? I suppose the answer has to be, until we take care of the matter, until we no longer need to seek.

Zazen is the way to look inside, and it is also the way to make peace with our restless small mind. With zazen we can pierce through the conditioning that keeps us on the treadmill of wanting to understand. We can go beyond understanding to a deeper knowing, and this is the only way to attain true freedom. Actually, we don't become free; we discover that we never were bound. Our true nature—unknowable, ungraspable, and ever-changing—flows effortlessly through all the changes of life.

14

Dance with Life

> Liberation is living each day without a place to stand or ideas about who we are. That's when we can dance with life.

YOU AND I have our views of the world, but we tend to forget that they are only views. You have your perspective and I have mine, but we go through daily life thinking that what we see is reality and acting as if everything "out there" were solid and fixed. In fact, all the evidence points to the opposite. We only have to open our eyes to see that everything is in a constant state of change. Nothing is fixed. Of three marks that characterize Buddha's teachings, the first is *impermanence*. Seeing the truth of impermanence is the foundation for understanding the rest of Buddha's teaching; it is also the dawn of enlightened life.

We don't find it easy to accept the fact that all things are impermanent, but once we do, our lives are transformed. Where does our resistance come from? We can each discover that for ourselves by reflecting for a moment on the statement "Everything is impermanent." It doesn't take long to see that the very idea of impermanence brings up fear. We fear losing our homes, our possessions, our health, and our loved ones; but the most basic fear is losing the self. We take our self as reality, as something fixed and solid, when it is not. We can realize the absolute truth of who we are through zazen. Then we can live freely, without clinging to the illusion of self.

We begin to see through the illusion of self by paying attention to how we define this "me" and make it appear substantial. We are full of ideas, beliefs, and habits that serve to build up and protect our image of self. But which ones are most true? Are the positive ideas of ourselves closest to the truth, or are they simply the ideas we find most acceptable? What about the way our parents think of us? Do they see us as we truly are? And which of our habits give the most accurate picture of who we are? When we take stock of all these ideas, beliefs, and habits, we see them for what they are: constructs, figments of our imagination! By seeing that these things have no substance at all, we create the space to discover who we truly are.

Getting to know our true self requires a lot of looking in. Just think of all the different views and perspectives we can hold. Take, for example, the various responses we may have when confronted by an angry person. The way we view the anger itself will depend on the situation. The anger may seem reasonable if it's coming from our boss but completely unreasonable if it's coming from our child. Our perspective will then influence how we respond. The same thing happens inside ourselves: we judge our response based on how we view the entire scenario, and that view may change over time. The anger that seems so justified today may seem overblown tomorrow. The point is, our perspective is shifting all the time, even regarding the same event.

As we become more familiar with our ever-changing perspectives, it is harder and harder to believe in any image of self that we once accepted as "me." The self we've identified with is nothing but a bunch of perspectives, and these perspectives are in constant flux. If we try to say who we are, we are always one step behind our latest perspective. Of course, we could decide to drop all our ideas and to live without any fixed perspective; but that option brings up a lot of fear. Who would we be then? What would happen to our so-called identity? To realize that there is no thing called "me," no self, can leave us feeling very insecure. The whole world is suddenly unpredictable. There is no fixed me, no fixed you, and no fixed world. Even though this insight brings up insecurity, it is the truth. When we try to live in denial of this reality, we only cause ourselves more suffering.

Imagine what would happen if we stopped resisting impermanence and instead simply dealt with what came up from moment to moment. Certainly we would live more freely. Instead of reacting to what happens based on some idea, habit, or leftover perspective, our responses would be grounded in the here and now. Tremendous space would open up in our relationships if we always remembered, "Not only am I unfixed, but so is everyone else!" We could never again assume that we knew someone, and we would need to work harder to really listen and be present. Furthermore, since you and I are constantly changing, we can't really expect one another to live up to our expectations. If I don't know what to expect from myself, how could I possibly know what to expect from you? By relating to others in this way, we would avoid generating so much anger and resentment. When we are able to accept ourselves as dynamic and ever-changing beings, we create the space to express ourselves in the moment with more honesty and integrity. This transforms not only our relationships but also the karma we create.

In and of itself, karma is neither positive nor negative. It is simply the law of cause and effect. From the relative perspective, however, we can speak of both positive and negative karma. Negative karma comes about when we resist what is, when we ignore the fact that everything is changing and nothing can be held on to. By waking up to the impermanence all around us, we can break through our habits of relating to people and things as fixed objects. If we happen to forget, karma is always there to wake us up again.

By staying alert to impermanence, we can avoid causing a lot of unnecessary pain and suffering for ourselves and others. But because constant change is unsettling—it makes us realize how insecure and vulnerable we really are—we keep falling back into denial, trying to find something fixed to cling to. These efforts are doomed from the start; we will always need to let go. We can help ourselves stay awake by considering some basic questions. First, can we truly afford to live in denial? What consequences do we cause for ourselves and others when we cling and try to hold on? What karma is created when we struggle against the flow of change? We can also look at the benefits of acknowledging impermanence, the positive karma we would create by living without clinging. Imagine how much freedom would open up if we stopped trying to solidify ourselves and the people around us! And by not clinging to our ideas and preferences, we could release our regret and resentment about the past and open up to the future without fear and anxiety. True peace of mind is achieved when we learn how to accept what is.

We practice meditation in order to see ourselves as we truly are and life as it truly is. When we are suffering, we can look inside to find the cause—always some form of clinging. By noticing how quickly we attach to new ideas and perspectives, we can begin to unlearn the habit. One trick is to watch for moments when we feel the need to defend ourselves or our point of view. Defensiveness is always a red flag; it shows that we have once again become stuck in a point of view. We are pretending to be solid, and we want everyone else to go along with it. With a little honesty and effort, we can determine where we are stuck and then choose to let go. Gradually we become more flexible, finding it easier to let go of our perspectives. We take this "me" less seriously, appreciating instead our dynamic and unfixed true nature.

With practice we begin to see the world from the perspective of Big Mind, which can see all perspectives but clings to none. We learn that it is possible to return to the view of Big Mind whenever we've become stuck. It's easiest to assume that we're stuck somewhere; we only have to figure out where and then let go. Liberation from the self is living each day without a place to stand or ideas about who we are. That's when we can dance with life.

15

The Greatest Gift

> Awareness is the foundation for appreciating life—and we are most aware when we are living in the moment.

WHAT IS the best gift you have ever received? For me the answer that comes up is, my life. Without this life, I couldn't appreciate any other gift. Still, life is both a blessing and a curse. Every birth comes with its own death sentence, and the years between birth and death are guaranteed to hold many experiences of pain and suffering. Pleasure and pain, good times and difficult times, are all simply part of life. How can we face life and all that it holds with equanimity? There is a famous saying: Zen is about resolving the great matter of life and death. This means coming to terms with our own life and our own death. When we honestly accept the fact that we will die, we can drop our resistance to life. Then we can discover true appreciation for this life.

Most of us take life for granted; we don't see our own life as fragile and impermanent. But at some point, a wake-up call will remind us that life is a terminal condition. It could come when someone close to us suddenly dies or when we begin to lose our own health and abilities. Such wake-up calls can open our eyes to the wonder of being alive. Perhaps for the first time, we can appreciate some of the simple things, like taking a breath or seeing the face of a loved one. But why wait to be hit over the head before waking up? We only need to remember that everything, including this life, could be lost at any moment.

I would like to live my life like the man in this story. A man living at the foot of a mountain likes to hike and explore. He is happily hiking along one day, when he trips and falls over the edge of a cliff. Miraculously, he manages to stop his fall by grabbing a branch of a scrawny tree with his teeth. He knows that he is doomed. Either the branch or his strength will eventually give way. The guy is just hanging there when he spots a juicy, red strawberry growing on the cliff. He reaches out, plucks the strawberry, and pops it into his mouth!

Can we appreciate each moment the way the hiker did? Truly life is always precarious, whether we are aware of it or not. If we are willing to look, we can see death and loss all around us. But are we able to live with that awareness? I remember meeting a remarkable woman years ago. She had studied for a long time with Yasutani Roshi and Yamada Roshi, and she was much more experienced in Zen training than I was. She was talking about what it was like to have cancer when she said something that really surprised me: "This illness is teaching me many things. Although I'm seeing some ways that Zen practice has prepared me to face cancer, I'm learning even more from the cancer about facing my practice." She had practiced Zen for thirty years, somehow denying all along the reality of her own death. Surely her practice had helped her lay the groundwork necessary to appreciate her illness and how much it was teaching her. But it was cancer that made her face death squarely. That's when her practice became true.

Zen practice is about seeing what is and then acknowledging that truth. An inevitable part of that process is returning to square one. Even after many years of practice, we discover that we are just beginning. This Path is a never-ending process; we continually discover and rediscover what practice is. Returning to square one doesn't mean that our practice is immature or incomplete somehow. Returning to square one is absolutely fundamental to Zen. Beginner's mind *is* Zen mind,[1] just as Suzuki Roshi said. We return to the mind of a beginner again and again because this practice goes beyond any understanding. No one can tell us what Zen is, and there is nothing in this practice that we can cling to or grasp. Instead, we must keep rediscovering practice for ourselves. There will be different phases, of course, times of progress as well as times of stagnation. As long as we keep going, we will always encounter times of renewal, when we rediscover what practice really is. And in those times of rediscovery, we always find new appreciation for life.

What does it mean, to appreciate your life? When you first look into that question, you see the concepts, ideas, and beliefs you hold about what makes life worth appreciating. And if you look a little deeper, you will probably realize that many of those ideas are actually false. Having been raised in our materialistic culture, we pick up a lot of fairy-tale notions about life: that it should be full of pleasure, that our dreams will come true if we work hard enough, that there will be a happy ending. Shakyamuni Buddha saw that suffering is an inevitable part of life and that resisting this fact only leads to more suffering. That's why, as the first noble truth, he taught that life is suffering.

If we want to free ourselves from suffering, we have to begin with acknowledging the truth of suffering. Every life contains pain, illness, and death; and happy endings are rare. For most people, old age and death are a very sad ending. With my own mother, I witnessed the suffering that often accompanies old age. She spent the last few years of her life in a nursing home, and I visited her almost daily. Many of the people living at the nursing home were suffering. And yet, if they had been given the choice to end their lives voluntarily, I believe that most of them would have chosen to keep living despite their suffering. Of course, the fear of death and the unknown would influence their decisions, but so would the fact that life in itself is such a tremendous gift. The abilities to see, hear, touch, and breathe are truly wondrous—even when we no longer see or hear very well. Even at the end of our lives, we can appreciate simply being conscious and aware, alive.

It's strange but often true that we don't appreciate life when it is most complete but instead take it for granted. Maybe this explains how a serious illness or injury can suddenly open our eyes to a new and deep appreciation for life. Yet for most of us, the question is, how can we appreciate life regardless of whether we are going through good times or bad times? We can be sure of one thing: in order to appreciate life through all its ups and downs, we need to notice its gifts, including those that are most basic.

Always, awareness is the foundation for appreciating life—and we are most aware when we are living in the moment. When thoughts about the past and the future are not distracting us, we can notice what *is*, right here and now. Sitting in zazen is the best way for us to cultivate awareness of the moment. Just sitting, we can enjoy being truly present. Thoughts slow down and the mind becomes still. It is like taking a glass of water from a muddy pond and setting it down on a table: after fifteen or twenty minutes, the sediment falls to the bottom, and the water becomes clear and transparent. Zazen allows the busyness of the mind to settle. Then the mind can simply reflect, like a still pool of water, whatever comes into our awareness.

The awareness that we cultivate in zazen allows us to simply be with whatever is in the moment. And because we don't attach to or follow the thoughts that bubble up, we can experience the fluidity that is our true Mind. Thoughts come and go, sensations come and go, things come and go. We practice not clinging to anything, neither pleasure nor pain. In this way we train ourselves to stop resisting life. And we learn something wonderful: the mind can be at ease regardless of what is happening. At last, we are liberated, free to enjoy and appreciate the greatest gift of all—this life.

16

Looking for Confirmation

Our skills and knowledge aren't very helpful when it comes to the study of the self. So although it may seem a little strange to look outside for someone to teach us how to look inside, it actually makes good sense.

WHENEVER AN INTRODUCTORY COURSE begins at Kanzeon Zen Center, I like to ask the students what they hope to gain by attending. It's interesting to look into that question, because usually students come not so much because they want to learn more about Zen but because they want to learn more about themselves. They have come to the right place. Dogen Zenji summed up Zen practice very well when he said, "To study the Buddha Way is to study the self."

People from all walks of life sign up for the introductory classes. Many of them are already quite accomplished and well established, with careers, families, and homes. From the surface you would expect them to feel contented and complete. Their lives truly seem to lack nothing. And yet they come, hoping to learn more about themselves and to feel more complete and satisfied with who they are. It's amazing how similar these desires are to the desires that prompted Siddhartha Gautama to drop everything and begin his inward journey. Like him, some of us may need to experience a certain level of success in life before we realize that worldly gains will never bring us true contentment.

At the crossroads, when we begin to wonder if there might be more to life and ourselves, many of us realize that we are at a complete loss: we don't have the tools we need to look inward. The skills and knowledge that we've picked up along the way aren't very helpful when it comes to the study of the self. So although it may seem a little strange to look outside ourselves for someone to teach us how to look inside, it actually makes good sense. Of course, we don't want to turn to just anybody; we want to find someone who has credentials, someone who is qualified to show us the way to the truth about ourselves. In the Zen tradition, we go to the lineage of Zen ancestors who have been confirmed, teacher to successor, from the time of the Buddha. We put our trust in the tradition. Nevertheless, when we first meet a teacher, we really don't know whether he or she deserves our trust. We have to go by our guts as well as his or her credentials. We have to listen to ourselves and trust our instincts. With luck, we find a teacher we can connect with.

Ultimately only you can confirm the truth about yourself, and only I can confirm the truth about myself. But of course, we can easily deceive and fool ourselves, especially when it comes to aspects of ourselves that we don't like. So when we first embark on the journey of self-discovery, we have to ask, "When I look inside, how will I know that what I see is the truth and not self-deception?" That is where a qualified teacher can be very helpful. A teacher can help you judge whether you are seeing with clarity and wisdom. To be able to do that, the teacher already must have that understanding. He or she needs to have gone through a personal process of self-discovery and to have had the clarity of his or her vision confirmed by a teacher. And of course, before he or she can teach, that person must demonstrate his or her ability to guide others. Confirmation within the Zen lineage is like a "seal of approval" that the teacher has met those standards.

The Zen tradition has been around long enough for us to know that there is something about this process that works. We make an agreement with a teacher that gives him or her the authority to judge and confirm the understanding we gain about ourselves. But we both know that ultimately the confirmation comes from inside of oneself.

We create an outside authority only temporarily, a Buddha to go to for guidance.

Perhaps what I've said makes you wonder about the way the word *Buddha* is understood in Zen. Certainly how you understand *Buddha* can make a critical difference in your practice. If I say that Buddha is the Enlightened One who lived twenty-five hundred years ago, who can argue? Shakyamuni Buddha is the historical Buddha who first awakened to his true nature. But if I limit my understanding of Buddha to Shakyamuni, to whom can I go for guidance in this day and age? One option is to go to Buddha's recorded teaching, the sutras, to help us clarify and confirm our understanding. That is the path of the Theravada school of Buddhism. Thus, the Theravada tradition is similar to the tradition of Christianity that relies on the Bible, and the tradition of Islam that relies on the Koran. If we want to determine whether we are following the Path of Shakyamuni Buddha, we can turn to the sutras. The Theravadin tradition is strong and well grounded, but it is also limited to the Dharma as it has been preserved in written form for more than two thousand years. And from that point of reference, the teaching can't be alive today because Shakyamuni Buddha is dead.

Zen Buddhism has a different view of Buddha's teaching. We say that the recorded teachings of the Buddha are not the only sutras: the Dharma is being expounded today by living Buddhas. This Zen view was expressed beautifully by Hannyatara, Bodhidharma's teacher. When Hannyatara was asked by the king to recite a sutra as a blessing before a meal, he did something amazing. Standing before the king and his guests, Hannyatara said, "Every time I breathe in, I recite the eighty-four thousand sutras. Every time I breathe out, I recite the eighty-four thousand sutras." He knew from his own realization that the Dharma abided within his very breath. Hannyatara was telling the king's guests—and he is telling you and me—something very profound and very simple: If we want to understand Buddha's teaching and learn the truth about our nature, we don't need to look any further than our own breath. Breathing in, breathing out, we express the Dharma perfectly. And in zazen, when we focus our mind on the breath and become one with it, we become one with Buddha.

In the samadhi of zazen, we receive the wisdom of the Buddha. We receive it directly from Buddha Mind, Big Mind, the Unborn. And when we return to this Heart-Mind, our understanding is confirmed. So the process of going to a teacher is a little ironic. First you confirm yourself by realizing your own Buddha Mind. Then you go to a teacher to confirm what you have realized. The teacher's confirmation is like frosting on the cake when your realization is clear. You know and the teacher knows. There's not even much to discuss. The two of you have simply been working together to confirm yourself. You gave away your authority so that you could receive it back. If you only confirm yourself, you may be deluded.

Working with a teacher is a lot like going to a doctor: you go in order to confirm your illness and to find out what to do about it. Maybe you're not sure there is a problem, but you go to the doctor because you want to know the truth. Then it becomes the doctor's job to make the diagnosis and to share it with you. The doctor will report the truth, but you don't have to accept what he or she says. You can choose to accept the diagnosis and to follow through with the treatment, or you can choose to ignore or deny the diagnosis and do nothing about it. Similarly we go to a Zen teacher because we want to know the truth. Maybe we have a hunch that something is not quite right. The teacher accepts the role and agrees to tell us the truth. We can walk away at that point, or we can decide to begin the treatment. If we stay, the teacher becomes our authority until we both know the illness has been cured.

When a student and a teacher have agreed to work together, the first task is neither easy nor pleasant. Who wants to hear that they are responsible for creating their own problems? We are much more comfortable when we can put the blame somewhere else, onto anyone or anything that is handy. So we might resist accepting the diagnosis "I am the problem." But that diagnosis is actually good news. If we are the problem, we are also the cure! We need to accept this before we will give up trying to fix the problem "out there."

What is the problem? This "me." The self that we have created is causing our troubles. After accepting this diagnosis, we may hope that the cure will follow along quite easily. "If this self is the problem, all I need to do is stop creating it." Yet when we try, we find out that we can't do it. Life has conditioned us to create and protect the self, and this habit doesn't die easily. Still, we can begin to let go of this conditioning by paying attention to the behavior patterns that serve to keep the self intact. With practice, we can become aware of conditioned responses before acting on them. In Buddhism this is the point of liberation. The moment a thought or desire pops up, we can choose to respond in a way that is different from our habitual, self-serving response. Mindfulness allows us to seize the moment between the impulse to act and the action itself. We can choose to respond in a new and creative way, or we can choose to simply watch as the impulse fades away. Either way, we have claimed our freedom.

To break free of conditioning takes time and practice, and the best place to practice mindfulness is on the cushion. But of course, we can practice mindfulness twenty-four hours a day by simply paying attention to whatever we are doing. If we commit ourselves to regular practice, it won't take long before we can see some of our habits and patterns. At first we notice the patterns after the fact, after falling into them. Sometimes we don't realize we've fallen back into our habits until we sit down on the cushion or lie down to go to sleep. Maybe a day or two will pass before we notice, "Yeah, I did it again." But each time we notice a pattern, we have the opportunity to study the details. We learn to spot the habit more and more quickly and to catch ourselves at the moment of action. Gradually the space between the impulse and the reaction lengthens; and in that space we are liberated, free to choose how to respond.

Freeing ourselves of conditioning, we become more spontaneous. We may surprise ourselves, as well as those who thought they knew us. The self that seemed so solid and predictable begins to melt, and we become more comfortable with our true self, which is fluid and unfixed. Our own experience confirms that our true Self is no-self, our true nature is no-nature. We are completely free.

17

Working with a Teacher

> A teacher never loses sight of our true Self. And because the teacher is not deceived by the ego, nor fazed in the least by its manipulations and selfishness, we find the courage to be curious, to wonder what lies beneath our facade.

ZEN HAS a reputation of being a challenging path. Knowing this, some of us are drawn to the practice out of curiosity or to test our mettle. Even so, when we actually are tested by the rigors of Zen, we may find ourselves unprepared. My first experience with Zen was nearly the last. If not for a few words from the man who would become my teacher, I wouldn't be here today. Before attending my first sesshin, I had read some works by D. T. Suzuki and Alan Watts, and I thought I knew what Zen was. But it was that weeklong sesshin in the spring of 1972 that really introduced me to Zen practice. Koryu Roshi was leading the sesshin, and Maezumi Roshi was assisting. On the morning of the third day, I went to Maezumi Roshi and said I would be leaving. He asked me why and I gave him an answer, but now I can see that I wasn't being completely honest with him or myself. The real reason was that the sesshin was so damn difficult. I was experiencing a lot of physical pain, especially in my legs. But the psychological pain was even harder to bear.

Sesshins are intensive training retreats that emphasize zazen and often include eight or more hours of sitting each day. They also include periods where mindfulness is practiced in some form of work. I was assigned to help Maezumi Roshi build a rock garden in the backyard of the zendo. My athletic training set me up for the job of moving big boulders wherever he wanted them, and that meant placing them "just so." The problem was, I had done some reading and I already knew what it meant to place things "just so": after raking up the leaves, you shake the tree so some leaves can fall naturally into place. But Maezumi Roshi had his own ideas, and I was becoming very irritated. This guy was tying up a lot of my time in order to place the boulders "just so."

Moving those stupid rocks around was just one thing bugging me about the sesshin. Another problem was the ritual. It seemed as if every time I turned around, we were making bows, first to the altar, then to the cushion, then to the teacher. My family was Jewish, and I learned at least one thing from that tradition: don't worship idols! But that is exactly what all the bowing looked like to me. Bowing wasn't supposed to be part of Zen training anyway—at least in my mind. D. T. Suzuki was emphatic about such matters, and he said that Zen has no ritual or idol worshiping. I was too green to know about the different forms of Zen training. I didn't realize that D. T. Suzuki came from a strictly Rinzai background. I just happened to be attending a sesshin in the Soto tradition. But I was twenty-six, and I had just spent a year reading and meditating in the mountains. I knew what Zen was supposed to look like.

When Maezumi Roshi asked why I was leaving, I told him that what they were practicing wasn't Zen. Suddenly boiling, he shouted, "What is Zen?" It seemed like the perfect opportunity to show what I knew. I thrust the trowel that was in my hand into the ground, "Just this!" He replied, "Your Zen eye is only partially open." That first cut went deep, but he wasn't finished. "Where have you studied?" "Nowhere, I have no teacher." I went on to tell him about the books by D. T. Suzuki and Alan Watts that I had been reading. Maezumi Roshi didn't miss the opening, "Alan Watts? He's not Zen!" The ground I had been standing on vaporized, and I had nothing to say. I was caught off guard, completely unprepared for his final blow: "I don't want you to go." He looked me in the eyes and repeated it:

"I don't want you to go." It felt as if my heart were in his hands and he was squeezing it. A third time: "I don't want you to go." His honesty and vulnerability cut through me, and I stayed.

I'm sharing this story because it is typical of first meetings with a teacher. We come to a teacher with a lot of ideas about how we should relate and what we can expect to receive. Yet we can't really meet the teacher until those ideas have been cut to shreds and our hearts and minds lie exposed and vulnerable. In the beginning we fear this exposure and what might be revealed. But something inside tells us that this is exactly what we want to occur. We go to a teacher in order to be seen through. The self has become too heavy to carry any longer; it has become our prison. We hope the teacher can help us cut through the bull to find what is real.

It's scary to begin working with a teacher, but when suffering becomes great enough, we find the courage to push beyond fear. I want the cure, so I accept the treatment. That openness allows the teacher to begin to reveal how attached we have become to this notion of self. Our lives have revolved around this "me," building up an identity and then maintaining it; and definitely we will not let it go unless we see for ourselves that it is the cause of our suffering. So the teacher becomes a mirror that reflects how much we cling to the self. Self has become an obsession; everything we do centers on *me*, *my*, and *mine*. Even when we try to be altruistic, in the back of our minds we want to know what we will get out of it. The deluded small mind can't operate in any other way because it always feels insufficient. The wanting simply won't go away.

Looking for something to make the small self feel whole has been our problem from the beginning. Ego tries to fill itself up by growing bigger and more solid; it lays claim to new skills, knowledge, and possessions. But ego is insatiable; it can never acquire enough to feel complete. The only way out of this trap is to transcend the small mind and look at it from the perspective of our true Self, Buddha Mind. From there we can see how the ego operates and just how much suffering it causes. We sit in zazen so that we can step back from the ego and view it without attachment. We learn how to witness thoughts, emotions, and sensations as they arise, without having the ego involved. When the ego isn't involved, we have no need to judge what goes through our mind. Buddha Mind knows no preferences, so we can simply be with what is.

Over time our identification with the ego starts to fade, and we become more identified with our true nature, this Heart-Mind. Preferences and judgments continue to pop up during zazen, but after we have seen that ego is not our true Self, the delusions of ego become less compelling. And there's no need to form a preference for no preferences; when they come up, we can simply notice what is happening: "Ah, judging again," or "I don't like that, but so what?" Buddha Mind is free from the influences of the ego. We don't need to figure out how to get the boat out of the bottle; we only need to see that there never was a bottle to begin with. That is instantaneous awakening. Walls that appear solid one moment can dissolve in the next moment because they are only aspects of the apparent reality, the realm of the ego. Beyond appearances lies no-self, our boundless Buddha Mind. Our true Self has always been free.

Our deepest longing is to reveal what is true, but that is also our biggest fear. We don't really know who we are, and we are afraid of what might be lurking inside. Who am I if I am not this easygoing, happy-go-lucky person that I try to be? A teacher can help us in our search because he or she never loses sight of our true Self. The teacher is not deceived by the faces of the ego, or fazed in the least by its manipulations and selfishness. And because the teacher is not repulsed or afraid, we find the courage to be curious, to wonder what lies beneath our facade. Smelly things may lurk inside; after all, we have spent years trying to control and hide away our ugly aspects—our selfishness, ignorance, and hatred. We don't want to look at them, and we certainly don't want to show them to others, but that is what the teacher asks us to do. It's the only way to come to terms with who we really are. We must see through the illusion of self in order to discover our true nature. Because the teacher already sees the truth, he or she can help us reveal the truth to ourselves.

Zazen is where we begin to see through the illusion. We quiet the mind and find the courage to look at what is really going on. Slowly we tackle the fear that has blocked us from revealing the truth to ourselves. The teacher is not shocked when we uncover ugliness, because it is no different from his or her own ugliness. Everyone is in the same boat. You and I are just as self-centered as anyone else, so who can be looked down on or up to? Trying to deceive one another is ridiculous; we are all motivated by self-interest. When we can get past our discomfort and admit that, it's a big relief. We can let go of our delusion—the self that we created and then took as real. There is no self! There is absolutely nothing solid to hold on to or claim. Our task is to look beyond the illusion, to our true essence. The teacher's job is to always point to the deeper truth, our Buddha nature.

To belong to a sangha, a community of Buddhist practitioners, can add tremendous depth to our practice because it provides opportunities to come together and practice being who we truly are. We can create a context in which it is OK to drop our facades and defenses and reveal our garbage to ourselves and to one another. We practice together so that we can discover who we really are and then live it. If the small mind tries to assert itself through opinions, judgments, shame, and pride, we can remind one another to return to Buddha Mind, our true nature, which is big enough to embrace it all. By supporting one another in this way, we become fearless.

Some Zen centers offer the opportunity to work with a teacher on koans. Koans have a way of bringing forward aspects of the small self that otherwise might remain hidden. We all have blind spots and hang-ups, but we won't know how much they burden and inhibit us until we experience freedom from them. Koans are especially helpful in teaching how to break through our fears of making mistakes and looking foolish. They give us practice in reclaiming control from the ego and in expressing the freedom that is our true nature.

The moment we shift from resistance to willingness to face our garbage, we become bigger than it. Our capacity to witness becomes larger than our fears. We experience our greatest capacity to witness when we sit in zazen, and there we can cultivate the equanimity that will sustain us through difficult times. The posture of zazen imparts great strength because it allows us to tap a special kind of energy, joriki, the power of samadhi. In zazen, we develop trust in our capacity to face anything, even our own deaths.

Difficult times are actually some of the best times to practice zazen. Rather than ignoring or suppressing what is troubling us, we can witness suffering as an aspect of the small mind. Moving beyond our resistance, we can take refuge in our own Buddha Mind, thereby becoming less fearful and more self-reliant. Our confidence grows because we learn that we can always return home to our true nature. Buddha Mind is right here! Breaking free of the world of delusion, we become masters of our selves.

18

Just One Mind

> In the realization of Mind, we leap beyond all duality. There is no you or me, this or that, affirmation or negation. There is just One Mind.

KOANS are like can openers for the mind. Our minds are stuck in duality, and koans pry them open to a new way of seeing the world. I would like to share a few koans with you as a way to explore how they work.

The word *koan* usually refers to a problem, a question, or a dialogue that cannot be resolved with the rational mind. In order to resolve a koan, we have to leap beyond the dualistic logic that we typically use to solve problems. Life presents us with numberless naturally occurring koans, yet within our tradition of Zen, about seventeen hundred koans are officially recognized. We study koans not because the dualistic perspective is somehow wrong but because it is limiting to have only that perspective. From the dualistic viewpoint, there is always more than one; there is you and me, this and that, self and other.

Our dualistic, rational mind can take us quite far in appreciating certain aspects of life, reality, philosophy, and so forth. But as the Buddha discovered when he attained enlightenment, the dualistic view is only one side of reality. Obviously the other side of reality would be nondualistic, and it would rely on a nondualistic view or understanding. According to Western thought, if an understanding is not dualistic, it can't be logical. The great minds of the East, however, have long known that there is another logic that stems from a nondualistic perspective. This so-called Buddhist logic relies on the enlightened view: everything is really One Mind.

Siddhartha Gautama was troubled by the suffering of the world. He wanted to find the root cause of suffering so that we might learn to free ourselves from it. After searching for many years and practicing various yogic disciplines, he realized that those methods could take him only so far. He remained stuck in duality, unable to break through. Intuition guided him to sit still and focus his mind inward. So he threw away the other practices and directed all of his energy into looking into his own mind. It worked! He broke free of the dualistic mind. That's what koans can help you and me to do. Koans are devices that teach us how to access the nondualistic view. They spark openings to the enlightened mind.

The first koan I would like to share is simple, and it gets right to the point. The koan is: How do you hide yourself in a pillar? When you are given this or any koan, you first have to sit with it; and in this case, you would need to begin by imagining a pillar. Next, you explore the pillar and come to know its nature intimately. The process is similar to that shown in the *Ten Ox-Herding Pictures*. First, we see the tracks, then we get a glimpse of the ox. If we are going to be able to capture the ox, we must draw closer and closer to it. As we get closer, our perceptions become clearer; we may even begin to smell the ox. The same thing happens with the pillar. As you get closer, your perceptions get clearer and more distinct. Suddenly you disappear; only the pillar remains.

We will come back to this koan a little later. For now, let's look at another koan. An Indian yogi, famous for his occult powers, traveled from India to meet a Chinese Zen master. The master wanted to test the abilities of his guest—Zen masters are always looking for the gold—so he asked the yogi to read his mind and try to figure out what places he was visualizing. The yogi agreed. The Zen master said, "OK, where am I now?" The yogi replied, "What is your reverence doing walking by the Tenshin Bridge?" "Right! OK, where am I now?" "What is your reverence doing watching a monkey show at the Seisen

River?" "Excellent! Where am I now?" The yogi couldn't find the master anywhere. The koan asks: Where is this no-place where the master was? You see, the Zen master had a few occult powers of his own. Just through basic practice in Zen, he became one with the yogi.

To *be one* is the whole point of Zen practice. Each koan presents the opportunity to be one with that koan; and because this seems impossible to the rational, dualistic mind, we are pushed in a new direction, toward the nondualistic mind. Perhaps you're wondering, "What good is the ability to be one? Maybe it would make a neat party trick, but does it really help someone in life?" To answer this question, let's look at another koan, one based on a dialogue between a monk and Zen Master Baso.

The monk asked, "What is Buddha?" Of course, the monk knew who the literal Buddha was, so he was asking about the experience of Buddha or buddhahood. Baso gave a straightforward answer: "Mind is Buddha!"—a koan to help the monk realize the answer for himself. That koan can work for us, too. You begin by asking yourself, "What did Baso mean, 'Mind is Buddha'?" We may have our doubts about this: "Definitely *my* mind is not Buddha!" Yet what else can we do but use this ordinary mind to look into the koan? Shakyamuni Buddha had to use his ordinary mind to look inward and discover the liberation from suffering. Just like you and me, he had only this very ordinary flashlight.

If you want to discover what Mind is, it only makes sense to ask the question "What is Mind?" In *Genjokoan*, Dogen Zenji wrote, "With your own mind, turn your light inward." Zen Master Bassui said that looking into the mind is the first step toward realization. Go ahead and ask a few more good questions while you're at it: How big is my mind? What shape does it have? What color is it? Get closer and closer to your mind until you can no longer find it. In that moment you become Mind. You can't find *your* mind, only One Mind.

This Mind is the same nondualistic Mind discovered by the Buddha. In the realization of Mind, we leap beyond all duality. We don't find you or me, this or that, affirmation or negation. There is just One Mind, Buddha Mind, appearing at all times, in all places, and in all forms, including you and me. There are no exceptions. Everything is a manifestation of One Mind. Koans help us open up so that we can experience this Mind. Then they help us clarify and confirm our realization. Koan practice is very simple in a way because every koan is about this Mind. Yet because the pull of dualistic thinking is so strong, we revert back to dualistic thinking almost automatically, koan after koan. In order to present and "pass" a koan, we must, for a few moments at least, let go of the dualistic mind.

Basically, the same process can be used to work with each of the koans we have been exploring here. When you get very close and intimate with the pillar, you disappear because you are the pillar. If you were working with the *Ten Ox-Herding Pictures* as koans, you would need to become the ox in the same way. And when you look deeply into your mind, mind disappears because you are Mind. But I must caution you: when it comes to the ego, beware! We always have a hard time seeing our own ego, and we may begin to hope or believe that we have become egoless. In fact, that belief is just a trap—a very deep trap. Instead of attaining buddhahood, we have attained egohood! It is much wiser to keep our ego out in the open where we can observe it. Watch it and stay awake!

A hazard of koan practice is to believe that the point is to pass many koans. But passing a koan isn't worth much if you can't apply that realization to your life. To know how to *be one* is a tremendous gift when we put it to practice in our daily lives. Imagine what it would be like to become one mind with someone you love: you would be able to see through his or her eyes, and that person would be able to see through yours. Amazing things would happen if you could extend that oneness to your family, friends, and coworkers. Luckily we don't need a koan in order to work on that skill. Working on our ability to listen is enough.

Listening is the first skill taught to new Zen students—not just how to listen with our ears but how to listen with our whole being. Harada Roshi and Yasutani Roshi stressed listening in their teaching. Instead of giving talks in the traditional way—with students sitting in zazen and facing the walls—they had everyone turn around and face the speaker.

Here's another trick that can help us learn to listen with total attention. Whenever we are part of a group listening to a talk, there is an unconscious tendency to divide the responsibility of hearing among everyone present. I fall into this trap whenever I am with my wife, Stephanie, and somebody tells us their phone number. I don't even hear it because I've come to rely on her amazing ability to recall phone numbers. When we are part of an audience, we can avoid this laziness by imagining that we and the speaker are the only two present. Then we feel 100 percent responsible for receiving the information.

Listening to the sounds while sitting in zazen is a wonderful form of meditation and a great way to practice listening. In a way we could say that Buddha's teaching always comes back to the practice of complete listening. When we sit in zazen, we open ourselves to whatever is going on. We practice listening and receiving with our whole being. When our mind is so open that thoughts, sounds, and other perceptions can just come and go without interference, the illusion of separation dissolves: the one who is listening and the sounds become one. This is the point at which koan practice and shikantaza become indistinguishable. Master Bassui knew this, and so he used listening as a koan. First, he tells us to look into our minds and ask, "What is this mind?" Then he encourages us to question further: "What hears the sounds?" By going deeply into that question, we move closer and closer to the sounds. Suddenly the listener disappears. Only sound remains.

In zazen, whether we are working on a koan or listening to the sounds, we can have the same experience: our small mind disappears and we awaken to One Mind. By realizing this One Mind, we discover the liberation that Buddha found. There is no separation, no mind, no one doing zazen. The illusion of separation has dissolved.

Bodhidharma is famous for bringing the Dharma from India to China. Maybe you have heard the story of how the emperor of China received him. As the most powerful man in China, the emperor rarely bothered to listen to anyone. Yet he had asked one of his priests for an appropriate question to ask the great Bodhidharma, and he felt prepared. When Bodhidharma arrived, the emperor asked, "What is the supreme meaning of the sacred Dharma?" Bodhidharma's answer was clear and direct—but the emperor couldn't hear it. "Vast emptiness, nothing holy." The emperor thought, "This guy must be an imposter! Certainly the great patriarch of India wouldn't give such an answer." He demanded, "Who is this standing before me?" At the time when this story took place, Bodhidharma was a very old man, and he had been practicing since childhood. His answer came directly from his realization: "I know not." Again, the emperor missed the teaching entirely. He sent Bodhidharma away!

Bodhidharma could see that the time was not ripe for transmitting the Dharma in China, so he found a cave where he could practice zazen. Nine years passed before the student who would become his successor finally arrived. That story gives us one of the most famous koans. Eka was a scholar of Taoism, Confucianism, and Buddhism; but after many years of study, he realized that the problem remained: his mind was not at peace. To find the old master in the mountains of China must have been tough. After finally reaching the cave, Eka cried, "My mind is not at peace. Please, master, I beg you, give it peace!" Bodhidharma replied, "Show me this mind!"

What a strange thing to say! Eka must have gone away scratching his head. Still, he was desperate enough to try to look for his mind—and that is exactly what Bodhidharma wanted Eka to do. It was a great trick, a skillful means. Eka went out into the snow and meditated for ten days and nights, "How do I show this man my mind? What is it? Where is it?" He went back finally and said, "I have searched everywhere for my mind. At last I realize it is ungraspable." Bodhidharma answered, "Then I have put your mind to rest!"

Bodhidharma and Master Bassui were great teachers, and they were able to convey the Buddha's teaching in just a few words. The story of Eka and Bodhidharma holds profound wisdom for us, too. We often look at life as just one problem after another, each one demanding its own resolution. Bodhidharma encourages us to focus instead on the source of our problems. What is this mind? Go to the root instead of playing around with the leaves and branches! When you look into the mind to discover the mind, you are already almost there. With sincere effort and the willingness to keep looking, you will finally see, beyond any doubt: this Mind is truly ungraspable.

Unless we thoroughly realize the ungraspable nature of Mind, doubt will keep coming back. Zen uses the analogy of being stranded on an island: before we can feel safe enough to rest, we have to search the island for dangerous animals and headhunters. Until we search behind every tree, on every shore, and in every cave, doubt will keep coming back. Our search has to be exhaustive; no stone can be left unturned. Eka searched everywhere until all traces of doubt were gone: he would *never* grasp the mind.

Mind is completely ungraspable. If we find something that can be grasped, it's not Mind but rather one of the infinite manifestations of Mind. By seeing through the manifestations of apparent reality to the Truth that is all things, the mind can find peace. Our restless searching for something to hold on to can be given up. Koans push us to search the entire island until no doubt remains. Rest comes when we know deep in our bones, there is no self or other, no inside or outside, no this or that. Just One Mind.

19

Staying in Tune

Boredom is a natural part of practice, but it can also be a warning that our sitting has become too routine and mechanical.

SOME ACTIVITIES we do purely for the pleasure they bring. We may forget that in the beginning they weren't pleasurable at all. Learning complex skills can be demanding; but after an initial investment of time and effort, we can relax and enjoy performing these skills with ease. Driving a car, cooking a meal, playing an instrument, and many athletic skills are like that; after we've attained a certain level of mastery, we can perform them almost automatically. Zazen is different. Zazen is quite simple and easy to learn, but it never can be mastered in a way that allows complacency. By its very nature, zazen is dynamic. It brings our attention to the present, where we must reckon with forces of constant change. The events and environment around us are always in flux, and so are our minds and bodies. So when we sit in zazen, we are always brought face-to-face with the truth of impermanence.

When the Buddha was asked about zazen, he likened it to playing a sitar. Sitars are notorious for going out of tune. Even the greatest sitar player can't simply sit back and play but must remain alert and ready to make fine tuning adjustments at any time. Sitars have many strings, and the tension of each string must be perfect, neither too tight nor too loose, for the sound to be harmonious. We find ourselves in a similar situation when it comes to zazen; we must continually tune the mind and body so that they work together in harmony. The mind needs to be held in a state of concentration that is focused and yet fluid, and the body needs to be held in balance so that the spine is erect but not tense.

We can use a simple movement at the beginning of each sitting to find that point of balance with our spines. The ancient Chinese knew about this movement and incorporated it into the martial art of taiji, but I learned it from a doctor when I was having back problems a few years ago. You start off with the lower part of the spine and gently sway side to side. Let your movement be sinuous like a snake, not rigid like a pendulum. Continue to sway while slowly moving the center of the swaying up your spine to the base of your head. In essence, this movement restacks one vertebra on top of the other so that they come to rest in proper alignment.

After reaching the top of the spine, you can turn your attention to the particular zazen practice you are working on, whether it is counting or following your breaths, a koan, or shikantaza. But don't forget about your posture altogether. Periodically, as you sit in zazen, bring your attention back to your posture to see if your spine has shifted out of alignment. Sitting should never become static but should always be a process of refinement. Just like a sitar, we are always going out of balance; and to sit well, we need to continually refine our posture.

The correct posture is a tremendous advantage in the practice of zazen; it gives our body the stability we need to sit for long periods of time with very little effort. But it is much more than that. The posture of zazen is itself a mudra. Mudras have both symbolic and esoteric significance and they help us connect with the inner states that they represent symbolically. In Zen we hold our hands in a circle, the cosmic mudra, in order to help us realize our true nature, our oneness with all things. The zazen posture has been called *mahamudra*, the "great mudra," because it embodies Buddha Mind.

Maezumi Roshi often talked about the "perfect" posture of zazen. The *perfect* that he was referring to comes from the Sanskrit word *samyak*. *Samyak* implies several meanings, including "true," "supreme," and "perfect." When the Buddha spoke about the Path to liberation, he used the word *samyak*. Thus, the disciplines of right view and right understanding are really samyak-view and samyak-understanding, meaning "supremely right and true." But *samyak* also means "sameness" or "oneness." So right understanding is to be one with what you are trying to understand or perceive, and perfect posture is to be one with your posture and with this existence. Whenever Maezumi Roshi was asked, "What is the point of practice?" he always replied, "To accomplish *anuttara-samyaksambodhi!*"—in other words, to accomplish the "supreme and perfect way of wisdom," to actualize Buddha Mind. We can begin to realize that supreme wisdom in zazen, when body and mind rest in perfect balance and stillness.

Zazen is not at all entertaining. The simplicity of zazen allows us to learn its fundamentals early on, especially the fundamentals of posture and breathing; and over time in our practice, we will inevitably go through periods of boredom. Boredom is a natural part of practice, but it can also be a warning that our sitting has become too routine and mechanical. The more we do any one activity, the greater the risk of shifting to automatic pilot, where habits and routine take over and our mind becomes disengaged from what we are doing. It's ironic, really. We practice zazen to become more alive and present in each moment; and yet if we grow complacent, our sitting can become dead and lifeless. For zazen to remain a vibrant and energizing aspect of our lives, we need to continually renew our practice. In that sense zazen is really not different from other lifelong activities such as work, family life, and staying fit. Stagnation and burnout can creep in when there is no movement or growth.

Surprisingly boredom is often a side effect of accomplishment; it could even be called a by-product of realization. To explain this, let me digress for a moment to the very beginning of practice. Curiosity is one of the basic motivators that brings us to Zen. Perhaps something we heard started us wondering what Zen is all about. Maybe we wanted to find out what sitting could do for us. Some of us came to Zen searching for answers to big questions: What is life all about? Who am I? Why am I here? Curiosity, the opposite of boredom, gives us a desire to explore, a passion to discover something. Yet in zazen practice we eventually realize that desire is the problem, even when the thing we seek is noble and grand—realization, enlightenment, freedom, truth. Craving anything keeps us on the wheel of samsara. After seeing this truth, we are able to put aside our seeking for a while and just sit in zazen. We may get a little bored, but at least we're not suffering. Yet until we realize beyond a shadow of a doubt that there really is nothing to seek and nothing to gain, our curiosity and seeking will rekindle again and again—and along with them our passion for practice.

Each of us will go through dry spells if we continue in meditation practice for any length of time. Still, as I mentioned before, boredom can be an even bigger obstacle *after* realization—when we have clearly seen that there is nothing to grasp. Then the desire to gain something—anything at all—is no longer available to help fuel our practice. Nevertheless, boredom is the window that we have to go through if we want to get to the bottom of our seeking. Even in the midst of boredom, we need to realize that there is absolutely nothing to be grasped. Hearing me say that and experiencing it for yourself are worlds apart. Understanding this realization conceptually doesn't come close to feeling it in your bones.

With enough time in this practice, each one of us will have a number of realization experiences. Regardless of the depth or extent, each realization brings the danger of getting stuck. We might mistake the realization for the end point of practice and stop practicing. Even a shallow experience of our intrinsic wholeness—of no need to seek anything—can become a trap if we cling to it.

When I was living and practicing at the Zen Center of Los Angeles, there was a group of university students who came to Maezumi Roshi to work on the koan *Joshu's "Mu."* They worked very hard until they passed Mu, and then they left. I wondered what was going on and asked one of the students about it. They were all students of a particular professor who had sent them to Maezumi Roshi just to pass Mu. Apparently they believed passing Mu marked the completion of Zen training. Incredible! Passing Mu is just the beginning! Mu is your first glimpse, your first opening into what practice is all about. Up to that point your practice is based on trust, almost a blind faith in zazen. With that glimpse you receive a confirmation of sorts. For the first time you can say from your own experience, "Aha. This is what it's all about!" A glimpse can leave you feeling as if you've won a race, but it's really only the first lap.

No matter how wonderful something is, when we can't let go of it, it will eventually become stale and lifeless. Zen practice is about living life fully, being one with life—and that means letting go moment by moment. As long as we hold something in our grasp, we can't be open and receptive to what appears in the next moment. Although we may understand that, we often continue to cling. Why? We want to feel comfortable and safe, and when something is familiar, we feel more at ease. Our tendency to cling can be extended to just about everything, including our ideas, experiences, and realizations. We can cling to things long after they have dried up and started to rot.

If we want to keep our zazen alive, we need to watch for sticking places. When we find them, we can practice letting go. You see, it takes courage and integrity to keep going with this practice. We can easily think we're not stuck when in fact we are. We may be feeling quite satisfied or even a little smug with ourselves and what we are accomplishing in practice when actually we are only trying to hold on to an experience or a realization. The people around us are often aware of this problem long before we are. The odor can be quite obvious. Eventually we will trip over the karma we've been creating with our clinging. A lot of problems can be avoided by making a habit of asking ourselves, "Where am I stuck?" If we're feeling really brave, we might even ask our loved ones or our teacher to tell us what they see.

We manage to get stuck in places we'd least expect, including our reasons for taking up a meditation practice. Those reasons can easily become something we strive after and try to attain, like a trophy. Many of us were drawn to meditation because we wanted to gain some understanding about life and ourselves. Zazen *does* bring about understanding—but not the kind of understanding that can be held on to. The understanding we gain through zazen is *right understanding*, like the Buddha talked about in the Eightfold Path to liberation. Remember, that *right* comes from the Sanskrit word *samyak*, which means "to be one." The only way we can experience true understanding—being one with—is to let go of everything. By letting go of our desire to understand, we can open ourselves to Oneness, the absolute unity of all things. We may have practiced for many years and had many realizations, but we still need to drop it all.

In a way, Zen practice is never mastered. Instead, we practice becoming more fluid, never settling anywhere. We will go through times when we feel the need to search for something and times when we discover a fresh understanding or insight. Regardless of what we've discovered, we almost inevitably turn it into a concept, something to hold on to and cherish. So when boredom comes up in our practice, it can be a gift. We can use it to wake up and see where we've become stagnant and disconnected from life. Buddha saw that the tendency to cling is the cause of suffering, *duhkha*, which literally refers to a wheel that won't turn. Our practice is to recognize when we have become stuck and then to choose to let go. By allowing the wheel to turn freely, we come back into harmony with life.

Dogen Zenji described Zen as continuous practice. When zazen has become a regular part of our life, we learn for ourselves that practice is a never-ending process of refinement and staying in tune. Practice is actually an ongoing refinement of who we are. Through zazen we first become familiar with our many aspects. Then gradually we learn to bring balance to all the dimensions of our being—body, mind, and spirit. The self that we begin to recognize as our true Self is unfixed. We can have many glimpses into this great mystery, but we will never come to know it. Our life becomes an adventure when it is fed by the limitless Source of our true nature.

PART THREE

RETURNING HOME

REALIZATION

Realizing the Truth always comes as a surprise. We discover our true nature, our Buddha nature, and realize it has been with us all along. Buddha nature has always been our real home, but somehow we have forgotten. Over time we have replaced our true Self with a concept, notions of who we are based on our conditioning. Zazen helps us to slowly strip away these notions so that the inner Truth begins to shine through. At first we catch only brief glimpses of our true nature. But as we continue in our meditation practice, our faith in what we have realized deepens. The realization of our true nature as no-nature becomes clearer, and we begin to carry that awareness into our daily life.

20

Returning Home

> Our deepest longing is to return home, to go back to our original nature.

YOU ARE BORN with the unborn Buddha Mind. It is your birthright, intrinsic to your very nature. Everything that exists is a manifestation of this Mind. Not everyone realizes that their life is an expression of the Unborn, but each one of us is trying to experience that natural state of mind. We are on our way back home.

The unborn Buddha Mind has been called by many different names—Buddha nature, true Self, true nature, the absolute, Source—but no name can ever reach it or describe it. All names fall short. However, when you experience It, you feel a sense of recognition. We left home earlier than we can remember, and over time the experiences of life have led us far away. Years may pass before we realize that we are lost.

The good news is, there are many ways to return home. In the Zen tradition alone, we have many ways. Zen students commonly learn meditation practices such as focusing on the breath or a koan; some learn the practice of shikantaza. All of these methods teach how to focus and concentrate your mind. Counting the breath is one of the easiest meditation forms to learn, so many people begin with this practice. The amazing and truly wonderful thing is, even though learning this method is quite easy, you can go the whole distance and return home simply by counting your breaths. So in this important way, there is no difference between practices that we call beginning or advanced. But different forms of meditation do require different degrees of concentration, so there are various levels of difficulty. As you gain experience with the various meditation practices, you begin to see that they share the same essence: they are tools to experience becoming "one with"—one with the breath, the koan, or just sitting. Being *one with* is the key to returning home.

When you become one with each breath, you suddenly realize that you have already returned home. At first it may last only a moment, but for that moment you recognize your true nature, the Unborn. You are One; there is no gap between you and your breath. The dichotomy of subject and object has disappeared, so there is no longer anywhere to go or anywhere to arrive. There is no coming or going. You are home.

Our deepest longing is to return home, to go back to our original nature. But that longing can become buried by other desires, hopes, and dreams. Through meditation we learn how to trim down our wish list, but this process takes time. As desires for the things of this world drop away, we begin to see that they never could satisfy our basic hunger, the desire to realize this Buddha Mind.

Meditation practice leads one to a strange and amazing discovery: you are and always have been the unborn Buddha Mind. And when you look from the perspective of that Mind, you experience the highest truth possible, the absolute reality. You realize that mind is nothing but the unborn Buddha Mind. There is nothing to seek, nothing to gain. But to know this in an intellectual way is not enough. Contentment will come only when we *experience* our wholeness, and that means that each one of us must realize the truth directly. If I told you that you are complete and whole and you simply accepted this, you would never realize for yourself your intrinsic completeness. One's own poverty can't be relieved by counting a treasure that belongs to another.

In the experience of nonduality, we see with our own eyes that all opposites are one. We may call it Mind or no-mind, Self or no-self, Dharma or enlightenment, but the experience is always the same. This is the only truth to teach, so after hearing about the same thing for many years, we can become a little sleepy and inattentive. One way to spark new insights is to play with various opposites and notice where we get stuck.

There are opposites of male and female, life and death, nirvana and samsara, and many more. Maybe we haven't yet experienced the oneness of those dualities, though we can accept on faith that in truth they are one. But when it comes to the opposites that are most familiar to us, the ones that we experience every day, that's when we run into the most difficulty. Take stupidity and intelligence, for example. We all know that they are not the same, right? There is intelligence, and then there is stupidity. How could they possibly be one? Any duality that appears to be obvious and true can be used to play this game with yourself. Flip the duality, or turn the table: in this case, consider and explore how stupidity *is* intelligence, and intelligence *is* stupidity. Then apply this new insight to yourself. Now, that doesn't sit so well, especially if we view ourselves as intelligent.

Actually we stupid ones are the intelligent ones, and the so-called intelligent ones are really stupid. When I point out how true this is, some students start looking for bricks to throw. It is strange that we can accept what Dogen Zenji tells us—that samsara is nirvana and nirvana is samsara, and that Buddha is a sentient being and a sentient being is Buddha—and still have a hard time accepting that intelligence is stupidity. Why is this so hard? The difference seems to hinge on what we can identify with. When we consider familiar dualities such as active and lazy, smart and stupid, the opposites are something that we can relate to. Most of us are personally identified with our intelligence, but not with being enlightened or deluded. From childhood on, society teaches that intelligence is a valuable and basically fixed personal characteristic; we work hard to bury our stupidity.

To accomplish in Zen practice, we have to become rather stupid. Why would an intelligent person sit counting his breath seven hours a day? After practicing for some time, many of us do such things without question because we have already met this requirement. Still, we like to hold on to the illusion that we are basically intelligent. It's hard to let go of that illusion because we've invested so much in our intelligence. To drop it all, you have to believe that there is absolutely nothing to lose. And that's true—there really is *nothing* to lose.

When you practice letting go of ideas about who or what you are, the apparent separation between self and others begins to dissolve. Meditation practices are like maps that help you find your way to that nondualistic place. Counting your breaths, working on a koan, and chanting a mantra can all lead you there. But the amazing thing is, just sitting and doing nothing will get you there, too! That's harder to swallow, isn't it? But sitting and doing nothing is what we try to do in the practice of shikantaza. Dogen Zenji said shikantaza is the ultimate meditation. Do you want to know the secret of why this is true? Sitting and doing absolutely nothing *is* there. You don't have to *do* anything because sitting and doing nothing is *already* there or here or It. Shikantaza is the unborn Buddha Mind in manifestation!

Students who are just beginning meditation practice are usually very happy to hear that sitting and doing nothing actually works. It sounds so easy. But in fact, it is very difficult. Try it, even once, and you will see why it is so difficult: things keep coming up in your mind. Thoughts creep in: "This can't be enough. How could I ever realize anything this way?" Or, "Not again! I'm supposed to be meditating, not thinking about work!" And, "I have to stop thinking so much!" All kinds of doubts arise, and they block us from just sitting. To just sit, to just be, is the hardest thing to do because it demands tremendous faith and trust.

Every great Buddhist teacher since Shakyamuni Buddha has taught that there is nothing to do and no place to go. But because our grasping mind wants to have something to grasp, we would rather believe that there is someplace to go and a way to get there. We also want to believe that there are teachers who can lead us to that special place. But all of this is delusion. Manjusri, the bodhisattva of wisdom, wields a sword that cuts through the delusion of duality. Manjusri's sword cuts two into one! If you use your own sword of Manjusri, you will see that there is no place to go, there is nothing to do, there is no way to get there, and there is no one who can lead you there. When you put that sword to use, you realize that you are completely on your own. And as you cut through even more, you will begin to see that there is no enlightenment and there are no enlightened ones. Rather, you will see that the enlightened ones are those who realize there is no enlightenment. Of course, we would like such enlightened ones to lead us there, but no one can lead us to where we already are!

As we continue to look deeper, each one of us discovers the simple truth: we don't want to stand alone. It feels so much more comfortable and secure to try to hold on to someone who we believe can guide us. We even hope they can confirm our attainment and enlightenment. That would be great because then we could cling to an even stronger illusion: "I have arrived!" Instead of settling for what feels comfortable and secure, Zen practice holds a big surprise: when you get there, which really is nowhere, you *know*! You *really* know! Beyond a shadow of a doubt, you know that you have attained nothing. You went nowhere and attained nothing, so why would you need someone to verify that?

To make the discovery, after years of practice, that there never was anything to attain or anywhere to go may sound like a big disappointment, but the experience is liberation. You realize that you had the unborn Buddha Mind all along. Looking back, you can see how deluded you have been: thinking your mind was so small, stuck in duality and concepts, completely selfish and egocentric. Of course, all of that is true, too! The "you" that you think you are has only this small mind. Our true Heart-Mind, the unborn Buddha Mind, manifests this small mind—lots of them, all over the place. You have the same small mind that you had all along, even though you were trying to get rid of it somehow (which is asinine). Without your small mind, you would be hopelessly stuck! We all need to be able to think dualistically. We need to be able to distinguish between intelligence and stupidity.

In this life all of us have it ass-backward or, as Buddha said, topsy-turvy. What we think is reality, actually is not; and what we can't possibly conceive, is reality. What we think of as sanity, is not; and what we fear as insanity, is true sanity. We think that knowing or understanding is the Buddha Way, but the Way is beyond knowing and understanding. We really do have it all upside down, so how can we call ourselves intelligent? True intelligence is not-knowing. When I think that I know something, all I have is a concept.

To live with not-knowing is to live as the unborn Buddha Mind. Then we are free to be anything. Your true identity is no-identity. Your true Self is unfixed; therefore, it can be anything and everything. And it *is* anything and everything. You have the freedom to be small mind, Big Mind, egoless, ego-centered, stupid, intelligent, enlightened, deluded.

My kids say, "Been there, done that," and that phrase describes Zen practice very well. Been there, done that? Then *let it go*! If you are thinking dualistically, let it go. If you are thinking in a nondualistic way, let it go. Then you're free, you see? No matter which one it is, if you cling to one way of thinking, it will become a burden. One way of thinking is not better than the other, and a Buddha is not better than a sentient being. Why have a preference? Sometimes you appear as a Buddha; sometimes you appear as a sentient being. Sometimes you appear as enlightened; sometimes you appear as deluded. You can appear as intelligent or stupid. So what? All of these are manifestations of your unborn Buddha Mind.

People may think that meditation will help them find their so-called true Self, and many people start on a spiritual path for that reason; but this goal really doesn't make sense. Who is it that is looking for the true Self—the false self? If we think meditation will help us find our true Self, certainly we are deluded; the last thing in the world that the false self wants to find is the true Self. Actually it is more likely that the false self, the ego, is using the search as a distraction to avoid finding the Self. Do you think ego wants to evaporate? Of course not! That's why it sends us on all these wild goose chases. We're so gullible, we will keep running around endlessly. Finally we wake up and realize we've been on a detour all along.

What is it that we hope to find? To search for yourself seems pretty silly, doesn't it? In every moment you express yourself exactly as you are. When you sit in zazen, you express yourself. When you walk, you express yourself. When you sleep, you express yourself. You are expressing yourself all day long. It's impossible not to.

In order to discover that there was nothing missing in the first place, it somehow seems necessary for each one of us to embark on the search for the Self; but really, it's just a big detour. Your unborn Buddha Mind is discovered when you are One—just sitting, just breathing, just sweeping the floor. In that moment, there is no one sweeping, no one breathing, no one sitting. You are one with whatever you are doing because you are that to begin with. You were born free, and your very nature is free and unfixed. The unborn Buddha Mind is always manifesting as you.

21

Big Mind

> Big Mind is without size, without limits, and is utterly ungraspable. Big Mind has no beginning and no end, no birth and no death, no boundary and no center. We can verify this for ourselves by simply looking in.

SUFFERING has always been part of life. The Buddha saw that human suffering stems from the perception that something is missing, either within ourselves or in our lives. It doesn't matter whether we're rich or poor, gifted or ordinary, when we believe that we are lacking something, we suffer. We envy people who seem to have what we lack: better jobs, homes, or families; more money, happiness, or intelligence; and on and on. Similarly, resentment and fear come up when we interact with people who have more authority or power. This can happen even with our best friends. If our friends appear to have more peace of mind, more clarity, more of anything at all, we can feel angry and jealous. There seem to be countless reasons for our resentment, fear, and anger. Unless we deal with our underlying sense of insufficiency, these negative emotions tend to fester, leading to chronic unhappiness and stress.

The surprising fact is, we are not born with that kind of suffering. Instead, we are born with the unborn Buddha Mind, what I like to call *Big Mind*,[1] an inner knowing that we are connected with others and our environment—literally, One Mind. When we know that we are one with everything, we do not struggle against what is. But something happens as we grow up: we begin to make distinctions and to separate ourselves from the rest of the world. A concept of "me" begins to form—an identity apart from everyone and everything. Soon this is the only way we see ourselves. It is as if we trade the Big Mind that we were born with for another mind, a mind that centers around the small self. That self then becomes our preoccupation. Our number one concern becomes *me* and *mine*—who I am, what I identify with, and what I possess. Anything not identified with this "me" is a threat and a potential enemy simply because it is outside, apart from me.

We create such separations all the time—and often not rationally. Sometimes we identify with our nation or country, and sometimes we don't. If we strongly identify with our country, we will die for it. If we don't, we may see it as an enemy working against us. If we identify with our family, we will do anything to protect our children, partner, or parents. But if we become disenchanted with our family members, then they become burdens. We even split ourselves from our physical bodies. Sometimes we think of the body as "me," and we go to great lengths to protect and care for it. Other times we see our body as only a source of pain, another problem to struggle against.

The small mind always looks at the world from the center called "me." The arrow points "out there," so everything else appears to be outside. And when I look "out there," I feel rather empty, unimportant, and incomplete "in here." Naturally, wanting arises: I want to feel better, more OK, and complete. Wanting or neediness is the basis of our greed and the endless striving to gain the things that we desire. But gaining all of the material and immaterial treasures of the world will still leave us feeling incomplete and inadequate because they can't fill the hollowness inside. As long as we believe that something outside of ourselves can satisfy our hunger and make us feel whole, we will be driven to grasp at things. Feelings of dissatisfaction and anxiety will haunt us because we have traded Big Mind for a narrow, self-centered mind. This unrest is what the Buddha called *ignorance*. We ignore our intrinsic wholeness.

The point of Zen practice is to return to our original mind, which is One Mind, not divided. When our mind is divided, we have all kinds of conflicts. When our mind is not divided, there simply is no conflict. To find the way back to original mind, various methods have been used over the centuries. One of the methods that we use in Zen originated with Master Bassui. He told his students to look into their own minds and ask the question "What is it that hears the sounds?" To find such an "it" is not really what Bassui was getting at. The point is to look directly into your own mind. Dogen Zenji taught exactly the same thing. He said, "Turn your own light inward!"

An easy exercise can give you a glimpse into the true nature of your mind. Take a few moments to look inside and ask yourself the simple question "How big is this mind?" After really looking in, can you find a size of this mind? Can you find a shape? The only way you can find a size, shape, or color for the mind is to *imagine* what the mind is, and this is how we invent the idea of the self. We create and reinforce the idea of a self continuously—a process that has become so habitual that we don't realize what we are doing. We've been inventing the small self as far back as we can remember and now take it as fact that a boundary exists between this self and everything else.

We imagine many kinds of boundaries to help define this entity called "me." The body appears to be a rather obvious boundary, and it seems only reasonable to think that we end at the surface of our skin. However, some people see auras that extend beyond the body. Where do auras end? And what about your mind? How far does it extend? Does it have any limits? Does your mind include only what you can see, hear, or feel, so that everything lying beyond the reach of your senses is not you?

Another way that we like to define ourselves is by what we know—and these can be the hardest illusions to drop. We find it difficult to identify with something we don't know. For example, consider life itself: we know life as it is, but we don't know death, so how can we personally identify with death? We may think that we only know ourselves as alive, so death seems outside of us, a definite threat to the familiar self. To investigate how death, too, is "me" is something we would rather avoid.

Sometimes people say that they don't fear death itself but rather the suffering that they might experience before dying. But why would we fear that suffering? It's interesting to think about that. When we look inside, we can see that whatever we don't identify with, we fear; and for most of us, suffering is one of our strongest fears. We don't want to identify with suffering, so we resist our own pain. We certainly don't want to be one with our pain! A good friend of mine is a dentist, and daily he sees the tremendous fear of suffering that we all share. The moment his patients hit the chair, they beg him to make the visit "as bearable as possible." We will do almost anything to keep our suffering at bay, to avoid experiencing it fully.

If we are willing to look into ourselves, we can see that anything with which we don't identify ends up causing us more fear and suffering. So why is it so difficult to stop resisting and allow ourselves to experience our pain? Simply because we don't like pain. It hurts! So once again, we trade Big Mind for our separate small mind, which fears pain and suffering. Our whole life can be spent fearing pain and trying to avoid it at all costs. Instead, why not take care of the matter and accept that pain is unavoidable? Why not admit and identify with whatever pain you are feeling now? Be your own pain! Buddha taught that life *is* suffering. John Lennon said that the only thing we've got is our own pain. If pain is unavoidable, why do we try so hard to distance ourselves from it? Fear! We don't have the courage to allow ourselves to experience our pain. It's as simple as that.

History tells us that pain is actually one of the more common catalysts for awakening. Many Zen ancestors attained enlightenment through pain, and it is interesting to look at how that happens. Master Ummon's leg was crushed when his teacher slammed it in the door. At that moment Ummon became one with his pain, and that sparked his realization. When pain becomes so great that it can't be resisted, the separation between pain and self disappears. There is just pain. There is no one experiencing the pain, only pain. And when you're one with pain, there is no fear.

It is easy to go through life fearing the painful things that might happen, but to live in that way is a waste of energy. Dread prevents us from living! To be alive means that we will suffer, so to avoid experiencing suffering is to avoid experiencing life. Only a fool would waste energy trying to resist life, but that's what we do. We can spend a hundred years in hell resisting life rather than surrendering to pain and suffering; no wonder delusion is also called folly or stupidity. When we open ourselves to pain and suffering, we actually experience *less* stress in our lives. Resistance is stressful. If I limit myself to this small ego entity, then the whole world is a threat and I must constantly be on guard. I sit with my back to the wall, afraid to move. To live in resistance to the full spectrum of life condemns us to a tiny, limited existence. We are viewing the whole world from a personal point of view, so of course, we feel very small. How big is a point? In this immense universe with no beginning and no end, a point seems very tiny and insignificant.

When you limit yourself to a point of view, a personal perspective, you will necessarily feel inadequate and threatened. Although you may think that you have an open mind and a broad perspective, you can have only one point of view. Maezumi Roshi used to put it this way: he would hold up his clenched fist and say, "Whatever we hold on to, that's what we've got—only that much!"

By looking inside, anyone can come to know Big Mind. Over time we can use our meditation practice to undermine the egocentric, small self and to open ourselves more completely to our limitless true nature. You can begin this exploration right now. Take a few minutes to look into your own mind and ask, "How big is this mind?" Really look! Don't imagine what you think you should find; look for yourself. What do you discover? Can you grasp the size of your mind? No. It is ungraspable. Can you find a beginning? No. Can you find an end? No. Can you find a birth or a death? No. Anything that you find has been invented by the small mind.

Big Mind is without size, without limits, and is utterly ungraspable. Big Mind has no beginning and no end, no birth and no death, no boundary and no center. We can verify this for ourselves by simply looking in. But even though we begin to see through the illusion of the small self, we can continue to hold on to an even more insidious illusion: the idea of a big "other," something or someone bigger than ourselves. The problem is, this belief implies separation, a "this" and a "that," so it is just another delusion created by our dualistic small mind. To create a "this," a center, you have to set a point; and whether you make it small or big, it's always just a point. It will never encompass the whole.

In meditation we can experience no separation, no duality. Big Mind has no outside and no inside, no point and no center. It is completely beyond our grasp. Even though we experience this incomprehensible Heart-Mind, our separate and frightened small self wants to believe that something or someone bigger than ourselves has everything in control; so we keep looking for God "out there." Yet the moment we even use the name *God*, we create a limitation. In the mystical tradition of Judaism, uttering the name of God is forbidden because God is limitless and no name can possibly fit. To use a name is really just a subtle form of control. The secret known by all the mystics is that God can be found only when we give up our efforts to control.

To try to understand life is also just another attempt by the small self to control life. Such striving is really unnecessary. When we give up our small perspective and come from Big Mind, what is there that we don't know? When we live in the present, in Big Mind, everything is known. But when we try to live in the future or grasp at the past, everything seems unknown and fearful.

When we look inside and let go, we can come from Big Mind and see that life is going perfectly. There is no need to try to control any of it. When we allow everything to just be, it all functions perfectly, exactly the way we want because we give up wanting it to be any other way. The trick is to let go of wanting. When we give up our preconceptions of where the snow should fall and let it fall where it falls, then there is no question about what to do. Grab a shovel! Instead of fighting and resisting, we can simply take care of each situation as it happens. So take a vacation. Put the car in neutral and give up trying to control. Relax and let be. Appreciate how everything is functioning perfectly.

Maybe it is hard to imagine not feeling inadequate or insufficient in some way. But when you see your completeness, striving to attain anything is nonsense. Striving just doesn't come up. So what's left? In the absence of our neediness, what remains is nirvana, peace. If we can accept what happens, even our feelings of grief and pain, then resistance doesn't come up, and things don't feel out of control. From that space we can simply live life, taking care of things as they come up. When the snow falls in the driveway, shovel it up. When the dishes are dirty, wash them.

Our most precious gift and birthright is the One Buddha Mind, but we all fall into ignorance and exchange this Mind for a tiny, self-centered mind. No matter how hard the small mind tries, it can never understand or control this life because in our ignorance we see ourselves as separate and limited. With his enlightened view, Buddha could see the way to end suffering, and he gave us the remedy in his teaching of the Eightfold Path, the fourth noble truth. The first step on the Eightfold Path is *right view*, the enlightened view. When we know Big Mind, we can rise above the small mind and cut through the illusion of separateness.

22

Nothing to Grasp

Regardless of how long we have been practicing or how many realizations we've had, the task is the same: to give up our beliefs.

WHAT IS IT that you really want out of life? It can seem like a simple question until you try to find an answer. Personally, I spent many years in denial before admitting that I really didn't know. Yet when we embark on a spiritual practice, it seems as if we already have some inner wisdom pushing us forward. Then, in the course of our practice, we become clearer about just what it is that we are seeking. Some people say they want to find peace or happiness; others say they seek freedom. Some are looking for a certain kind of spiritual experience. We may use different words—*peace, happiness, freedom, enlightenment*—but what we are all seeking is absolute truth, the Truth that goes beyond conceptual understanding. Rest won't come until we have encountered this Truth for ourselves. We long for the experience of One Mind.

In this tradition we say, "To experience Truth is to experience Zen." Buddha called it nirvana. The first step toward experiencing "It" is to realize that this is our quest. By admitting this, we are also revealing an underlying belief in the possibility of experiencing Truth, nirvana, for ourselves. But to believe in "something" is a form of dualistic thinking. Belief always implies separation, some "one" believing in some "thing." Believing in Buddha, God, or nirvana is not the same as being one with It. So we need to find a way to move beyond belief if we want to have the experience itself.

Most religions are based on the belief that there is something outside of or beyond one's self; and from that perspective it can be quite difficult to think about letting go of our belief. It may seem wrong or even sinful to consider this possibility. But Zen encourages us to give up our beliefs—not because beliefs are somehow wrong or bad but because believing in something and directly experiencing it are entirely different things. Zen teaches us how to become empty and receptive.

We choose the Zen path because we want more than an understanding of Buddha's teaching: we want to experience enlightenment for ourselves. But to have that experience, we first must give up all beliefs and concepts because they separate us from experiencing things directly. This is a frightening process, yet as we continue to practice zazen, we gradually learn how to simply let go into pure faith, which doesn't rely on any beliefs. One of the first things that we learn through zazen is that our ideas about something are not the thing itself. We begin to see how our beliefs and ideas just get in the way of experiencing something directly, so we understand more and more clearly the value of giving up our beliefs and concepts.

Sooner or later the realization flashes: "Concepts are all that I have!" This realization can be very funny and incredibly liberating; and yet, when it comes to personal beliefs, we can still have a very hard time admitting that they, too, are concepts. Beliefs lie close to the heart, close to what we wish to be true. Beliefs are often deeply integrated into our identities, so we can practice for years before seeing what beliefs we hold. Our deepest beliefs are adopted early in life—so early, in fact, most of us can't remember where or when it was that we first picked them up. So it's understandable that fear should come up when we see that in order to experience what we have been searching for, the price will be nothing less than all of our ideas, concepts, opinions, and beliefs. Just the thought of losing them brings up tremendous fear. But really, what is there to fear? Ideas are not solid, substantial, or real. However, they confine us just like chains. We can't see how much we are burdened by our ideas because we've been carrying them around for so long. To let them all go is like setting down a heavy load, and it opens up a freedom that we've never imagined possible.

Even though concepts and beliefs are not real, the fear that comes up seems very real. In fact, it is the fear of death, because letting go of all concepts and beliefs means that we must also let go of our ideas about who we are. Lose those ideas, and we lose the self that we know. What we fear even more, perhaps, is to let go of the belief that there is something "out there" to rely on. Letting go of this belief brings true liberation and freedom: at last we can stop trying to hold on! If there is nothing to grasp, then to continue trying to grasp is ridiculous! This is exactly what Buddha realized. Grasping causes all of our suffering. To stop grasping is nirvana.

We must go beyond a conceptual understanding of Buddha's teaching in order to experience One Mind. According to the dualistic, conceptual mind, we need to work toward stopping our suffering so that we can arrive at nirvana. But that approach is really just another attempt of the mind to gain some kind of understanding or control over what can never be understood or controlled. It is another form of grasping, and it will only lead to more suffering. So how can we relate to our suffering in a nondualistic way? When there is suffering, just suffer. When we are experiencing nirvana, just be nirvana. After all, samsara is nirvana. Problems arise because nirvana feels so much better than suffering. Once you've had a taste of nirvana, you want more. We try to grasp nirvana, and in doing so, we step back onto the wheel of suffering.

The way to break out of this pattern is simple—but not easy. *Stop caring!* Stop having a preference for nirvana and an aversion to suffering. When we stop picking and choosing, we no longer fall into dualistic thinking: we experience One Mind. But to believe that not picking and choosing is nondualistic is itself dualistic thinking. It is an example of how we can solidify an experience into a belief: "Not picking and choosing is liberation." And if we believe this is true, we will struggle to stay in the experience of not picking and choosing. It's so easy to slip back onto the wheel of samsara! We are freed from this trap when we realize that there is no way to be free of it. Only then do we stop trying to attain freedom. When we give up all of our efforts, in that moment we are free! In that moment, there is no experience apart from what is. There is no seeker trying to find something; the two have become one. Nothing exists outside of this One. One Mind embraces everything.

Although suffering is always a part of life, it is possible to discover liberation within our suffering. One Mind has no preferences: it embraces both nirvana and samsara. Therefore, nirvana can be realized within any experience, including suffering. We experience liberation, One Mind, when we stop resisting and become one with suffering. Likewise, when we become one with breathing, that's It. When we become one with sitting, that's It. Become one with sweeping the floor, that's It. Become one with fear, that's It.

Zen is all about having a direct experience of this One Mind. We emphasize the practice of zazen because it is the easiest way to experience being "one with." When we are sitting still, we have the greatest ability to focus our mind. Then the task is simple: be one! One with what? Whatever! If you are angry, be one with your anger. If you are feeling jealous or fearful, that's OK; be jealous or fearful. When doubt comes up, be doubt. Dualistic thinking? Be dualistic. Enlightenment doesn't mean that doubt and dualistic thinking disappear. That would be dualistic.

Regardless of how long we have been practicing or how many realizations we've had, the task is the same: to give up our beliefs. No matter how subtle or sublime, a belief will always be a hindrance, a barrier; so regardless of what it is, we must give up whatever we have become attached to. But don't try to live without attachments. That would be just another kind of attachment, an ideal to strive toward. We practice so that we can live freely. No longer enslaved by fear or clinging, we open ourselves to whatever life holds. There is no greater liberation.

23

To Live in the Moment

When we embrace both faith and doubt, we open ourselves to the unknown. By living this experience from moment to moment, we manifest the unknown, our unfixed Buddha nature.

HAVE YOU ever noticed how difficult it is to live in the present? Instead of being with what is, right here and now, our minds are usually occupied with thoughts about the past or plans for the future. We often miss the moment entirely. When we look into this habit, we can see it for what it is—just another form of grasping. The ego doesn't want to live in the present because in the present there is no ego. The present moment is gone in a flash, so living in the moment requires continuous letting go of what has been and continuous opening up to what will be.

Because we never really know what the next moment will bring, staying aware in the moment can feel like standing on the edge of a cliff. There's bound to be fear. What has already happened is now in the past, and what will be hasn't yet arrived. It's natural to wish we could count on something that we think or hope might happen, but any expectations just create a false sense of security. Something opens up inside when we find the courage to leap into the unknown. We open up to and experience a glimpse of a different reality—the realm of nonduality. When this first happens to us, it's easy to believe that something has been accomplished. We might even tell ourselves, "I've experienced 'It,' and now I can relax!" But we're only fooling ourselves. We've fallen back into the habit of grasping. We are trying to hold on to an understanding instead of living in the moment, in not-knowing. In a way, living in not-knowing *is* a kind of knowing: it is both absolute knowing and absolute not-knowing. The trick is not to form a preference. If we have the slightest preference for either knowing or not-knowing, we fall into grasping and lose touch with the present moment.

Shakyamuni Buddha was sitting under the bodhi tree when he awakened to nondual awareness. In that moment, he saw through the conventional understanding of reality, in which there is either this or that. He realized that Self is really no-self, and no-self is Self. From the nondual view, if there is a Self, there has to be no-self. If there is enlightenment, there has to be no-enlightenment; if nirvana, also no-nirvana. Now, we can easily get caught up in our heads trying to figure out which is true: is this enlightenment or delusion, nirvana or samsara? We can spend years contemplating such questions, but the mind will never grasp nonduality. However, when we *experience* nonduality, it's quicker than instantaneous, and we no longer have any doubts. How can this be? Because you are already awakened; you simply haven't realized it yet. Buddha said it this way: "I and all sentient beings simultaneously attained enlightenment."

There are two ways we can relate to Buddha's declaration: with faith or with doubt—and they are not mutually exclusive. We can practice with faith that we already have Buddha nature. It really doesn't matter whether we've realized it yet or not. Because it is already so, there is nothing to attain. Practice is simply *being* it. This approach is used by many in the Soto school of Zen. But some of us find it difficult to practice with that kind of faith, and we may prefer to doubt and question. In this case practice means facing our doubts and striving to realize it for ourselves. Many in the Rinzai school of Zen emphasize this approach to practice.

With such different approaches to the practice of meditation, it's tempting to ask which way is better, but there is no answer. In our lives every moment is different. Our faith may be strong at certain times, and doubt can arise at other times. Either way, we don't need to make ourselves wrong, wondering why we don't feel more doubt or faith. When we have faith, we can follow that direction. When we have doubt, we can go into that doubt and question everything and everyone.

Faith and doubt are really inseparable; we are born with the unlimited Buddha Mind, and we naturally embrace both sides. But we don't usually live that way. Instead, we pick and choose, favoring one thing over another; and as we go through life, we tend to become more and more narrow. If we try to separate faith from doubt, we create problems for our practice. We may want to embrace only faith, but then we live in fear of losing it and falling into doubt. When faith can be lost to doubt, what good is it? Some of the great mystics have described what it is like to lose *all* faith, and it's a discovery each one of us can make. To lose what we think of as faith is really to lose *belief*—belief in something. And when that happens, instead of falling into confusion and despair, we discover true faith—faith that doesn't depend on anything.

When we embrace both faith and doubt, we open ourselves up to the unknown. By living this experience from moment to moment, we manifest the unknown, our unfixed Buddha nature. Sometimes fear will come up, but instead of suppressing or running away from it, we can learn to surrender and just be with it. Living with our fear of the unknown means admitting our vulnerability: we can't understand this life, and we really can't count on anything. Nothing abides. Anything we grasp is just an idea, a temporary illusion of security, and to attach hopes to it will only lead to more suffering.

Siddhartha Gautama's illusions were shattered when he left his protected life behind palace walls. He was nearly thirty years old when he was first confronted with the harsh realities of life: sickness, old age, and death. This dark side of life shocked and horrified him, but it also drove him to search for the way to end suffering. Maybe because his search was so down-to-earth, Siddhartha was able to break through conventional reality. He wasn't a philosopher trying to answer the unanswerable; he focused on the basics and asked, "How do we go beyond suffering?" He discovered an amazing and simple truth: we suffer because we see things dualistically.

Buddha taught that we can liberate ourselves from suffering by following the Middle Way. We could mistakenly picture this Way as a narrow path, exactly in the center between two extremes. Then practice would become the struggle to walk a straight line between faith and doubt, enlightenment and delusion, right and wrong. What kind of freedom is that? To make such distinctions is the activity of the dualistic mind. Dualistic thinking leads us to desire one thing and to avoid something else, and this is always the root of our suffering.

The Middle Way is the way to liberation, but that doesn't mean we can avoid all suffering. Buddha's teaching goes beyond a dualistic understanding of suffering and liberation. When Buddha tells us that there is a way out, he is also saying there is no way out. He is telling us to embrace everything, the entire mandala. When you can swallow this 100 percent, you're free. When you try to grab hold of it, you will suffer. We suffer whenever we deny one side or the other. The only way to go beyond the extremes is to embrace both sides. So rather than being narrow, the Middle Way is infinitely wide. The Path has no breadth, no shape, and no form. And yet the opposite is also true: the size, shape, and form of the Path are *your* size, *your* shape, and *your* form. You are the Path! So there is really no need to struggle; when we let go moment by moment, the Way opens naturally before us.

24

Sudden Enlightenment

Instant enlightenment sounds almost too good to be true. But if one person did it, it's possible for others to do it, too.

AROUND THE WORLD Buddhism is practiced in many different ways, but the foundation of all the traditions is the same—the realization experience of Shakyamuni Buddha. Zen, however, stands apart from other Buddhist traditions in the degree of emphasis it places on personal realization. Zen teaches that realization is the most direct way to liberate oneself from the world of suffering, and therefore, comparatively less emphasis is placed on religious practices, codes of conduct, and the intellectual understanding of Buddha's teaching. And because zazen is the most direct path to realization, it is the heart of Zen practice.

Many people are drawn to Zen Buddhism because they want to experience what the Buddha experienced. But before long even newcomers can see that Zen practice doesn't end with realization. Instead, Zen is a lifelong practice of deepening one's realization and integrating it into daily life. Even knowing that, most beginners want to know how long it will take to have a first opening or glimpse of Buddha Mind, what we call a *kensho* experience. Of course, there is no simple answer; each person is unique and must walk his or her own path. But we can take heart and remember that the cornerstone of Zen Buddhism is *sudden* realization. Realization happens in an instant.

Zen Buddhism is known as the school of sudden enlightenment. That is our practice and our experience. Still, the Zen school hasn't always been so confident about this matter. Historically there were five major schools of Zen. Two of them died out, and now only three exist; the largest are the Soto and Rinzai schools, and a small remnant of the Obaku school still exists in Japan. Each of these three schools belongs to the larger school of sudden enlightenment.

Early on, only one school of Zen existed in China. In the seventh century, the school split over a debate on the nature of realization. The mother school included teachings of both sudden and gradual realization, but gradual realization was emphasized. It was the sixth ancestor after Bodhidharma, the great Zen master Hui-neng, who shifted the emphasis. In the southern part of China, he founded what is now known as the *sudden school* for the emphasis it places on instantaneous enlightenment. Eventually the northern or *gradual school* died out; so today the Soto, Rinzai, and Obaku schools all trace their lineages back to Hui-neng.

The sixth patriarch's influence on the course of Zen Buddhism is evident to this day. Apparently Hui-neng delivered his message with tremendous authority. That kind of authority can only come from one place: experience. Hui-neng embodied the teaching of instantaneous enlightenment because that is precisely how it happened to him. Hui-neng was not a monk, nor was he practicing any formal discipline when he attained enlightenment. He was a simple woodcutter, selling firewood to support himself and his mother. One day Hui-neng was in the forest when he happened to overhear a monk chanting the *Diamond Sutra*. Simply hearing a phrase of that sutra, Hui-neng awakened.

The enlightenment story of Hui-neng reads like a fairy tale. It's hard to believe that you can be an ordinary guy from no place special one day, and the next day you're a Buddha! But Hui-neng didn't have to believe it; and he didn't waste time trying to fit thoughts about sudden enlightenment into a bunch of other beliefs and concepts. Enlightenment just happened. The day began like any other: Hui-neng was cutting wood in the forest when he heard someone chanting in the distance. *Bam!* His life took an about-face. Everything that he had believed was important, real, and substantial—his entire reality—was flipped upside down. Suddenly he realized who he really was.

The sixth patriarch was the first person to awaken without even sitting down. All of the previous ancestors attained enlightenment after practicing long and hard, so some doubt about this so-called instantaneous enlightenment is understandable. Sure, the experience itself happened suddenly to each ancestor, and then he could see that none of his previous work was really necessary—but he couldn't convince anyone else of that fact. One after the other, the ancestors remarked, "Having attained the Way, I now see that all my efforts were in vain." How could they make such an incredible statement? They all discovered the same thing: there was never anything to be attained. If there were something to be attained, then, of course, it would take time to attain it. Instead, each ancestor experienced that nothing was lacking to begin with.

As deluded beings, we see ourselves as incomplete and inadequate, a little confused, and definitely dualistic. How can we possibly hope to discover that we truly lack nothing? We would need to be a complete package, already having everything, and that's not how we appear. We don't feel complete, whole, or perfect, and we certainly don't look like Buddhas. In fact, we see ourselves as ordinary jokers, inadequate, incomplete, and riddled with problems. We may long for wholeness and to be at peace with ourselves and our lives, but to actually attain that state sounds impossible.

Somehow we need to realize that it is our *concept* of wholeness that blocks us from the experience. We may have confusion, feelings of inadequacy, and a bunch of other problems, but if the point is to experience wholeness, how can any part of ourselves be left out? To be perfect and complete *as we are* is not the same as having only the nice bits. By definition, perfect wholeness has to include and embrace all aspects of ourselves. Yet we go on trying to eliminate the disagreeable parts while hoping to attain the experience of wholeness. This simply makes no sense. We're not the first ones to have such convoluted thinking; it was also prevalent in the days of the sixth patriarch. Hui-neng was a revolutionary; he broke new ground. He was the first to teach the Buddha-dharma in the way we now call *Zen*.

When the sixth patriarch began teaching sudden enlightenment, he was labeled a heretic. All the ancestors before him taught that long years of practice were necessary before someone could awaken. That became the common teaching because it made sense to the rational mind. People couldn't accept that enlightenment didn't require any time or any prerequisites. Even today instant enlightenment sounds almost too good to be true, but if one person did it, it's possible for others to do it, too. This teaching is what makes Zen unique.

Hui-neng's story may be incredible, but it is also very encouraging. Imagine yourself walking through the forest, minding your own business, when you hear a voice in the distance: "Let your mind flow freely without dwelling on anything." *Bam!* You awaken to your intrinsic wholeness and perfection. You *know* you are Buddha! When this happened to Hui-neng, he was compelled to go to the source of this teaching. He found the monk who had been chanting and asked, "What are you chanting, and who is your teacher?" The monk replied, "My master is the fifth patriarch, Hung-jen, and he told us to practice reciting the *Diamond Sutra*." Hui-neng sold all the wood he had gathered, gave the money to his mother, and set out to find this man called the fifth patriarch.

It must have been a long journey. Hui-neng was from the south of China, and the fifth patriarch was in the north. After walking hundreds of miles, he finally arrived at the temple of the fifth patriarch. In those days the people of northern China were aristocratic and well educated, and they looked down on the southerners as illiterate barbarians. Imagine, here comes this nineteen-year-old kid dressed in rags. He doesn't know how to read; he doesn't know how to do much of anything except chop wood. He's just a poor, humble, ignorant, young guy. The monks must have had their doubts, but they led him to their teacher. Hui-neng explained that he had come from the south and he wanted to enter practice there at the monastery. Did the master welcome this naive but sincere boy? No, he replied, "Those southern barbarians don't have Buddha nature!" Hui-neng's answer was simple and direct, and it revealed the depth of his realization: "Buddha nature knows no north, south, east, or west."

Perhaps his ignorance was an advantage. Hui-neng didn't enter the Way with a truckload of preconceptions. We tend to be more like Eka: we first have to empty our minds of loads of accumulated garbage. Remember, when Eka went to Bodhidharma, he had been searching and studying for years. Despite all his knowledge of the Buddha-dharma, he still felt confused and dissatisfied. His mind was crowded and busy, almost ready to explode, and he was desperate for peace of mind. Bodhidharma could easily have told Eka, "Go empty your mind," but he did something amazing instead. "Show me your mind!"—he gave Eka a koan. How do you present this mind that is brimming with ideas and concepts? In order to present it, you have to be able to grasp it. Bodhidharma was essentially tossing Eka out on his ear, pushing him—if the guy had any bones at all—to go out and find his mind.

Eka was sophisticated enough to know that he wouldn't find the answer outside of himself, so he sat down and turned his mind inward. He started searching for his mind with his own mind—an impossible puzzle! Eka was already in despair; now Bodhidharma had managed to make matters worse. Eka sat in the snow for ten days and nights searching all of his understanding and knowledge for the answer.

How long did it take for Eka to awaken? We could say that after spending ten days and nights searching with all of his might, he still failed miserably. Nevertheless, he did learn something very important in the process. Eka knew that although he had given absolutely everything to the search, he failed anyway. Thus, he realized it was impossible to grasp the mind. If he had not given his all to the search, doubt would have kept coming back—along with his despair. Eka searched everywhere and found nothing at all.

Eka went back empty-handed. "I've searched everywhere, and now I realize that my mind is ungraspable." Bodhidharma replied, "Then I have put your mind to rest!" Bam! If there is no mind, what is there to suffer? In that instant Eka woke up.

How long does it take to attain enlightenment? It takes no time and it can take lifetimes; it all depends on how much we cling to our ideas and concepts. If you say, "I don't have enough time to practice," you're deluding yourself. Realization doesn't depend on time. If you say, "I don't have enough years of practice," that's bull. Realization has no prerequisites. If you say, "I'm not ready to drop all my ideas and concepts," that may be true! Excuses just cover up this fact. Nobody needs to sit for a hundred hours or a hundred years; anyone can awaken once they are ready to drop their ideas and opinions.

We all cling to our ideas and opinions because our ego is invested in them. We want to be *right*. Everyone else may be stupid or in denial, but the way I've put things together, the way that I understand reality, can't possibly be wrong! My whole way of life is based on what I think and believe, and to consider being wrong is just too scary. Ego hates to fail or appear foolish, so it keeps trying to get things right.

To admit that I am creating the problem is a life-changing step. It is always easier to blame others—especially the teacher who sends us back into the cold with no answers. Yet Bodhidharma was showing compassion when he stripped Eka of his knowledge and sent him away in confusion. Eka may have mastered the Buddha's teaching, but he had not digested it. Conceptual understanding would never satisfy his hunger—and it will leave us just as empty. Ego wants to understand, regardless; so it raises all sorts of doubts: letting go of understanding could lead to chaos, anarchy, possibly insanity! Perhaps a little insanity is the best place to start. By losing his mind, Eka found freedom.

The humble beginnings of Hui-neng must have been some protection from accumulating a lot of conceptual and egocentric baggage. When he overheard the sutra that day in the forest, his mind was already a clean cup and the Dharma poured right in. Eventually Hui-neng went on to become the next ancestor, but not through conventional channels. He may have revealed his own clarity and cut through the fifth patriarch's criticism, but Hui-neng was still an uneducated, ragged kid. No doubt the master recognized the gem standing before him, but he also knew that the monks would never accept this upstart. So he put Hui-neng to work in the kitchen pounding rice.

Hui-neng lived at the monastery for some time, but he was never allowed to take vows or to practice as a monk. He just labored in the kitchen until the fifth patriarch was approaching death and needed a successor. Then, rather than bringing forth this gem for everyone to see, the master secretly gave Hui-neng the bowl and the robe that signified successorship and told him to run for his life! When the monks found out about it, they were angry. A group chased after him, hoping to kill the imposter and bring back the bowl and robe. Hui-neng lived in anonymity for fifteen years before finally declaring that he was the true successor and beginning to teach. Hui-neng was master enough of his ego to be able to wait. He didn't fight for what was right or deserved; he simply devoted himself to deepening his understanding until the time was ripe for him to teach.

In Zen we honor what the world considers ignorance and insanity. Instead of building a secure bridge that leads to accomplishment, Zen pulls out the rug from under our feet. From the groundless position where ego has dropped away, anything can spark an opening, a glimpse into our true nature. Our practice is to chip away, bit by bit, the conditioning that blocks the enlightened view. The challenge is to stay open and honest about what tools seem to work best for us. Teachers are helpful for shaping our practice to our needs, and especially for chipping away at our blind spots. Ultimately, however, we must each accept responsibility for doing our own work. We build the walls that block us from realization, and only we can tear them down.

25

Form Is Emptiness, Emptiness Is Form

> Avalokitesvara Bodhisattva, doing deep prajna-paramita, clearly saw emptiness of all the five conditions, thus completely relieving misfortune and pain. Form is no other than emptiness, emptiness no other than form.
>
> —Opening lines of the *Heart Sutra*

IN THE BEGINNING of practice, we focus primarily on learning the form of meditation. We learn how to work with our bodies so that we can sit comfortably in zazen with good posture and natural breathing, and we learn how to work with our minds so that we can focus our attention. At some point we experience an opening to our true nature. We call that first experience of nonduality "the shift" because it is a shift from our usual way of perceiving reality. Suddenly, instead of perceiving only the apparent reality, what appears to be so, we have a direct experience of the absolute reality that underlies and pervades all things, including the self. Once we have glimpsed the Absolute, the self never again seems so solid or permanent. Our usual way of perceiving the self and the world has been cut through, even if only for an instant, and it becomes easier to remember that duality is just one side of reality.

The shift marks a turning point in practice. We now want to clarify what our true nature really is. By "true" nature, I don't mean *true* as opposed to *false*. That dualistic understanding would imply that practice is a process of leaving behind what is false and claiming more of what is true. Yet if we use our own experience of zazen as a guide, we can see that true nature goes beyond any such descriptions or categories. True nature is no-nature, or emptiness, and what we experience is the *absence* of specific or identifying characteristics. So, of course, true nature can't be described; but we can use different names to try to point to the experience of it, such as Heart-Mind, Buddha Mind, Buddha nature, true Self, and no-self. Each of these names has meaning once you have experienced your true nature. They all point to Mind, which can never be expressed in words.

The experience of Mind is like dividing a number into zero: it doesn't matter what number we start out with, we always end up with zero. Similarly it doesn't matter what person is sitting in zazen, the experience of Mind is the same: we experience *being* no-self, zero. This is the shift. Then, as we continue our meditation practice, we begin to see that the opposite is also true: this no-self is nothing other than "me," and it is nothing other than all beings and all forms. We could say the experience is like dividing this self—or any being—by one: we always end up with what we had in the beginning. You get you, and I get me. But don't imagine that the true Self that you discover is the same as what you typically think of as "yourself." Your true Self is Buddha.

True nature is no nature, no fixed nature, emptiness. Thus, it is able to manifest as all things and all beings; the possibilities are infinite. Buddha manifests as all things, yet in our case it manifests as our life—this very life, in this form, in this body! You—exactly as you are—are nothing but the manifestation of Buddha Mind.

We all share this same root nature, but like the leaves on a tree, each manifestation is absolutely unique. Zazen opens our eyes to this wonderful mystery; then practice becomes a process of closing the gap between what we have realized and how we live that realization. The *Heart Sutra* relates the story of Avalokiteshvara Bodhisattva, who through meditation realized the inseparability of emptiness and form and thus transcended suffering. We seek the same realization and liberation for ourselves and for all beings. Through practice, we, too, can come to appreciate all life as the manifestation of Buddha Mind. We continue to practice in order to express this realization more clearly in everything we do. Closing the gap is a big job, and it may take lifetimes to accomplish. Yet how long it takes doesn't really matter. Zen practice is not about arriving at a finish line but about seeing that the process is It. This life *is It!*

Form is emptiness, and emptiness is form. They are the same, and yet they are also very different. Form has no fixed nature; all forms appear as *this* form, "my" form. The true nature of this very form is no-nature, emptiness, Mu. Whatever you do from morning to night is nothing but the form of emptiness, emptiness manifesting as all things, the ten thousand dharmas. Because form is empty, life can appear in all of its forms. You realize this for yourself when you experience Buddha Mind, your true nature. You divide yourself by One and end up with your Self! The concept of the small self drops away, and what is left is your true Self.

It's not necessary to try to become your true Self. You can't be anything else. It's impossible to be other than what we truly are—and what we are changes moment to moment. But because our tendency to grasp is so strong, it may take us some time to learn to trust and relax into our unfixed nature. Ego wants to be substantial and special, and it will try to possess each new realization and insight. When ego grasps at the gains we've made, we will suffer the consequences. Most of us fall into this trap many times before finally seeing that grasping is futile and admitting to ourselves, "Ah, maybe I really am zero, nothing special!"

When we make practice our life, we can expect to encounter many traps and sticking places. Yet we can make this an honorable part of our practice by remaining watchful and letting go each time we become stuck. By returning to zero again and again, we gradually close the gap and actualize our unfathomable true nature.

26

Mountains and Valleys

Why is it that we can't hold on to the experience of Oneness? Why must we return to our doubts about who we really are?

WHAT EVENTS have brought you to this moment of your life? This question could be answered superficially by listing such things as daily tasks and recent events. But it also could be answered at a deeper level by looking at the larger and more mysterious forces that have influenced the direction of your life. Think about it. What aroused your interest in something as crazy as Zen? How did you become curious about Buddhism in the first place? Most of us were not raised in a Buddhist culture, and for some of us, it hasn't been that long since we didn't know what a Buddha was. Maybe some unusual karma is at work here.

Somehow the events of your life brought you the rare opportunity to learn about the Buddha-dharma. And if you have studied the Buddha's teachings, perhaps your mind has been opened to the possibility that there are Buddhas living today. Maybe you doubt that you've met a real Buddha yet, but still you believe that there could be modern-day Buddhas, awakened ones who have realized the truth. To arrive at this understanding is in itself a catalytic event. Your life is headed for change when you leave open the possibility of living Buddhas.

When somehow you have realized that Buddhas are here, *now*, it's just a matter of time before the direction of your life changes and you embark on a search. You may not know exactly what those enlightened ones have, but they must have something, right? And maybe what you've heard is true: they found liberation or even nirvana. If we sit for a moment with that thought, something immediately comes up. Desire! Who knows what all this enlightenment stuff is about, but if someone has found it, we want it, too. This desire pushes us forward to the spiritual journey. We step onto the Path. Is that good karma or bad? Perhaps it's both.

Buddha taught that everything changes, and you and I are not exceptions. Each one of us is continually changing, transforming, reforming, conditioning, and reconditioning. Are you who you were five years ago? What about five days ago or even in the last moment? By investigating in this way, we realize that this so-called me is transforming continuously. Nevertheless, we like to think of ourselves as rather solid and unchanging. How do we manage to deceive ourselves? If we look below the surface of what we call "me," we will discover a collection of ideas: concepts of who we are and beliefs about what our life is. By clinging to those concepts and beliefs, we create an illusion of form—a structure of sorts that we identify as "me." Then you and I go on to label ourselves: "I am a student," "I am a father," "I am a woman."

So in a way we become our understandings. I begin to live according to an image of myself, whoever I understand myself to be. I don't even notice that this image of me has become a box—a prison, really—that causes a great deal of unhappiness. When I try, but fail, to live up to my ideas of who I am, I feel disappointed. We do this with ourselves and with others. We want the people in our lives to fit into the boxes that we've built for them, and we can become quite upset when they don't.

Each one of us carries this kind of baggage when we begin the spiritual journey. We gather up all of our expectations and set out on a search for a Buddha that looks like a Buddha. We may not have a clear picture of what a Buddha looks like, but we believe they must be extraordinary somehow. After all, Buddhas are the "awakened ones"; they've realized Truth! And since you and I experience so much confusion and doubt, we believe that Buddhas must look very different from us. A Buddha should look like a Buddha—maybe jolly and fat like Santa Claus. So we begin the journey looking for something outside and very unlike ourselves. It never even crosses our minds that you and I might be Buddhas.

The spiritual journey surprises us because it turns out to be nothing like what we expected. It can even be a big disappointment in the beginning. The Path is full of hope and disappointment, confusion and pain. We can't seem to find a Buddha anywhere. In despair, we may decide to step off the Path for a while. But disappointment and despair are essential steps along the way because they force us to stop looking outside ourselves for the truth. When we give up all hope of finding Buddha "out there," we can finally be with *what is*. From this position of openness, we can finally realize *"I am It!"* At first we were sure that we were not the Buddha; but after encountering a word or event, we make a 180-degree turn. Suddenly we are filled with light: "I am It!" Yet when that side is light, what side is dark? What kind of blindness have we attained?

In order to have the experience of being Buddha, we have to stop being stuck in the rational mind. That's the point, really. The rational mind sees this and that, me and other. You know who you are and who you are not; it is all logical and rational. But the mind that is logical, rational, conceptual, and dualistic must get out of the way in order to experience Oneness. When duality disappears, the experience is, "Well obviously I am the Buddha." You never think to ask yourself, "What am I not seeing?" Any rational person can see that we now have a dangerous case of blindness. But in that moment you are not rational.

The more complete the experience, the more total the blindness. The dark side is ignored, and we fall into a deep trap. We experience complete freedom when we are stuck in the side of Oneness. Inevitably the karma of ignoring the relative side catches up with us. Doubt arises, and we begin to question our realization. We aren't so sure anymore just what we experienced; and no matter how hard we try, we can't make our doubt go away.

Nobody likes to go through this. We all want to stay in the realm of Buddhas. Why is it that we can't hold on to the experience of Oneness? Why must we return to our doubts about who we really are? Truth always goes beyond duality. Knowing can't be separated from not knowing, and certainty is not opposed to uncertainty. So doubt comes back. Actually doubt is the seed of truth. That's why we resist it so much. Doubt makes us finally face the relative truth: "I am *not* Buddha!" We are Buddha, awakened, and yet we are not Buddha. The ego is not Buddha Mind, yet Buddha Mind does manifest as the ego.

What happened? We have gone full circle and arrived back where we started. Nevertheless, something is different this time around. Something lingers. The experience—no matter how dim or bright, no matter how brief or long—lingers like an itch. The itch that won't go away is Bodhi-mind, the mind that seeks the Way. We had the experience of being Buddha, but now we can't see it. Now it seems obvious that we are *not* Buddha. We think, "There must be *truly* enlightened beings out there, Buddhas and ancestors who really embody 'It'; I'm just a fake, an incomplete Buddha, a bad copy."

No, you are not a bad copy, and you are not the exception. If someone is a bad copy, then everyone is a bad copy. Everyone is imperfect. Now hold on a minute, how can that be? Buddha is perfect, right? That's what we've been told, and that is what we experience. Realizing "I am Buddha" means that we experience complete and perfect wholeness; we see that we lack absolutely nothing. What about our imperfections, the stuff that we need to work on? When we look at ourselves, it can seem as if we never have a moment of mindfulness, that our mind is forever wandering. And then the thoughts that come into our minds are the wrong kind of thoughts—all sorts of fantasies and desires. This mind of ours is definitely not the mind of a Buddha! Or so we think.

What does the mind of a Buddha look like? A koan gives us some clues. The *Mumonkan*, or "Gateless Gate," is a collection of koans put together by the Chinese ancestor Mumon. This koan, "Case 18" of the *Mumonkan*,[1] is about a monk meeting the great Zen master Tozan.

> A monk once asked Master Tozan, "What is Buddha?"
> Tozan said, "Three pounds of flax."

What does the mind of a Buddha look like? Isn't that what the monk is asking? In a way Tozan is answering, "Everyone and everything." He doesn't say, "I am Buddha." Of course, Tozan knows that he is Buddha, but saying it in that way would be too green for Tozan, too obvious and too limiting. Tozan was a very accomplished master, and his answer goes far beyond that.

When we first step onto the Path, we trust our rational mind and believe that it is capable of determining what is true. You know who you are, and I know who I am. I would never say that I am you, or that I am the Buddha or God. But then everything flips: my mind opens, and I realize, "I am the Buddha; I am the whole universe; I am It!" And although this experience is absolutely true, we soon find out that very few people want to hear about it. We may turn to books about meditation or Buddhism or possibly a Zen center or monastery. If we're lucky, we find a place where we can simply admit this truth we've discovered.

It doesn't really matter which side of reality we find ourselves on, the Path stretches before us. We may wish that we could stay in one place, but the view changes continuously, and we must let go of each vista. Some people manage to stick to one place for years, clinging to a realization that felt really good. It's possible to stay stuck for a long time and to build up an elaborate new image of our self—one that is great, complete, and whole. After having a glimpse of the Truth, we can identify with the words of Shakyamuni Buddha—"I alone am the revered one, the world-honored one"—and of course, we don't want to let go. But when we stick here, the realization has become the illness—and we need powerful medicine.

Only one medicine is strong enough to cure this illness: doubt! Doubt may begin small and nagging like a mosquito, but it can grow to become complete, all-encompassing and all-embracing. If doubt is incomplete, if there are limitations to how far it extends, then we are able to imagine something beyond the doubt, and maybe that something will be true. As long as there seems to be a choice, we will hold on to this hope. Doubt then becomes the killing sword of compassion. No stone can be left unturned, and only complete doubt can negate everything. Our experience, the realization itself, was true; but our clinging turned it into an understanding. We've created another concept, a bigger and better "me." This concept can grow to such gigantic proportions that only absolute doubt can cut the monster down.

Once doubt has done the job, what happens then? Do we find liberation and freedom, the end of the journey? No, we learn that the journey is to go through this process again and again. We keep taking the detour. Our question creates the problem. It doesn't matter whether our question is "What is Buddha?" or "Why am I here?" Any question will lead the rational mind on a goose chase. The mind *always* tries to understand. That's its job. Perhaps you wonder whether it might be better to not ask any questions at all, but would you be where you are now if you had never questioned?

We're all curious about our lives and where we're going. We would like to know whether we have good karma or bad, and it's easy to slip right back into looking for an answer. But Tozan is asking a different question: can we live without knowing? In the town where Tozan lived, the people grew flax for a living. Although Tozan was a great master, he was still just an ordinary guy, and he worked with flax like everyone else. One day a monk walked by and asked, "What is Buddha?" Tozan just happened to be weighing flax: "Ah, three pounds!" He didn't fall into the monk's trap; he transcended it. He didn't come right out and say, "I am It," but he also didn't leave himself out of the picture. He was manifesting Buddha's activity in his ordinary life—weighing flax. No longer stuck in "I am It" or "I am not It," Tozan goes beyond. He just is.

Hearing this story we might think that we should try to act like Tozan: to just do what we do from morning till night. We may hope that whatever we do will be Buddha's activity. If you believe that, you're in serious trouble—even though it is true! Everything you do, from morning till night, *is* nothing but Buddha's activity. That is the absolute truth. But something is missing from this picture; we are ignoring the relative side of reality: no matter what we are doing, it's *not* Buddha's activity! Maybe I've realized that everything I do is a manifestation of Buddha; yet if I stay there, my realization has become a concept. I'm stuck, and I'm probably creating lots of karma.

To release the absolute and to embrace the relative again is painful because then we have to admit that our activity is just one mistake after another. We don't need to stop there, though. Which mind prefers to be stuck in the Absolute, and which mind doesn't care? Look at Tozan. Was he worrying about the monk not "getting it"? No, he was simply manifesting Buddha at that moment. If on another day the monk had asked, "What is Buddha?" Tozan would have said something else. Tozan was far beyond trying to figure out whether or not he was Buddha.

I'd like to share a poem about Tozan.

> Time passes without hesitation;
> There is no gap between the question and the answer.
> To meet Tozan in this way never happened again.

This poem illuminates both the absolute and relative. It describes the impermanent nature of our experience, the fact that everything changes moment to moment. Time passes quickly, and our lives will come to an end. Each one of us will die. Do we really appreciate this truth? To live completely, we need to live with the awareness of impermanence.

"There is no gap between the question and the answer." This line refers to the absolute side of reality. The moment you ask the question "What is Buddha?" you also create the problem. You are bitten by the question, and it becomes the koan of your life. As long as you live in your rational and dualistic mind, you will have to answer this question.

Why are you here? Just possibly, on some level, you are here to take care of the question "What is Buddha?" The amazing thing is, the question is already the answer! But to know this, you must look inside and see for yourself who is asking the question. You may answer, "I am!" but simply accepting this without truly realizing it is a trap.

"To meet Tozan in this way never happened again." Tozan changes continually. He can't help it—he manifests Buddha in every moment. What about you? When is your chance to answer the question? The window can close at any moment. Tozan: here today, gone tomorrow. This opportunity doesn't come along very often, and life is quickly passing by. Faster than we can snap our fingers, gone!

Still, there is no need to worry, because the question is already the answer. If you have the question, you have the answer. Yet for this to be true, it must be complete. This becomes perfectly logical when you drop the conceptual dualistic mind.

27

The Middle Way

Not grasping or resisting, we walk the Middle Way.

SHAKYAMUNI BUDDHA'S teaching is called the *Middle Way*. Conventionally we understand *middle* to mean "in the center," like the line that marks the middle of a road. Based on this understanding, to follow the Middle Way would mean that we should find a path in the center and not deviate to either extreme. Our actions and thoughts should be neither too disciplined nor too free. Many religions support following such a limiting path, and even some Buddhists think like that. What Buddha meant by the Middle Way, however, is to transcend the opposites by embracing them without attaching to them. So, you see, the Middle Way is actually a very broad and inclusive path.

How do we work with this realization in everyday life? Let's take the practice of "no-self," one of the three essential points of Buddha's teaching. To embody no-self means to act selflessly, without regard for yourself. But this basic teaching can become problematic or even dangerous when it is taken as a fixed truth. Then practicing no-self may become a form of self-neglect, not attending to the well-being of the body and mind. Basic needs for proper diet, exercise, and rest might be ignored. We might disregard our needs for shelter or for medical care when we are sick.

We also can neglect the requirements for a healthy mind. One of the most insidious ways to neglect the mind is to keep it distracted. Our society actually encourages us to keep our minds distracted with desires, especially desires for wealth, position, and entertainment. We can easily forget to focus and take charge of our mind. Undisciplined, the mind is like a runaway horse or a wild monkey. If we give it free rein—which we often do without noticing—our crazy mind can have us going in circles, chasing every desire, every hope, every possession, while trying to avoid anything that causes pain, suffering, or fear.

How do we become the master of our mind? First, we have to notice there is a problem, and the best way to do that is to sit in zazen. In zazen we clearly see how little control we have over our mind. Buddha taught the Middle Way so that we could learn how to master the mind, and the most essential point for achieving this mastery is to transcend duality. We need to realize the Oneness beyond all the dualities of our conceptual mind, such as good and bad, male and female, enlightened and deluded, life and death.

Let's look at a duality that we usually see as fixed: life and death. How can we transcend the apparent opposites of life and death? Is it possible to go beyond the extremes of being utterly and completely dead and being fully and completely alive? We could try to practice something in between—not quite dead and not really alive—but this kind of practice would rely on a limited and conventional understanding of the Middle Way by simply avoiding the extremes. To *transcend* rather than avoid the extremes is the ideal in Zen. That means, when you're alive, be completely and fully alive; and when you're dead, be utterly dead! Don't mix them up into a lukewarm soup.

The teachings of Dogen Zenji come from the view beyond duality, and they can sound quite extreme, even radical. Take this world, for example. Anyone with their eyes half open can see that this world is full of problems. It's a big mess, and things need to get a lot better before we can reach nirvana. Many traditions agree with this and teach that the only way we will ever be liberated from this world of suffering is for a God-like being—possibly the Messiah, Christ, or Maitreya—to come and change everything. Dogen Zenji taught something entirely different. He said that nirvana and the world of samsara are not two. This existence *as it is*, is already nirvana. Nobody has to save us. This is it!

Hearing this, we can question whether it is really possible to live such an understanding. How can the inseparability of nirvana and samsara be manifested in ordinary life? Dogen Zenji taught that *shikan*, "just," is the key to manifesting this truth. That is, whatever you are doing, just do it! When you are walking, just walk. When you are eating, just eat. When you are dead, just be dead. Dogen Zenji's entire teaching can be boiled down to this one word, *shikan*. What makes this shikan so profound? It is Buddha Mind in manifestation, the mind that transcends duality.

We manifest Buddha Mind when we sit in shikantaza, even if we have not yet realized this truth for ourselves. Dogen Zenji's instructions for how to do shikantaza are simple: practice nonthinking. Now, this does not mean that we should try to stop our thoughts. Nonthinking embraces both thinking and not-thinking; it's not something in the middle, and it's not either extreme. He said, "Sometimes you study the way by casting off the mind. Sometimes you study the way by taking up the mind. Either way, study the way with thinking, and study the way not-thinking." [1]

Our approach to shikantaza has to go beyond the conventional way of understanding thinking and not-thinking. In school we are taught that thinking is a good thing, maybe even the best tool for life. Then, when it comes to meditation, the common understanding is that it is all about learning how to stop our thoughts. Unless we find a way to move past these perspectives, our ordinary life and our meditation practice will always be separate things. One of our first realizations when we begin to meditate is that our mind generates endless thoughts. Eventually it dawns on us what the real problem is: we don't know how to shift gears. We haven't found the clutch that will help us to move our mind smoothly from one view to another, so we keep getting stuck. Imagine only knowing about fourth gear. You probably wouldn't even be able to start moving. And if you were stuck in reverse all the time, it would be hell to get around! The same kind of thing happens when our mind gets stuck in one perspective. Instead of experiencing the free and fluid nature of Buddha Mind, we cling to a narrow perspective, judging all other views as wrong. We have given up the intrinsic freedom of our natural mind. With discipline and practice, we can learn how to shift the mind into neutral, and from there we can choose any gear.

It's amazing how meditation can change the way we look at ourselves. Most people imagine that they are flexible and free—at least until they start a meditation practice. Meditation makes our lack of freedom painfully obvious. To sit with your legs folded up in the lotus posture is especially effective! From there you can't possibly ignore how stuck you really are. The mind churns through its habitual patterns over and over and over again: how we view ourselves and our lives, the way we look at the world, how we judge others. We may have some great videos, but eventually even the best ones drive us crazy. When we are no longer entertained by the show, a little space can open up for something new. We begin to experience the gaps between our thoughts, moments of spaciousness, glimpses of Buddha Mind. That's when we get a taste of true freedom. Compared to being stuck, it feels great. Before we know it, we've set up a new goal: to experience this freedom all the time. We're stuck all over again!

It may be hard to believe, but there is no bad place to be stuck. There's also no good place to be stuck. Some stuck places may appear to be bad, but that's only because our view is limited. Other stuck places feel so good, it's easy to think they must be good places to stay. But anyplace will become stagnant and painful when we stay too long. Sooner or later we have to admit that we've become stuck again, and we really need to move on—this is our practice. The mind naturally grasps at things, especially our concepts and understandings. What can we do about it? Follow the Middle Way and keep moving.

Does following the Middle Way mean that there are no understandings that we can trust and hold on to? Well, we could try to hold on to "no-understanding," but that would be only another understanding, an idea about holding no view. Can we embrace the extremes of all understandings and no-understanding? If we tried, what would we look like? Flexible? Foolish? Insane? To embrace all views without holding on to any of them, perhaps you have to be a fool—or a Buddha.

At first glance, it may seem as if living the Middle Way is living without faith, but this is not true. The Middle Way simply goes beyond placing faith in this or that. We put our trust in no-thingness, emptiness, the absence of an intrinsic identity in anything, including ourselves. In other words, we have faith in our own Buddha nature.

I remember a time when someone confronted Maezumi Roshi with the statement "Buddhists don't believe in anything." That made Maezumi Roshi angry, and he shot back, "Buddhists have faith in the Three Treasures!" It took me a long time to absorb what he was saying. To believe in no-thingness is not the same as nihilism, the belief that nothing exists. All things are the infinite manifestations of Buddha, emptiness. So we put our faith in the Three Treasures: Buddha—emptiness; Dharma—the manifestations of Buddha, all forms; and Sangha—the inseparability and absolute harmony of emptiness and form.

If we have faith in the Three Treasures, does that mean we should never experience a lack of faith? When we go through periods of faithlessness or doubt, it may seem as if we have fallen off the Path; but that is not so. The Middle Way has to include both faith and faithlessness. Thus, no matter where we find ourselves, we are still on the Path. We only have to remember one thing: *keep moving!* Never stop letting go of your understandings and views. As one ancestor said, "Dwell in non-dwelling. Don't alight anywhere."

The Middle Way excludes nothing, and becoming stuck is the only way we detour from the Path. So "don't alight anywhere" is a good motto to follow. Buddha taught another important guideline for following the Middle Way. He said, "Be a light unto yourself." When we are a light unto ourselves, we take responsibility for our practice. Instead of trusting in an authority outside of ourselves, we place our trust in our own experience. We pay attention to whatever our experience is and embrace it—but without clinging. We don't try to hold on to it, and we don't try to push it away; we just let it be. Everything is allowed to simply come and go of its own accord. All of our thoughts, emotions, understandings, and realizations are like bubbles, arising one moment and disappearing in the next moment. Not grasping or resisting, we walk the Middle Way.

28

The Path of the Human Being

We have to get down to the earth, into the mud.
That's where the bodhisattva can make a difference.

THIS ANCIENT tale is a good metaphor for our journey in Zen practice. The story of Enyadatta was told by the Buddha himself and is recorded in the *Lotus Sutra*, but I like to give the story a little twist. Enyadatta lived an ordinary life with her husband and children. Like many of us, she was a bit vain and rather obsessed with her appearance. She often looked into the mirror to admire herself. One morning her children decided to play a little joke on her. They turned the glass of the mirror around so that when she woke up and glanced into it, there was no reflection. Maybe she was groggy, or maybe she had a rough night; we don't really know what the circumstances were—but when Enyadatta looked into the mirror and saw no head, she freaked out. Thinking her head was lost, she searched the house from top to bottom but couldn't find her head. So she began to look outside, again with no success. Poor Enyadatta, frantic to find her head, ran through the neighborhood, screaming and crying. "I've lost my head! I've lost my head! Please help me!"

Some friends finally caught up to Enyadatta and asked what was wrong. "I can't find my head!" she cried. "Your head isn't gone; it's right there where it's always been." "No, no, no! I've seen for myself that it's missing, and I've got to find it. What will I ever do without my head?" The friends saw that Enyadatta was in a strange state of mind, to put it mildly, so they tied her to a chair and tried to convince her that she was not really missing her head. Still she struggled and fought, desperate to break free. "Let me go. I've got to find my head!" Her friends tried everything they could think of to calm her down, but nothing worked. Finally one of them slapped Enyadatta, and at that moment she realized her head was right where it belonged. She started shouting all over again—only now she was completely ecstatic. "My head, my head, I found my head!" Still fearing for her state of mind, Enyadatta's friends kept her tied to the chair, hoping she would calm down. They told her, "Just sit there!" and then they left for a while. She sat for what seemed like a very long time and gradually returned to her usual calm self. Then her friends let her go.

Enyadatta went home and continued her daily routines, yet she was still in a state of bliss. She was so happy to have her head back. Over time she began to notice that everybody had a head and that she had never really lost hers. So the excitement faded, and eventually she was able to move on. She returned to her ordinary life, almost as if nothing had happened. But of course, something had happened: she had gone through an incredible experience.

In the earlier stages of our practice, we are like Enyadatta before she looked in the mirror on that fateful morning: we see things in a dualistic way. When we look at ourselves, we feel either good or bad, adequate or inadequate, superior or inferior. When we look at other people, we judge them to be either better or worse than ourselves; we elevate others or put them down. We can't seem to stop comparing and judging everything we encounter. This habit comes from our state of delusion, the way we look at the world. We're slaves of our dualistic minds, caught up in our thoughts, feelings, and emotions. On and on, we pass from one realm to another, from happiness to depression, and from contentment to frustration, anger, and resentment. This suffering is created by our own minds. When we feel that we can bear it no longer, we begin to search for a way out.

One morning Enyadatta looked into the mirror and couldn't see her head. At some point in our lives, we also may realize that something is off, something seems to be missing. We try many different ways to lessen our pain, hoping to somehow make our lives work better. Sometimes things actually seem to go better for a while. But it doesn't last, and sooner or later we fall back into our discontentment and frustration. Inwardly we still feel incomplete, so we keep searching for a way to feel whole. We begin by looking nearby, in places that are familiar. Later on, our search may lead us far away from home, even to other countries and cultures. We can end up traveling thousands of miles trying to find "It."

Our destiny changes when we finally encounter the practice of zazen. We learn to sit down and shut up long enough to turn our light inward. In the beginning, though, it's a struggle. Our mind is undisciplined; it seems to have a mind of its own. It creates all kinds of ideas and chases after all kinds of things. We realize that instead of riding the waves of life, we are being tumbled and crushed by our thoughts and emotions. In despair, we may wonder if we will ever find peace of mind. We obviously have no control over our experience, and we don't have a clue how to become the master.

With perseverance and a little luck, we may meet someone who says, "You don't lack anything. You are complete, whole, and perfect as you are. In fact, you are Buddha!" But at first we can't hear this because our own experience tells us that we are incomplete. Every time I look at myself, I see how inadequate I am. Other people appear to be much better off than myself—more together, more confident, more enlightened. Any trust or confidence that I manage to build is easily shaken. When life puts me to the test, my self-confidence is exposed as the act it really is, and I'm reminded again just how incomplete and insufficient I am. From this perspective, to believe that nothing is lacking seems like fantasy.

The turning point comes when life slaps us in the face. In that moment, we cut through the apparent reality and realize that nothing ever was missing. Our deluded view only made it seem so. Suddenly we can see our wholeness and perfection—the absolute side of reality.

Just a glimpse of the Absolute makes us ecstatic. We get high on the experience and forget all about the relative side of reality. So the next thing to arise is arrogance. We believe that we can see something that others can't. Our view seems so profound, we doubt that anyone has ever experienced anything like it. When this happened to the great ancestor Hakuin, he proclaimed, "Since the time of Shakyamuni Buddha, nobody else has had such a clear experience!" Even the Buddha announced, "I alone am the world-honored one." Yet the Buddha's realization was unique because it was complete. He could see that not only was he perfect and whole, so was everyone else. For most of us, it takes a lot of time and practice to go from the realization "I am It" to the insight "so is everyone else."

Even after realization, sitting is essential because we can easily get stuck in the absolute perspective. We're no longer stuck in the delusion before enlightenment; we are deluded *in* enlightenment. We are living in a state of grace where everything is perfect as it is. Every snowflake falls on the right spot because we have no preconceived ideas of where it should fall. Everything has meaning because we're not looking for any meaning. In this state we can do no wrong; everything is perfect.

Now, if you think about this while you are in a relative state of mind, red flags pop up right away. It's dangerous to believe that everything you do is perfect, somehow beyond all judgments of right and wrong. Yet from the absolute state of mind, this is the simple truth. So in this phase of our practice, we fall into a big trap—the delusion of enlightenment. Everything we do is in harmony with the Buddhadharma. We disregard dualistic views such as right and wrong, good and bad; and we easily ignore the law of cause and effect—karma—which operates on the relative level. In the absolute, there is no cause and effect. Yet the absolute and the relative are two sides of the same coin, and they can't be separated. If you screw up in the relative world, the absolute won't save you.

From the perspective of this delusion-within-enlightenment state, nothing seems to matter, and we think we can do whatever we want; but we are ignoring the relative side of our existence, where what we do really does matter. Everything counts—not only our actions and words but also our thoughts and attitude. Still, we go on blindly, creating more and more karma.

It's inevitable that at some point we will have to let go of the absolute state. But it's also inevitable that we will become attached to the absolute state of mind—and this attachment stops us from moving ahead willingly. The enlightened view that everything is perfect as it is, is now our delusion. Why let go of bliss when the memory of hell is so fresh? We recognize that other people are still living in duality—judging, evaluating, comparing, and condemning, and literally creating hell for themselves—and we remember it well. Now that we've made it to the top of the mountain and tasted realization, we don't want to go back down. Just the thought of returning to the world of samsara and all the suffering that goes with it brings up fear. Yet life goes on, and eventually we see that there is really no choice. Karma catches up with us, and we can't ignore any longer the harm that we've been causing. It's time to pay for all those vittles we've been eating.

It takes tremendous faith and courage to release the enlightened view and to go back into a state of complete delusion. The enlightened view is a higher view; it goes beyond all dualistic thinking, beyond our normal state of delusion. Although we may still experience pain and suffering, we are liberated because we know there is no self and no one to suffer. Yet finally we return to our ordinary view. We go beyond delusion within enlightenment and arrive at delusion within delusion. Conventional perception returns, and we see things just as everybody else sees them. We're back to square one, zero, the world of suffering. But there is a subtle difference: we remember the enlightened perspective. After going through this process many times, we learn how to move freely between the dualistic and the nondualistic views.

Zen practice goes in circles; one phase simply follows another. When we look ahead, there is always further to go. Even if we're only one step away from returning to square one, square one is still ahead of us. And if we've reached the summit, there is always another mountain to climb. We have to descend and climb up the next one, over and over again. Dogen Zenji taught that the first step is to raise the Bodhimind, the mind that wishes to clarify this life. Like Enyadatta, we need to see that something is missing. Our feelings of incompleteness become the motivation to practice. Then a slap in the face brings us awakening, liberation, and peace. But we can't stay there, and eventually we have to return to zero. Raise the Bodhi-mind, practice, realize, drop it—on and on.

Because the deluded mind can think only in limited terms, it wants to find a conclusion or finish line. The mind is simply too small to fathom infinity or eternity. So when we *can* fathom infinity, we're not using the deluded mind; in fact, we're completely out of our mind. When the small mind lets go, we experience Buddha.

Some spiritual paths seem to end at the top of the mountain, and perhaps some people manage to stay there. But the Zen path is the practice of the bodhisattva—what I call the path of the human being. After realization, we knowingly choose to return to being human. We didn't really have a choice before; we were stuck in duality and the realm of suffering. After we have traveled the entire circle, we can make a conscious choice to be just an ordinary human being. A bodhisattva is someone who has awakened and yet chooses to return to the world to help others. How many people can we reach from the top of a mountain? To meet other human beings, we have to get down to the earth, into the mud. That's where the bodhisattva can make a difference.

PART FOUR

WALKING THE PATH

MANIFESTING THE LIBERATION

Realization of our Buddha nature is just the beginning. Our practice now becomes one of manifestation, closing the gap between the truth we have experienced and how we relate to the world. If we are truly one with the universe, no other than this great earth and all it contains, how do we live this truth? As realization opens our eyes to interconnections and responsibilities that reach far beyond each of us as individuals, modern-day challenges can seem overwhelming. Yet we need not fall into despair. Practice has taught us how to return to the Source of wisdom and compassion. The more we let go of the small self, the clearer vessels we become for our boundless and intrinsically pure Buddha nature. In this way, our daily life is transformed into the Path of liberation.

29

Kanzeon Rising

All creations are the manifestation of Kanzeon. You are not the exception.

THE ZEN tradition teaches that everyone has faith—tremendous faith, really, whether we are aware of it or not. We call it Bodhi-mind, awakened mind, and it is the source of our impulse to practice. Not only do you already have the awakened mind, you already are the awakened one, the Buddha.

Now, of course, this sounds like pure nonsense. How could you be the Buddha? Shakyamuni Buddha lived twenty-five hundred years ago! He's long gone, right? He didn't look like you and he didn't dress like you, so how could you possibly be the Buddha? It seems impossible. And yet, do you know what Zen practice brings about?

Maybe we should start with the word *Zen*. *Zen* has been defined as "what is," but those are just words. Zen is to *realize* what is. To realize that you are the awakened one, the living Buddha, is probably the most incredible, mind-blowing experience that you could ever have. But in Zen we see it as just one step on the Path, a phase to go through. Something else is even more important. After realizing who you are, you have to manifest it; you have to embody the Buddha. That doesn't mean you have to act or dress like the historical Buddha. Buddha manifests in all forms. Everything you see, everything you hear, everything you touch, is Buddha. Everything is awakened mind. You said so yourself when you awakened twenty-five hundred years ago, remember? "I and all sentient beings simultaneously have attained the Way."

What on earth possessed the Buddha and caused him to make such an outrageous statement? Doesn't it sound like complete insanity or at least pure arrogance? Either that guy had a huge ego, or he realized something nobody else had realized. So what was it that you realized so long ago? Everything and everyone is Buddha! The only problem is that we see things upside down. Somehow sentient beings have it all backward, topsy-turvy: they believe they are sentient beings and not the Buddha. They are deluded.

So turn it over, inside out, or backward, and what do you get? Buddha! Now, maybe you're thinking to yourself, "Yeah, right! I don't know why I am here, and I don't know where I am going; obviously I am an ordinary sentient being. To think 'I am the Buddha' never even crossed my mind!" And yet, you sit like the Buddha. You do what Buddhas do, so you must be a Buddha. At some point in practice, you realize the truth of this, and then it becomes quite clear that your life is about manifesting the awakened mind.

A bodhisattva is a Buddha who postpones entering nirvana in order to help save all sentient beings. There are many different bodhisattvas, and they embody a variety of qualities. Avalokiteshvara is the Sanskrit name of the bodhisattva of compassion. In Japanese she is called Kannon or Kanzeon. She is often depicted with many heads and arms, which represent the infinite manifestations of the All-Compassionate One. Whether you're a man or a woman, she manifests as you; and she also manifests as a dog, a cat, and a fox. All creations are the manifestation of Kanzeon. You are not the exception. Kanzeon manifests as you—looking like you, acting like you. In other words, to manifest Kanzeon in your life, you have to act like you. Stop trying to be someone else.

If you try to figure out why you practice zazen, it may seem to make no sense. You practice zazen to realize not only who you truly are but also what your impulse to practice truly is. And once you know why you do it, you really have no choice but to keep on practicing. You just do it. But let's say you decide to stop practicing zazen. Does that mean you no longer are Buddha? No! How can you stop being who you really are? If you're no longer practicing zazen, you might think you're no longer manifesting the life of Kanzeon, yet how could that stop being true? Kanzeon manifests as all things. There is nothing conditional about it. You can stop doing zazen, and still you are Buddha. You may ask, "Why, then, does anyone practice zazen?" I have to admit that there is a catch: if you stop practicing, you may never realize who you are or what your life is.

Earlier I told the story of "The Beggar and the Gem" to help illustrate this point. The beggar had a precious jewel in his pocket, yet he didn't know it was there; so what good was it? Most people live their lives like beggars—trying to become rich, more popular, more successful, more secure. Always, more, more, more! We hope to find happiness and security by acquiring more things, more status, more relationships. We look everywhere outside of ourselves, while all along the most precious jewel is right here.

The story has a happy ending because the beggar finds the jewel. Still, most people live and die as beggars, never realizing they already hold what is most precious. On the one hand, we could say, *"C'est la vie,"* no big deal. On the other hand, it's tragic! It is tragic that people go through years and years suffering for no reason. Inwardly they are as poor as beggars, getting kicked around by all kinds of circumstances, while all along they could have had anything, they could have been anyone. The jewel is our birthright, and this practice is all about claiming that gem. My life, your life, *is* the life of Kanzeon, manifesting as all things. Everyone and everything carries this priceless jewel. All we need to do is find it. Then we can put it to use in our lives—or at least it can seem that way in the beginning. Eventually we realize that it doesn't really work like that. Actually, Kanzeon uses *you* to manifest as compassion in this world.

Maybe you already knew this to be true, but would you admit it? I've noticed it can be difficult for people to admit they are Kanzeon, even after they've had that realization. Why not admit it? Does it seem arrogant to admit the truth? In fact, the fear of looking arrogant is arrogance. If you can see that and admit it, then also you are admitting that you are Buddha, because Buddha is the one who knows this. In Zen we say, "It takes a Buddha to perceive a Buddha." Only Buddhas can see Buddhas.

Imagine that you go around telling people that you are the Buddha, what might happen? A psychiatrist would say you are delusional—and that would be true! So if you're going to admit that you're the Buddha, you have two choices about where to end up: in a psychiatric facility or at a Zen center. A Zen center is a great place to take refuge and give in to your delusion. You can be your true Self.

This truth can be scary, but isn't truth what you really want? Would anyone search for what is false, the big lie? Of course you seek truth, but can you admit the truth once you find it? What if admitting the truth also meant gaining the freedom to be your true Self? Perhaps this freedom would be even more frightening. Society can deliver all kinds of consequences to someone who behaves too freely. When you live the freedom that is your true nature, others may not approve. You might be rejected by some people, possibly even family and friends. Or you might be thrown out of a group or tradition. It can be scary and even risky to claim your intrinsic freedom.

To live with freedom does not mean that you will end up behaving in irresponsible or senseless ways. You already know how to function in society with the so-called sane mind, and there is no need to fear that you will lose that mind through this practice. In Zen, to lose your mind means that you lose all of your concepts. So of course, your life is transformed, but you don't forget how to function in society. You can still go to work, take care of your family, and brush your teeth. Yet when you let go of your mind, you *do* function more freely. You lighten up and have more fun playing the game. Before we realize that life is a game, we take the whole thing too seriously.

Earlier I introduced the characters Ganto and Seppo in the story about Tokusan carrying his eating bowls. I'd like to tell you another story that took place after Tokusan had died. Ganto and Seppo continued to live at the monastery a few more years in order to take care of Tokusan's remains. After fulfilling their obligations, Ganto and Seppo left on a journey to visit another famous teacher, Master Rinzai. As it turned out, Rinzai died before they arrived. Along the way, though, Ganto and Seppo probably walked many hours each day and went to bed exhausted. One night something woke up Ganto. In the light of the moon, he saw the silhouette of Seppo sitting in zazen. Ganto asked, "What are you doing? It's the middle of the night!"

Seppo probably thought that was a stupid question—after all, they were Zen monks—but he replied, "I'm doing zazen." Ganto pressed further, "Why are you doing that?" At this point Ganto must have seemed like an idiot. Seppo patiently replied, "I'm sitting zazen to become a Buddha." Seppo already knew that much, of course; he had been a Zen monk for years. But maybe you don't know. Or rather, maybe you don't believe it yet. You, too, are sitting to become a Buddha. Seppo knew: "I'm sitting to become a Buddha." Then Ganto tried to wake up Seppo: "Don't you realize that whatever gushes out of your heart is nothing but the Buddha-dharma?"

Kanzeon Bodhisattva is manifesting as you and me, and she is expressing the Buddha-dharma through our lives—but only if we let go and let it gush out. You can't control the situation, and you can't control what comes out. You have to relinquish and just let it gush out. Ganto is telling Seppo, "You already are so!" And he's also saying, beautifully, "But it's not true if you don't let it gush out."

Seppo sat there in the moonlight because he hadn't yet realized he was a Buddha, and he wanted to become free. And that is exactly why you and I practice zazen. Each one of us is like a seed: we already contain the whole tree, but the tree is not fully grown. In Tibetan Buddhism they call it *dharmadhatu*, the place or womb that holds the seed of the Buddha. Where is that place? Even though you look everywhere, you won't find it. It's not somewhere in heaven, and it's not in your head. When you drop your mind, you find it. Then you practice zazen because you realize it is the very best way to manifest Buddha.

30

The Price of Knowing Who I Am

Zen asks, "Do you want to know the truth about who you are?"

MAYBE YOU don't know it, but the voice of the Master is within you. It's within all of us. Most people never discover this master because they don't know where to look. The voice of the Master is the voice of the Buddha, and each and every one of us has it. Shakyamuni Buddha said that all sentient beings have the same Buddha nature, or the same awakened mind. It is intrinsic. This is the Mind that identifies with every voice and every thing, from a bee on a flower to the sun. Buddha Mind identifies with the universe, and it also identifies with a grain of sand.

By the time we become adults, most of us think we have a pretty good idea of who we are, a fairly concrete idea of "me." But sooner or later in Zen practice, that idea is destroyed. The image or notion of who we are drops. We lose it and can no longer recognize ourselves. We look in the mirror and think, "That's not me."

Hopefully we begin to ask ourselves, "Who am I, really?" Unless we return to that question again and again, we will eventually adjust to a new self and begin to think of it as "me." Maybe this new "me" seems like an improved self, more enlightened and wise than the previous one. Perhaps this new self can identify with all things and even feel some compassion. It doesn't take long to become comfortable and very stuck in our new identity. We have developed and attached to a new concept of who we are.

What happened to the previous identity, the one that used to seem so solid and real? It crashed! And inevitably, any new identity also must crash. The process of creating and destroying each new identity is difficult for anyone, but in Zen it is just part of the Path. Of course, we can wonder why on earth someone would choose to continually destroy his or her identity. But Zen approaches the issue a little differently. Zen asks, "Do you want to know the truth about who you are?" Maybe you do and maybe you don't—but it is a good question to ask yourself. If you answer, "Yes, I want to know the truth!" then the next question should be, "Am I really willing to pay the price?"

Are you willing to pay the price to know your true Self? When I was a student at Zen Center of Los Angeles, we had a saying, sort of a joke: "The price of admission is just your life." To realize your true Self, you must die. When people hear that, some feel like laughing and some feel like crying. But the truth is, you are not who you think you are!

You are not who you think you are; and to find out who you truly are, the one who you think you are must die. The illusion of self needs to die; and although this is only the death of a concept, it is a very deeply and dearly held concept. When the concept of self dies, we have to start over. We must return to the basic questions: "Who am I? Who am I if I am not who I thought I was?"

In Zen training we can go through the process of creating and destroying the self over and over. We're not this, but we're not that, either. Maybe we're all of the above; maybe we're none of the above. Maybe we are constantly changing. In Zen, even after years of training, *not knowing* who we are is the most intimate. Why? Because we *have* discovered something: we have discovered our unlimited true nature. Now we know that all of the selves are "me," and yet we're not limited to any one of them. Somehow we are the sum total and gestalt of the numberless voices of self. There is no true me; there is no real self. The true Self is not fixed. It transcends this and that. The true Self is no-self. Master Hakuin, one of the greatest Zen teachers, said it this way: "The true Self is to realize there is no true self."

To discover our unfixed nature can be a frightening process. When we first begin that journey, we feel ambivalent about finding our true Self. Somehow we seem to already know that when we find our true Self, there will be nothing left to hold on to, there will be no security. When we find our true Self, we lose all markers of who to be and how to be. All of our reference points disappear. We discover total freedom—but it may seem like more freedom than we bargained for. In a way, we are a lot like kids; we want freedom, but freedom within boundaries.

In 1986 I led a meditation retreat in Poland. At the last moment I decided to let go of the traditional sesshin structure and to have no rules, no regulations, and no schedule. At that time in Poland, the people were still ruled by Communism, and they wanted freedom more than anything else. There were about one hundred twenty people attending the sesshin, and it was fascinating to see how they reacted to this unexpected freedom: They begged for rules! They begged for a schedule, no matter how demanding or exhausting!

When we first begin a spiritual practice, none of us really wants the complete freedom that comes with the discovery of our no-self nature. The freedom to be anything appears just too frightening. We only *think* we want to discover who we really are when we believe that we will find something, especially an identity to hold on to. We want to believe that we are this and not that: if I am a man, I can't be a woman; if I am young, I can't be old. If we are a parent, a teacher, a good person, a whatever, we identify with that role. It's extremely difficult to let go of these basic identities, even though they are just concepts that we've created. If the role of "mother" is our identity and somehow that identity is taken away from us, we suddenly don't know who we are anymore. But not-knowing is a good thing! Until we give up our identity, *any identity*, we will not have the opportunity to be something else—our true Self.

Buddha called our world of suffering duhkha, which in Sanskrit refers to the broken axle of a wheel. When a wheel is working properly, it turns freely; it moves with the changing situation as the ground passes underneath. But we are like wheels that won't turn. Buddha saw that we create suffering for ourselves when we hold on to some aspect of our life—especially the concept of self. When we grasp on to an idea of who we are or what life is, we can't move with the situation. We suffer because we are not expressing our unfixed and fluid true nature. We're not flowing with life.

One reason we study koans as part of Zen training is to practice becoming one identity after another and then letting go of each identity. A koan may ask us to become something we have never identified with before, like Mount Fuji or a temple bell. Or we may be asked to become one of the great Zen ancestors, maybe Joshu or Bodhidharma. Many koans are stories of monks who start out a little stupid but who become enlightened in the end, and we can become one of those monks, too. All of the koans help us learn a skill that makes it possible to become anything and everything: we learn to drop the self. When we let go of the small self, we can be our true Self, unfixed and completely free.

Most of us find it relatively easy to see how someone else might be better off if they changed and gave up their familiar identity. If we return to the situation faced by a mother, we can see how the whole world would open up to her if she did not cling to her identity of "mother." Anything would be possible! But it is a very different experience to look at oneself and the identities to which we all cling. Suddenly letting go doesn't look so wonderful. It doesn't look like liberation; in fact, it looks like death! When we are going through the process of dropping the self, it can seem as if all the meaning and purpose in our life are evaporating.

With time and practice, the awareness of our unfixed nature deepens, and it becomes easier to unstick from each new concept of self. We become more natural and fluid in our lives. Eventually we can learn to let go continuously. Then we can experience the freedom and joy of manifesting our true nature. Koan practice is one way to learn how to move more freely from one identity to another and another. But daily life also can teach us how to do this. If we are paying attention, we will see that we never are, and never have been, just one self. This "me" is never stable; it is always in a state of flux. Our very nature is unfixed and dynamic. If we can't see that, we are ignoring the natural process of change. We are born and we die in every moment.

Maezumi Roshi had a favorite koan about Zen master Zuigan. Zuigan was a little eccentric. Every day he used to sit on a rock outside of the monastery grounds and call out to himself, "Hey, Master, are you in?" Zuigan would then reply, "Yes!" "Master, are you awake?" "Yes, I am!" Then he would say, "Don't be deceived by anyone!" "No, I won't!" Zuigan realized how easy it is to forget who we really are, so he called to the Master inside. Every day he reminded himself to wake up, to realize his true nature, and to listen to that wisdom. We can listen to the same wisdom: "Don't be deceived by anyone, especially yourself." You are not who you think you are! Your true self is no-self, ever-changing, and as vast and unknowable as the sky.

31

The Circle Path of Practice

> There is no place to go—just around and around and around.

WE ARE ALL conditioned beings, every one of us. We bear the marks of our conditioning in the ways we perceive and think about the world and ourselves, and in our responses to our perceptions and thoughts. We like to think we are open and free to respond in each moment, but sooner or later we begin to see how conditioned we really are. I'm not sure why we don't realize it sooner; it seems to be karma. But when we finally face the truth of our situation, the natural response is a desire to be free, and that's when we really begin on the Path of awakening.

In the beginning we see things in a particular way—dualistically. For example, when I notice I am in my small mind, my next thought will be, "I am not in Big Mind." And what usually follows is something like, "Since I'm not in Big Mind, I need to get into Big Mind." Likewise, when we realize that we are conditioned, our response will be the thought and desire to be free of conditioning. Do you see how the mind works? We begin on the Path and simultaneously set up a problem for ourselves. From a dualistic perspective, it looks as if we have been relatively unconscious up to this point. There seems to be a time before being conscious, so we think there must be another time of being conscious. The conventional mind believes we can be only one way or the other. We certainly can't be conscious and not conscious simultaneously, at least not from a logical point of view.

Through practice we experience the other side of reality—our nondual nature. And over time we become more accustomed to looking at things from the nondual perspective. We begin to see the unfixed nature of everything, including ourselves. This unfixed nature, the true nature of all things, is the manifestation of Kanzeon, the bodhisattva of compassion.

Kanzeon is a beautiful name, and it is the name we use for our sangha. I really love the name because it emphasizes the feminine. But actually Kanzeon is neither female nor male: she is both female and male. Kanzeon goes beyond duality; therefore, she is the manifestation of yin and yang, enlightened and deluded, conditioned and unconditioned. She manifests both sides. Although we may begin practice because we want to become less conditioned, we will never be free of all conditioning. Like Kanzeon, we always manifest both sides. The degree to which we leave behind our old conditioning and enter completely some new conditioning is the degree to which we are free. Do you get what I am saying? As we climb out of one box, we get into a new one. If you hoped to become unconditioned, I'm sorry to disappoint you.

Our practice is to let go of old conditioning, and yet we pick up new conditioning. Of course, we want to get out of the new box, too. So when we step out of the new conditioning, I guess there's only one place to go—back to conditioning! But something is different now. We may be back in the small mind, the old conditioning, but we did step out of it for a time. And the longer we stepped out, the clearer we become in our new conditioning, the Big Mind view, our original Mind. To step out for a quick glimpse helps a little; to step out for a few hours helps a little more. If we keep practicing in this way, our perspective will become fluid. Then even the old view is changed somehow. The ancestors said it this way: at first a mountain is a mountain; then a mountain is no longer a mountain; and finally again at some point, mountain is just mountain.

Dogen Zenji said, "Delusion is enlightenment." This deluded mind is enlightened—but that doesn't make sense. It's nonsense to the deluded mind, but to the enlightened mind, Big Mind, it makes perfect sense. Big Mind doesn't need to make sense out of it, and we don't need to comprehend or understand it. Why is this so difficult to accept? We stay stuck when we want to grasp and understand. I put my chains around me; you put your chains around you. Those chains are nothing but our conditioning: *my* understanding, *my* habits, *my* way of thinking, *my* emotional reactions. It all has to do with *me*. No one else keeps us chained.

Now stop for a minute and look in. What does the logical, rational mind want to do when it hears that? It wants to do something about it! Don't you feel the urge to do something, to drop your conditioning, throw off the chains, and be free? Next, we begin to look for someone who seems to be free, not caught up in the deluded mind. We want to find someone who has "It" so that we can receive It, or steal It, for ourselves. We start to look for a hero, a savior; and in so doing, we put the responsibility for our bondage "out there." But no one, living or dead, can free us. It's impossible for someone else to give us freedom, so we can't be dependent on anyone. We have to free ourselves.

Maybe the situation seems pretty bleak or even hopeless, but we *can* begin to free ourselves. Go back to the moment the desire to seek first arose. That little intention is really a doorway. Desire arises and our conditioning makes us want to fulfill the desire. It almost happens automatically, without any conscious awareness. Desire keeps us on a treadmill, running and running and running—but getting nowhere.

Imagine a big circle with each one of us someplace on that circle. Some of us are here, some of us are a little farther along, and some are far ahead. Now, the small mind is very nearsighted, but it doesn't realize this fact. So it looks ahead and sees Jack and Jill; it looks behind and sees Sam and Nancy. From this perspective the circle looks like a straight line. Everyone seems to have a place on the line, and that makes perfect sense to the small mind. A few people are in front, a few more people are behind, and each one of us is traveling from here to there. We're getting somewhere! But what happens when we look at the whole circle from the Big Mind perspective? The one who seemed to be in front is now far behind, and the one who was behind is now in front!

We practice in order to become more conscious. We work hard to let go of our conditioning and to leave behind the world as we knew it. We climb up the mountain and at some point reach the top. Then we must descend. The mountain is no longer the mountain. We must return to the conditioning, to the marketplace, the ground. This is where our delusion is complete. Dogen Zenji described this as delusion within delusion or delusion beyond delusion. Two are better than one! Only now there is a difference: we have been through the process, around the circle. We have gone through deconditioning and nonconditioning, and now we're back to conditioning. And here, we discover it's no biggie. It's nothing worth seeking! Is that a letdown? We have been seeking and striving and moving and working—all of it to become unconditioned. When we finally have an experience of being unconditioned, we realize it's no big deal! Of course, the first experience of freedom *is* a big deal. Any glimpse of freedom is a big deal when all we have known is bondage. At last we experience no limits, no fetters! But as with all new experiences, we eventually become accustomed to this, too, and then it's no big deal. When we have lived in the space of no-conditioning for a while, we get used to it.

So that's the end of the Path, right? Wrong! We want more. We begin seeking something clearer, better, greater. And seeking keeps the whole thing going, just as Buddha said. But in the gap between desire and striving to fulfill the desire, we can have some awareness and mindfulness. We can choose not to grab. Grabbing may look worthy—wanting to understand or to figure it out, wanting to have or to get, and wanting to become—but Big Mind doesn't care. Big Mind has no preference whatsoever. When we discover that self-involvement, our egoism, is the cause of the problem, the desire to become egoless or free of the self, naturally comes up. But we don't have to take the dualistic jump and think, "No-self is better than self." Still, most of us jump right in and tell ourselves, "If I am going to be spiritual, I should have no self; I should be free."

Why do that to yourself? Why not just be? The answer is, simply, it's difficult! To just be is the most difficult thing in the world. Even sitting in zazen, it's difficult to just be. But in zazen we can discover Big Mind. When we just sit, holding no preference, not craving or desiring, we *are* Big Mind. Anyone can do it; just sit! Of course, the small mind will creep in and say, "I'm not getting anywhere!" When that happens, just remember the circle. There is no place to go—just around and around and around. If you pass up someone, so what? From the bigger perspective, he or she is now in front of you. Try taking that into your relationships!

Just remember that there is no *right* way to do this. So obviously there is no wrong way either. Your way of walking the Path is the Buddha Way. The only thing we really need to do is just be. Then we're already there. Our small mind will keep whining, "I gotta get somewhere; I gotta understand," but the small mind never will. Is that a good thing or a bad thing? Big Mind doesn't know the difference. To Big Mind, it simply doesn't matter.

32

Life Is Practice

> Is Zen like a cup of coffee—something we can pick up, carry about the house for a while, and then set down to be forgotten until later? If this is how your practice works, let me set one thing straight: it's not Zen.

MANY OF US begin a spiritual practice like Zen with some kind of goal in mind, perhaps to help us understand or cope with a particularly difficult aspect of our life. Then, when we have achieved that goal or attained some resolution of the problem, we may want to broaden our practice to see if it can be helpful in other ways. Maybe we would even like to integrate practice into our life as a whole and wonder, "How can I bring Zen into my daily life?" It seems like a reasonable question, but if we look a little deeper, we will see that the question itself is the problem.

Is Zen like a cup of coffee—something we can pick up, carry about the house for a while, and then set down to be forgotten until later? If this is how your practice works, let me set one thing straight: it's not Zen. Yet we often think about practice in that way. What is it really that we are trying to bring into our lives? Perhaps we are holding on to some idea about Zen or about what it means to be spiritual or Buddhist, and we are trying to bring that *idea* into our daily lives. If so, this will cause us endless problems because ideas have very little to do with Zen.

The word *Zen* comes from the word *zazen*, the Japanese translation of the Sanskrit, *dhyana*. Maezumi Roshi used to translate *dhyana* as "quiet sitting" or "quiet thinking," but I prefer "silent sitting" or "sitting in silence." How can we integrate silent sitting into our lives without reducing Zen to a thing—something separate and apart from ourselves and our daily activities? The key is to take this question as a koan, a paradox that can't be resolved with the rational mind. As with any koan, we have to *become* this koan in order to clarify its meaning. Sitting in silence *is* Zen, and when we sit in silence, we *are* Zen. The *I* disappears and there is just Zen. Even when we are going about our lives, doing the different things we do, still we are Zen; there is no gap. Any notion about bringing Zen into our lives is extra.

There is a story about a meeting between a master and disciple that took place in China around the eighth century. The disciple's name was Baso, and his teacher was the great Zen ancestor Nangaku Ejo. One day Nangaku Ejo was walking on a path near the monastery when he found Baso sitting zazen under a tree. Of course, this is a common occurrence around a Zen monastery, but Nangaku Ejo asked, "What are you doing?" Right away we should realize that what he's asking is not just an ordinary question; he's giving Baso a koan. But Baso didn't get it, and he answered with the obvious, "I'm sitting zazen." Nangaku Ejo pushed a little harder: "Why are you sitting zazen?" It's good to know that Baso went on to become a great Zen teacher in his own right, yet here, he was as thickheaded as any of us, and he answered, "I'm sitting zazen to become enlightened, to become a Buddha."

Well, that seemed to satisfy the master, so Baso went back to his zazen. But moments later his silent sitting was interrupted again by an annoying sound: *tch, tch, tch, tch*. Looking up, he was surprised to see his teacher sitting nearby polishing one broken piece of roof tile with another. Eventually Baso just had to ask, "Master, what are you doing?" After all, Baso was trying to meditate. "I'm polishing this tile." "Why?" The master replied, "To make a mirror." This answer probably only added to Baso's exasperation. He blurted out, "You could polish that tile until you're blue in the face, and it will never become a mirror!"

That's when Nangaku Ejo cut through: "You can sit in zazen until you're blue in the face, and you will never become a Buddha!"

This koan is often misunderstood and misrepresented by people who don't see it clearly. Nangaku Ejo is not telling Baso that sitting is a waste of time; he's saying that sitting with the hope of enlightenment or the intention of becoming a Buddha is as ridiculous as polishing a tile to make a mirror. Why? Because to do that is to approach practice from a dualistic point of view, as something apart from who we really are. No matter how hard we try, we will never become something other than what we already are. Buddha doesn't need to try to become Buddha; enlightenment is realizing this fact.

Why, then, do we practice zazen? If you have any confusion or doubt about who you really are, then, of course, realizing that you are already enlightened, already Buddha, will have a profound effect on your life. But if you sit with this as a goal, you only create an obstacle, a hindrance to the realization itself. Sitting in zazen is already the perfect expression of your Buddha nature.

In approaching our practice of zazen, it is important to find the proper balance. Realization is important, of course; it is the foundation of Buddhism. The word *Buddha* comes from the Sanskrit root *bodh*, which means "awaken." So a Buddha is "one who has awakened," and the Buddha Way is the Way of Awakening. If we discount the importance of awakening, we are not practicing the Buddha Way, much less Zen. On the other hand, if we make realization the goal of our practice, we will never attain it. The goal of attaining enlightenment places realization somewhere in front of us, like a carrot in front of a donkey. When we focus our intent on arriving at the top of the mountain, we can't be truly present in every step. Yet we can also lean too far in the other direction and put too little importance on awakening and clarifying our realization. When we sit like a stone Buddha, that's what we are—a stone Buddha, not a living, breathing Buddha.

Zen practice is a paradox, a koan, and we need to embrace it like a koan. The question, then, isn't how do you take Zen into your life but how do you not? If you and I are Zen, then whatever we do is Zen. Walking, eating, talking, defecating, urinating, sleeping—it's all Zen!

You see, Zen is nothing special. If we think it is, we have only some idea about Zen, not the real thing. The difference can be very subtle. We can be thinking in our rational mind, "I haven't attained anything yet," while still holding on to the belief that we're doing something special. And if it seems special to me, just imagine how special it would be to share it with others, those poor unfortunates who haven't got it. Perhaps what we're really sharing is the stink of Zen. If truly you are Zen, and Zen truly is you, then what can you share with others? Not Zen and not your understanding. Share yourself.

When we think of Zen as a spiritual practice, and we hold on to some idea or notion of what spirituality is, we will strive to bring the trappings of spirituality into our lives. Perhaps we will even feel compelled to share our spirituality with others. It all stinks! Have you ever had someone try to share their spirituality with you? It's disgusting. In contrast, if you are offered a helping hand when you need it, that can be wonderful. Nothing in Zen says we shouldn't improve ourselves by becoming a better parent, a better friend, a better carpenter. When someone needs a carpenter and you give them your best work, you've shared yourself and made someone happy. To have Zen practice appreciated by the people in your life, maybe that is all you have to do: focus on what you're doing and do a good job. Taking Zen into your life doesn't have to be complicated.

Sometimes we overlook the most basic gifts of our practice. Take the ability to concentrate, for example. If you look around at work, at the gym, or at the grocery store, it's easy to see that most people find it difficult to simply focus on what they're doing. Being able to focus the mind is a natural by-product of sitting; and when we've been sitting a long time, being present in the moment becomes our natural state of being. Simply being 100 percent focused on our work—as a teacher, a carpenter, a whatever—can be the best way to communicate Zen to others.

Early on in zazen practice, we begin to see how everything changes continuously. We also begin to see that trying to control or interfere with the process of change only leads to disharmony, frustration, and conflict. As we learn to *let go* and *go with* the impermanence in our lives, we notice that change doesn't upset us as much as it used to. We begin to develop a certain fluidity and flexibility, and an ability to be *one with*, in harmony with the flow of change. This flexibility opens up many new ways to share our practice with others—not by saying or doing anything in particular but by sharing the gifts we've developed through zazen: calmness, the ability to focus and be present in the moment, and the ability to simply be who we are.

When we first come to Zen, we tend to think there is our life on the one hand and practice on the other. It may take some years before that separation dissolves completely. In the meantime, be patient and keep sitting; the illusion of separation will dissolve by itself. Go about your daily life and bring as much awareness as you can to whatever you are doing. When you're exercising, focus on your workout. When you're walking the dog, just walk the dog. When sitting zazen, be zazen.

In Zen we talk about *practice*, but really, any activity can become our practice. Maybe you are a student and you study very hard. Studying can be your practice. Maybe you are staying at home to raise kids. That, too, can be practice. Anything pursued with energy and focus can become your practice. Zazen is just the best way to dissolve the separateness that we've created. When the separation disappears, we realize the truth: practice is always our life, and life is always our practice. There never was a separation.

33

Life Just As It Is

> The Dharma, incomparably profound and infinitely subtle,
> Is rarely encountered, even in millions of ages.
> Now we see it, hear it, receive and maintain it.
> May we completely realize the Tathagata's true meaning!
>
> —Gatha on Opening the Sutra

WHAT IS the *Tathagata*'s true meaning? *Tathagata* means "suchness," "thusness," or we might say "as-is-ness," and it is one of the names of the Buddha. Shakyamuni Buddha embodied suchness. We may wonder how someone could embody suchness, but we might just as well wonder how anyone could *not* embody suchness. Doesn't everyone embody suchness just by living one's life? Buddha's enlightenment shows us the difference: some of us realize that we embody suchness, and some of us don't. Buddha also took the next step: he embodied and manifested his realization through his life. If it is to have meaning in our lives, we must learn how to manifest our own realization. But we will not fully manifest or embody suchness until we have truly realized it. One who realizes and embodies suchness is a Tathagata, is suchness.

Probably all of us have heard people complain that their lives feel incomplete or unfulfilled somehow; this sense of incompleteness seems to be common today. Perhaps this is because our consumer culture encourages us to seek fulfillment through things—a new car, home, job, or even a new partner. Self-help books are regularly found on best-seller lists, and many people read them hoping to learn how to give meaning and fulfillment to their lives. But even after searching for a long time and trying very hard, our feelings of incompleteness can remain unchanged. To find a path that actually leads to the fulfillment of our true nature is a rare and precious thing.

If we have been fortunate enough to have found a spiritual practice or path that suits us, most likely we first had to go through a long period of difficult searching. Many of us are drawn to a meditation practice because we feel that somehow we are not fully manifesting our lives. We may sense that our life is not whole, that something is missing, but we can't figure out what that "something" is. Or maybe, through a spiritual practice, we have had some realization of our true nature, but we have also seen the gap between what we have realized and what we are manifesting in daily life. It's only natural to want to close that gap. To reach this point of dissatisfaction may be uncomfortable or even painful, but actually it is a very good thing. Many people go through life without having even a glimpse of their true nature, so they never develop the desire to realize and manifest it. As it says in the *gatha*, the Dharma is rarely encountered. But we do encounter the Dharma and real fulfillment when we sit in zazen.

So what does "to encounter the Dharma" mean? In fact, it is rare to truly encounter anything or anybody. There is a koan that explores what it means to truly encounter the Dharma, and by working on this koan, we can develop deep appreciation for the opportunity we have. The koan tells a story about a confrontation between the famous teacher Joshu and a brazen young monk. The monk asked Joshu, "Did you really meet Nansen? You studied with him for forty years, but did you really encounter him?" It's a good question. To really encounter the Dharma, you have to *become* it; and to encounter the teacher, you have to meet intimately and become one with the teacher. How do you do that? *You* have to get out of the way! For Joshu to become Nansen, he had to drop Joshu. This is tremendously difficult to do because we are so full of ourselves there is simply no space for anything else.

All of us are stuffed full with our own opinions of the way things are—our ideas of suchness. If we can't drop our concepts and just be with what is, we create big problems for ourselves. When I come from my own perspective, I can easily mistake what I see as reality. And when I don't see and respond to what really is, things don't go very well. Reality hits particularly hard when we have been ignoring it. And what makes matters even worse is that other people are doing the same thing. Each one of us views reality from "my" perspective; so when we try to relate to one another, we can't. Most of us are thoroughly enamored with *my* view, *my* truth. No wonder we have so many relationship problems!

Our culture has helped to create this situation. Society conditions us to perceive the world dualistically. Conventional reality says that I am separate from everyone and everything. There is you, and there is me. There are trees, mountains, rivers, this whole earth—and then there is me. Buddha saw that we are deluded—our perception of separation is an illusion—and he taught the way that we, too, can see through our delusion. When we break through delusion, we encounter Oneness, wholeness, absolutely no separation. We have a direct experience of the Truth: you are me and I am you; this whole great cosmos is me, and I am it. Needless to say, experiencing this is mind-blowing and exhilarating. But the experience of Oneness is not the end of the story. We have encountered the Absolute, but that is not yet enlightenment.

When we experience our wholeness, it is as if we've returned home. With this shift in perception, we are filled with joy, freedom, peace, and love. Everything is me and I embrace everything. This experience of oneness with all things brings up feelings of compassion and the desire to help relieve the suffering of others. Our liberated view feels so good and right, we can easily try to cling to it. Of course we don't want to let go; we still remember how it felt to be stuck in duality. When we come from the absolute perspective, there is less suffering.

It's only human to try to cling to the absolute view of reality because it feels so good, but every perspective is limited, even this ultimate perspective. The absolute view that embraces everything and everyone is still only one perspective, just one side of reality. Even though it is the absolute truth, we have to relinquish this understanding. Someone who clings to this truth too long begins to smell bad. We call it "the stink of Zen."

The Ten Ox-Herding Pictures illustrate the process of Zen training and the stages of understanding or perspectives that we go through along the way. The first picture shows a young ox herder searching for the ox. This is when we first begin to acknowledge our basic dissatisfaction in life. We start to feel restless, hungry for some sort of change. In the second picture, the ox herder finds the tracks of the ox. This is when we stumble upon some promising tracks and start off on the search for liberation. We haven't actually found the way yet, but we have some hope that we will be able to find it. Perhaps we feel insufficient and incomplete. Maybe we have realized that the problem lies within. Our suffering pushes us to search for an answer, and this is when many of us become drawn to a meditation practice.

Meditation practice begins to open us to our true nature, and we begin to have glimpses into our complete and intrinsically perfect Self. This stage is shown in the third picture: the ox herder finally catches a glimpse of the ox. And because he's seen it, he starts to search in earnest. We have become convinced that liberation really is possible, so we go for it! We're like Indiana Jones: we put on our hat and go looking for the Ark of Truth.

Eventually we catch hold of the ox, our true nature. The fourth picture shows the ox herder having caught and roped the ox, but now he is struggling to control it, and he must use a whip. This is the stage of rigorous practice and discipline to tame the mind. Just because we have some kind of hold on our mind doesn't mean we can control it. At first we just get dragged around.

If we continue on with our meditation practice, our mind will become more calm and we can relax a little bit. But practice is still needed to tame the mind so that our true nature can be revealed. This is the stage shown in the fifth ox-herding picture, in which the ox herder is leading the ox with a rope. We have had some realization, some experience of nonduality, but we have lived most of our life coming from the relative view of the world. So at this stage we become acutely aware of how big the gap is between our true nature and our usual self. It takes time to let go of all the conditioning that causes us to see ourselves as separate from everything else. But with continued effort, we eventually become accustomed to seeing things from the enlightened perspective.

The sixth picture shows the ox herder riding the ox and playing a flute. Practice has become easy, and we are more comfortable with seeing our life and the world from the absolute perspective. We are beginning to trust the experience of our true Self. We don't have to work so hard to control it; we don't have to dig in our knees and struggle to stay on. We enjoy more trust and freedom, but there is a dark side to this stage of enlightenment: arrogance. This is another stage where it is easy to get stuck because arrogance feels so much better than inadequacy and incompleteness. At this stage I see that I am already complete and whole, so of course, there is no need to search for anything outside of myself. But when I look around, I see all those unfortunate others—those poor, unenlightened beings!—and I want to help them see what I see. After all, I know the Truth! I've got it! Can you smell the stink?

A big change has taken place in the seventh picture: the ox herder is sitting peacefully and all alone. The ox has disappeared. At this advanced stage, we have finally let go of the enlightened perspective. We can just sit like the Buddha, very comfortable, complete, and at peace. There is nothing special about me, and there is nothing to grasp. Even the enlightenment is gone. So what is left? Just me!

Maybe it seems that this stage would make a nice ending to the story, but there are three more ox-herding pictures. Even at this stage of practice, there is something extra—something still needs to go. The ox herder needs to lose the ox herder. The eighth picture shows the result: an empty circle. We have to lose our self—again. Now wait a minute! Didn't we lose our conditioned self already? Aren't we now able to identify with all things and all beings? Perhaps we didn't lose ourselves completely when we grasped the ox or when we let go of the ox. Maybe we simply traded the small self for a new self—a bigger and better one. Maybe we only expanded the self to include or embrace the universe, to become a superself! We can become so arrogant, our ego embraces the cosmos!

The ninth ox-herding picture shows an empty landscape. According to the great masters, this level is rarely attained. So few reach this level, it's not easy to talk about. It's hard even to imagine what someone would be like if they really lost the self completely. In many ways it's like dying. We lose everything because there is no self to hold on to and nothing apart from self to grasp. We become like Humpty-Dumpty: all the king's horses and all the king's men couldn't put Humpty together again. It all comes crashing down, and we can't put ourselves back together. We don't see ourselves or anything else because we embrace everything! There is just empty space.

From this experience of no-self and nothing else, there really is nothing left to do but return to the everyday world. The tenth picture shows the ox herder, now a ragged and barefoot old man, smiling and walking back into the marketplace with a sack of gifts slung over his shoulder. All perspectives have been lost; there is just manifesting what is. Suchness.

34

Your Life Is the Koan

As soon as we form the concept "my life," we have fallen into duality.

WE ALL have a problem, but some of us don't realize it. And of course, until we realize we have a problem, we will never begin to resolve it. Instead of resolving the problem of our life, we will notice all sorts of problems coming up: problems of those whom we care about and problems of our own. We can begin by focusing on each one of these problems: that's a legitimate way to go. But there's also a less complicated way.

The Zen tradition has its own problems. We recognize seventeen hundred koans: that's a lot of problems! In fact, it's too many, and no school works on all seventeen hundred. In the lineage of Maezumi Roshi, we work on about seven hundred koans; that means there are seven hundred different ways to look at our problem. It usually takes years for a student to go through each of these problems one by one; so of course, this is a gradual process. Yet Zen claims to be the school of "sudden" enlightenment. How can it possibly call itself "sudden" with so many problems and such a long training process? Zen must be able to show us how to go beyond trying to resolve each individual problem and to instead focus on *the* problem. What is *the* problem? I'll give you a hint. Do you remember the question "What is the koan?" The answers are the same: The koan is our life. The problem is our life.

As soon as we form the concept "my life," we have fallen into duality: my life as opposed to something else, my life as opposed to your life, my life as opposed to my death. Either way, it's a concept. Our life is a concept! Let me put it a little differently: it's inconceivable to conceive of our life as a problem. The problem always seems to be "out there," and the last place we want it to be is "here." We simply can't conceive of the nondual state. Anything that can be conceived is not nondual. Even the notion of dropping duality is duality. The duality that there is duality to drop is the last duality to drop. There is *nothing* to drop. There is *nothing* to do. Why do we find that so difficult to accept? We have so many different ways of doing, it's nearly impossible to give them all up. And when we try to give them up, we have to face our biggest fear: if we do nothing, we *are* nothing.

Can we really do nothing? I don't know. Do you? Can we really be nothing and do nothing? Obviously we've got a problem on our hands. The problem is our life, so what can we do about it? If we try to solve the problem, we only create another problem, another trap: our life becomes something to resolve, something to fix. In fact, there is *nothing to begin with*! So, of course, there's nothing to fix. But because that is inconceivable, we conceive ourselves as something—and that is what we try to fix.

We conceive of ourselves in different ways, first as a body, then as a mind. Don't you think you have a body and a mind? If so, you're in luck! We're in the age of fixin' and healin' the body and mind! Yet true healing is just being—and you and I can't do that. Healing takes place when we can just be, but *we* can't do it. If you or I want to heal ourselves, there's a "me" involved. Take the "me" out of the picture and then there's just healing.

When there is "me" and "my life," we've created a problem where a problem didn't exist. What can we do? We can go either the slow and gradual route or the sudden route; they're both kosher. If we go the gradual route, we'll keep coming up with more problems. We may realize eventually that we can't grasp it and we can't resolve it. As soon as we have this realization, though, we try to grasp it; and that only creates another concept. You can't have an answer. I also have no answer. If someone thinks they have an answer, it isn't the answer. You are the problem; you are also the answer. You're it!

If you can simply be one with that, there's no more problem. You're free. But if you try to grasp it, you've grabbed on to another concept, and you're stuck again. You may think you're free, or you may think you're not free; either way, you've created another trap. So what to do? There doesn't seem to be an answer—and in fact, there is nothing to do. We can't do anything, really, except take the next step.

Buddha saw that life is suffering, duhkha. So if we want to escape suffering, we've got a big problem. There is, however, a way to cope: we can *just be* the pain and suffering. Actually that's where compassion comes from. Life is pain, and all sentient beings have pain. Your pain and my pain is the pain of all sentient beings. Think about that for a minute. Admitting that we are our own pain is difficult enough; can we admit that we are also the pain of every other being? Now, that's hard to swallow! But if we are the pain of all beings, we are also the absence of pain of all beings—nirvana, the liberation from suffering, Buddha.

Try to conceive of that! If you can conceive that you are Buddha, you're not. Yet you are Buddha, even though it's inconceivable. The sudden path is to realize this in an instant, and that's really what Zen is about. It doesn't take time to realize who you are.

So what's the problem? There's a story of a monk going to his teacher and announcing, "I've resolved the koan; I have dropped myself." The teacher answers, "Then carry it on!" Don't create the problem to begin with; simply step off the one-hundred-foot pole! From the top every step looks fearful. All around is the abyss, the unknown. The only thing to do is take the next step.

No matter where we are, the next step is always *now*. The past and the future are only concepts. There is only now, the eternal present; and since we can't conceive of that, we have to *be* it. But how? The true present is no present. *No present!* There is nothing between past and future. What does that mean? Nothing! The eternal present is nothing. So why pretend to be something? There is absolutely no hope, no escape, no answer. There is no liberation; there is no nirvana. There is no suffering, no hell, no duhkha. It's all illusion.

Suffering is illusion, and freedom is illusion. To transcend these two, we need to embrace both. We have to be suffering *and* liberation, samsara *and* nirvana. As Buddha taught, attachment is always the cause of suffering—so don't attach to either one. Don't attach to any concept, enlightened or deluded. Still, if you think you're free of attachment, you are already stuck.

There really is no hope—that's what I'm trying to say. If you get it, that's it! If you get it and you're willing to live and manifest it, you're a Buddha. And if you choose to embrace the suffering of the world as your own, then you're a bodhisattva. We don't really have a choice, you see, so we might as well be big about it and choose it. At least then we're a true human being, living this life out of choice. We choose to suffer as a human being because all sentient beings suffer. No longer playing the victim, we become the master of our life.

Committing to our life, to being who we truly are, means we stop trying to escape our own suffering. We can have all kinds of suffering, or we can have just one big suffering. It can be gradual, or it can be sudden. We've got a koan: "Can I really do nothing?" If I become one with the koan, then I *am* nothing. Yet if I am nothing, I am also everything—Big Mind, boundless, infinite, unborn, undying. Big Mind embraces everything—every tree, every mountain, every insect, every person.

You are all beings, and all beings suffer—so trying to escape suffering is the same as trying to escape who you are. There are no sentient beings apart from Buddha and no Buddhas apart from sentient beings! When we open ourselves to the suffering of all beings, no division can be made between one being's suffering and another's. Then compassion manifests naturally. The moment we begin to create a separation, we fall into duhkha. Again, there is really no choice, so why not give up fighting and resisting? Why not choose to be it?

How does not-knowing fit into all of this? We already know that knowing is a concept, a delusion; but so is not-knowing. We need to go beyond the duality and embrace both aspects, knowing and not-knowing, without becoming attached to either one. Would that be sudden or gradual? It's both! Let's say you immediately get who you are; do you immediately manifest it? No, that's the gradual part. And when you look at how you came to your realization, did you suddenly get it without any groundwork? No, that's another gradual piece. Realization is always sudden, but all kinds of events can build up to it.

Maezumi Roshi used to say that Zen practice is all about growing up or maturing. One definition of maturity is to be responsible, or able to respond. Likewise, when we mature in practice, we become more able to respond to whatever situation is at hand. Yet that requires being truly present in the moment. Zen practice always comes back to the basics of being mindful and aware. When we're aware, we at least have the chance to respond appropriately. But when our response comes from self or ego, it's almost never appropriate. We need to take the self out of the picture for compassion to function freely. Zen practice teaches us how to do this, but of course, the self keeps coming back. That's why our practice needs to be continuous. Dogen Zenji described it this way: "Practice, realize, drop it! Raise the Bodhi-mind, practice, realize, drop it!" Endless practice—that's our life.

This life is truly endless and beginningless. We were never born; we are unborn—and what is unborn never dies. You and I never had a life to begin with. What, then, is born every moment? The illusion of self—and we can't hold on to that even if we try. To maintain the illusion of self just gets harder and harder. Aren't you already tired, exhausted, bored? Why not give it up? Then who created this world? "I did!" Not "We did." I did and you did. Who is destroying this world and all beings? "I am!" Who is reaching out to save all beings? "I am!" I am *the* cause—the principal villain and the savior, too. I am all of it.

35

Joshu's Stone Bridge

Joshu manifested just who he was—a true human being, far beyond human and Buddha.

I WOULD LIKE to share with you a beautiful koan about a monk meeting Master Joshu. Master Joshu is famous for his way with words; his spoken teaching is unsurpassed in the entire history of Zen. He is considered the greatest because of his unique gift for expressing situations or questions as koans, and many of his koans have been preserved in the major koan collections. This particular koan is a wonderful example of the genius of Joshu. On the surface it is very simple and clear; but at deeper levels it also contains the whole path of Zen practice, from the first ox-herding picture to the last.

First, though, a little background on Joshu can help us appreciate the situation described in this koan. Joshu began practice when he was eighteen, after meeting his teacher, Nansen. At that young age, he already had some understanding. Joshu's first question to Master Nansen was, "What is the Tao, the Way?" Although Joshu began his training with great desire and insight, he did not begin teaching until he was eighty-four years old. It wasn't that he was a slow learner—he became a successor in his forties—but he wasn't easily satisfied with his understanding. At the age of sixty-two, after Nansen had died, he left the monastery and sought teaching from many different Zen masters. It didn't matter whether they were older or younger than he was, Joshu vowed to learn from anyone who had deeper understanding and to teach anyone who could learn from him.

Now, imagine yourself in the shoes of a young monk meeting the venerable Master Joshu for the first time. At the time of the encounter in this koan, Joshu was a very old man, somewhere between eighty-four and one hundred twenty-four, the age of his death. Of course, the monk must have already heard about the legendary Joshu. And even before setting out to meet Joshu, the monk had probably developed a lot of expectations about what he would find. After traveling very far, the monk finally met the master face-to-face. What happened next? The monk blurted out, "I have heard of the wonderful and extraordinary stone bridge of Joshu, and yet I find only a plain wooden bridge!" Joshu answered, "It is because you see only the wooden bridge that you don't see the stone bridge of Joshu."

How can we use this koan for our practice? It's not very difficult to identify with the monk who was obviously disappointed in what he found. Maybe you have had an opportunity to meet with an accomplished teacher and can think back to your own experience. Or you can simply imagine what such an encounter would be like. But to really get to the heart of this koan, we need to ask ourselves, "What ideas do *I* have about such an awakened and accomplished individual? What are my ideas about what it means to be spiritual?" When it comes to ideas about what it means to be spiritual, we all have our preferences: either we want to be spiritual or we want nothing to do with being spiritual. Repressing such ideas won't make them go away; anything we try to repress only comes back later at full force. But the point is, ideas can blind us, just as they blinded this monk. Our notions can keep us from realizing or actualizing what we really want, so we need to look at our ideas about what it means to be spiritual, accomplished, awakened, and enlightened. Such concepts are tough and insidious—difficult to see and even more difficult to wash away.

Now, Joshu did not always appear to be a broken-down wooden bridge. There was a time in his life when he was manifesting a more noticeable magnitude and greatness. Early on, his teaching showed a certain kind of "greenness." We have a different way of keeping track of age in Zen. Basically we consider the first ten years of practice to be like infancy. The second ten years are like childhood, and the next ten years are adolescence. So reaching maturity can take forty years or more. At the time of the encounter in this koan, Joshu no longer needed to make a show of his greatness. He had gone so far beyond self-consciousness, meeting this monk was like playing with a polliwog. Joshu was being very nice, in a way; but he was also ripping the monk to shreds. Joshu's response fit like a glove: "Yeah, you don't see a grand bridge, but that is only because of your expectations."

Don't misunderstand where Joshu was coming from. He had been teaching for twenty years and studying the Dharma for nearly one hundred years when this brash young monk confronted him. Joshu wasn't giving the guy a watered-down teaching. A master of his accomplishment would never think that one occasion for teaching was less important than another or that one student was any less deserving than another. Every situation is a unique opportunity for teaching to occur, an opportunity to truly meet. So for Joshu, any discrimination between teaching and not teaching wouldn't make sense; he was far beyond such dualistic thinking. Similarly, Joshu's ordinariness was not because he wasn't extraordinary but simply because he had gone beyond needing to prove anything. He just revealed everything—who he was as a human being.

Joshu was an extraordinary teacher because somehow whatever came out of his mouth fit the uniqueness of each situation with great precision and insight. The circumstances were always changing, of course, and every student's question was unique, but Joshu's responses were always perfectly tuned. Why is it so different for us, when we are responding to the situations we find ourselves in? Why shouldn't everything that we say and do fit perfectly with the immediate situation? Well, just think about what it would take to get to Joshu's level of accomplishment. We would need to be completely in tune with the moment, one with the situation. And there could be no trace of self-consciousness or striving to meet some standard. If Joshu had been worrying about getting things right, he couldn't have made each teaching fitting and appropriate; his teachings would have been out of sync somehow. But remember, Joshu had worked many years in order to empty his mind. His mind was like a mirror, simply reflecting each situation perfectly. It was the same way with the Buddha. With such greatly enlightened people, every gesture is the Dharma. When the Buddha transmitted the teaching to Mahakashyapa, he simply held up a flower. In that moment holding up a flower was an ordinary and natural gesture; it wasn't planned. Buddha held up a flower, and Mahakashyapa got it.

In order to manifest such presence, Joshu first had to reach some degree of liberation from suffering, some lasting peace of mind; and along with such attainment comes understanding. Whenever we attain some new understanding, we tend to grab on to it. The monk thought he had attained some understanding; but really, he was just a beginner, still looking for special characteristics and marks of enlightenment. Joshu had already been there and done that; he had gone beyond holding on to any understanding. Joshu had accomplished something that is very rare, even among the historically great ancestors: he became completely plain and ordinary. That may sound like a simple thing to do, but it's not. To do it, you have to let go of everything!

Nobody wants to hear that, much less do it. After we have been practicing for some time, we want to have something to show for it. But if we really want to keep moving and growing, we have to be willing to look at the ideas, concepts, beliefs, and understandings we are holding on to, and then we have to let them all go. This is exactly what Joshu had achieved in his practice—and why so few attain it. Joshu had given up everything, particularly anything that resembled enlightenment. He gave it all up to become a plain, ordinary human being.

On one level we're all human beings, of course. Yet how many people do you know who have managed to become completely one with their ordinariness? The movie *American Beauty* illustrated the aversion we can feel toward our plainness. To the young woman in the movie, being ordinary was the worst thing she could imagine. Now, we may think we are ordinary, but to *settle* for ordinariness is scary. It's even un-American! Who wants to feel perfectly comfortable and completely at peace with being nothing special? Of course, before we can truly allow ourselves to be ordinary, we first have to be comfortable with who we really are. We have to go through, at least once, the experience of being whole, perfect, and unique. But after that experience, practice becomes a long downhill struggle to let go of it, every last trace! This becomes a lifelong practice, and Joshu used his long life to accomplish it.

I was fortunate to have a final meeting with Yamada Roshi just before he died. He was eighty something, and he had been practicing since his teens. He had studied with some great teachers, too, including Harada Roshi and Yasutani Roshi. At the time of our meeting, Yamada Roshi was himself a highly accomplished master. He told me something I will never forget. He said, "You know, it wasn't until I was seventy that I didn't give a shit anymore. Now, I don't care what people say or think about me. I just don't care!" Over the previous few years, people had been gossiping about all the strange things Yamada Roshi had been doing. Sometimes he even gave different students different answers to koans. Bizarre behavior! If you were one of his students, it probably looked that way. Maezumi Roshi did his share of bizarre and challenging things, too, some of which were embarrassing to me. Who wants to see their teacher making a fool of him- or herself? We want our teacher to make a good showing, especially when others are watching. Nevertheless, what we feel is bizarre behavior might actually be valuable teaching. Unless we stay open to this possibility, we might miss the point entirely.

When we come to Zen practice, we all have aspirations. We want to ascend the mountain—and of course, we have to! We can't really accomplish in this practice until after we have experienced the view of Big Mind. We need to experience our complete uniqueness and oneness, just as Shakyamuni Buddha did when he announced, "Below the heavens and above the earth, I alone am the revered one, the world-honored one!" But we also need to go beyond that experience. We need to ascend the mountain in order to have enough faith to let it all go again.

Yasutani Roshi used to chuckle and say, "After awakening, it took me ten years to let go of that enlightenment." In other words, even after ten years, he had not been able to let it all go. At first, when I heard him say that, I thought, "Wow, what a profound statement!" But it was not such a profound statement; it was the truth. He was just being honest: "Yeah, I had this experience ten years ago, and there are still strings of attachment."

On the one hand, we can get a little down and pessimistic about Zen being such a long-term practice. On the other hand, we can look at it as eternal practice. This practice goes on forever. Endless practice means endless life. Accomplishing the Way is eternal. I love what Bassui said: "You don't need to worry if you die before you reach so-called accomplishment; the work done in this lifetime will just continue on in a future time." Isn't it obvious? If you are building a bridge and you stop working for a while, you can get back to it a few days later. It's still the same project; we just lose sight of it for a while.

Even today we look to Joshu as an example of a highly accomplished person. But he lived a long time ago in eighth-century China, and we can wonder, what does it mean to be an accomplished individual in the twenty-first century? This is a very different container for the Dharma, a different culture and a different time. It is important not to hold on to any ideas or concepts about what Zen is, or we can end up like ice, unable to flow and take the shape of this new container. However, the intuitive understanding that we gain from our sitting can be used as a guideline. When we have experienced Big Mind for ourselves, we know that in order to live our realization, we have to somehow go beyond ourselves, our understanding, and our dualistic minds. We also know that enlightened life must include embracing ourselves and everyone else. Big Mind embraces everything, so to live that awareness means we have to embrace all aspects of life: our body, mind, and spirit; our strengths and our weaknesses; our masculine and our feminine sides; our brilliance and our stupidity; our enlightenment and our delusion.

Joshu embraced who he was completely. He had nothing to hide and everything to give. He was a fully integrated human being. We can romanticize what he must have been like, but what we really need to do is discover what it means to be an integrated human being right here and now. This is where zazen—lots of it—comes in. But in our day and age, most of us can't sit all the time. We have to go about our ordinary lives and get certain things done. That doesn't mean we can forget about being integrated when we're off the cushion. What good would that do? We must learn to bring integration into all of our daily activities, moment by moment and all day long. We also need to go beyond any ideas about how this should look. We don't need to be feeding the poor like Mother Teresa did in order to bring our realization into our lives. Walking my dog can be the most important thing I do in a day if that is when I am most integrated. Washing the dishes can be the most significant moment of our day if in that moment there is nothing but washing the dishes. We all want to do something really great, noble, exciting, helpful, and purposeful, but the dog still needs to be walked.

Any notions about doing something special or being someone special will become barriers to our practice. Another koan from Joshu talks about this, and it's a good example of the multilevel teaching Joshu is famous for. Here Joshu is meeting another newly arrived monk. Joshu asks, "Have you eaten yet?" "Yes." "Then wash your bowls." This is profound teaching; the great Master Joshu is telling us, "Wash up!" On one level Joshu is asking, "Have you awakened yet?" Yes? "Then wash it away!" Wash away all traces of our realization? That's tough!

Joshu's teaching is just as profound on the kitchen-sink level: "You dirtied some plates; clean 'em up!" Doesn't it seem as if we're forever cleaning up? There's always another dish to be washed, another counter to be wiped. But do you get what Joshu is saying? *That's it!* You don't have to look for anything more profound; just cleaning up after yourself can be a tremendous practice. Don't let a day go by waiting for great satori; it's here and now—cleaning up the kitchen, hanging up our clothes, putting our shoes away neatly. Living your realization can't get any clearer.

Joshu showed us what it means to be a *true* human being. This true transcends true and false, yes and no. At some point in our practice, we have the experience of no-self: being Buddha, an awakened being, not a human being. Then at some point we make a conscious choice to go back into the world of suffering, to become a human being again. Joshu embraced his humanness, not because he had no choice but because he had gone beyond resisting suffering and looking for liberation: been there, done that, gone beyond that. Joshu manifested just who he was—a true human being, far beyond human and Buddha.

36

The Global Sangha

> As our consciousness develops, we become more open and vulnerable to the suffering of the world, and there will be times when we try to close down. Yet our practice is to open ourselves up again and again.

ON SUNDAY mornings at Kanzeon Zen Center, in Salt Lake City, we hold a class that is open to everybody, from first-time visitors to old-timers in Zen practice. My goal for the class is to teach a little about Zen in a way that really speaks to the Western mind. The way I see it, anyone who walks in the door has already overcome a lot of obstacles, so I don't want to set up more barriers. My hope is that everyone will feel welcome and comfortable so they can relax and listen with an open mind.

There is a danger, however, in making things too comfortable. If we made everything about the Zen center completely familiar to the average American, would it still be Zen? How do we determine which elements of the tradition can be dropped in order to make it easier for Westerners to practice? Such decisions need to be made very carefully, and it probably is safest to take only small steps toward change. That way there will be less risk of losing anything that truly makes this practice Zen. We also need to respect the mystery of the Dharma and avoid trying to reduce it to something understandable. In the "Gatha on Opening the Sutra," an ancient poem chanted before teisho and Dharma talks, it says: "The Dharma, incomparably profound and infinitely subtle, is rarely encountered." We need to appreciate the Dharma in all of its mystery and profundity, and to truly value this rare opportunity to hear and practice the Dharma together.

The Sunday morning group is a particularly diverse bunch. Some people are dressed up; others are wearing casual clothes. Adults of all ages are present, and sometimes children are, too. People of different races and cultures are there. Obviously the sangha of today is very different from the sangha of the past, and it has different needs. The original sangha was made up of monks, or *bhikkus*. A little later the Buddha opened it up to include nuns, or *bhikkunis*. Because sangha was limited to monks and nuns, a lot of people were left out. The Buddha had thousands and thousands of followers, but compared with the number of people in the world, the sangha was only a tiny fraction. Nowadays sangha includes anyone who has received the Buddhist precepts, and men and women who have taken monastic vows. Even though there are now millions and millions of Buddhist practitioners throughout the world, I believe it is time to expand the meaning of sangha even further.

The modern world is certainly very different from the world at the time of the Buddha. Perhaps the most important difference is the fact that now so many things that we humans do have a global impact. It's more and more apparent that Earth is like a ship—Spaceship Earth. Together we face hazards like asteroids and comets, but we face equally dangerous hazards of our own making. It's been said that a butterfly fluttering its wings can change things at the farthest reaches of the earth. Modern technology has multiplied the potential impacts of our human actions infinitely more. Events happening on the other side of the globe really can and do affect us, and we can no longer afford to pretend that they don't. This earth of ours is actually a rather small and fragile boat.

For the first time in history, it's quite easy to be well informed about what is happening around the world. Nevertheless, being informed doesn't necessarily lead to sincere concern about what's going on. In reflecting on what it takes for us to develop genuine caring, I've noticed an interesting pattern: global awareness seems to dawn at about the same time we begin a spiritual search. The search for truth, meaning, enlightenment, and communion seems to appear simultaneously with an appreciation of the earth's interconnectedness, an awareness of Spaceship Earth.

There are some other interesting things that happen when we've begun to see the interrelatedness of all things and we've embarked on the search for Truth. For example, we become increasingly aware of karma, how our actions affect everyone, including ourselves. We also become more aware of the suffering of others. As our consciousness develops even further, we become increasingly open and vulnerable to the suffering of the world. At times the pain of it all can be overwhelming, and we may try to shut down and close our eyes for a while. Still, our practice is to open ourselves up again and again and to never forget our connection and absolute oneness with all beings. We practice stepping beyond the ego, beyond ourselves as individuals, in order to identify with the whole.

Buddha means "awakened one," one who is fully aware. In a nutshell that's what *Zen* means, too. The practice of Zen is to experience waking up, to become more and more conscious, to become a Buddha. From that perspective how many people are practicing Zen? We could say anyone seeking Truth is practicing Zen. Furthermore, all seekers are sangha because they are striving for greater awareness. Master Rinzai was speaking therefore to all seekers when he began his talks, "You followers of the Way . . ." All seekers are following the Way.

What *way* are we talking about when we say "the Way"? Here the word *Way* comes from the Chinese word *Tao*, as in Taoism. It means "the Way," but it also implies *your* way. To follow the Way is not what we might think; it does not mean that there is a narrow path to follow, like a little brick road leading to the end of the rainbow. *Your* way is the Way, and *your* life is the Path.

As followers of the Way, we are waking up—becoming more conscious and more aware of what this life is and how far it extends. This life is not nearly as small as we tend to believe. Think about how many family members and friends are affected by what you do in a typical day. Then think about how many people you connect with each day—and don't limit yourself to only those people with whom you connect consciously. Haven't we all had the experience of blissfully driving along when another car suddenly cuts us off? Often the driver of that car isn't even aware of what happened, and yet that action could have caused an accident. The point is, even our unconscious actions have consequences; the effects ripple outward and in turn affect how others respond. Sometimes we have little or no control over an event, but we always have some choice in how to respond. Awareness is key if we want to limit the karma we create. Every day we are tested in our ability to respond consciously. Each test is an opportunity to ask ourselves, "Am I really becoming more and more conscious, or am I simply reacting, responding habitually or mindlessly?"

We can know that our level of consciousness is expanding when our circle of awareness and concern grows wider and wider. This means we are developing true wisdom—the awareness of the interconnectedness and interdependency of all things. Our ability to act with compassion grows from this wisdom. When we come from the view of Heart-Mind, we see that not only is everything connected, everything *is me*! We are one, inseparable and identical. Thus, compassion is a natural outgrowth of our meditation practice. Ego-centeredness, on the other hand, doesn't simply disappear because we've had a glimpse of Big Mind. No, learning to come from Big Mind in daily life is a gradual process that takes persistent effort and a strong meditation practice.

Dogen Zenji urges us to practice as if our head were on fire. Yet very few of us actually apply ourselves in that way. When we look at ourselves, most of us have to admit that the fire within is more likely due to what Buddha called the *three poisons*: our greed, hatred, and ignorance. Once we see that, we may wonder if the statement "My life is the Way" really applies to us. But there is one thing we should have no doubt about: to be burning up with the three deadly poisons and yet *not* practicing as if our life depends on it means that we are living in denial. Basically we're ignoring the Buddha's teaching. Does that make us bad people? No, it just means we're being stupid; we are poisoned by ignorance.

Ignorance is found at the root of the other two poisons as well. Because of ignorance—seeing everything as separate from ourselves—we experience greed: we want, we need, and we will never be satisfied. The delusion of separateness also brings about fear. When others appear to be separate and different from "me," everyone is a potential threat, even loved ones. In fact, the more we love someone, the more vulnerable we are and the more easily we can be hurt. And once we've been hurt, our response is usually anger; we want to strike back. If we don't bring awareness to the situation and choose a different response, our anger can fester and grow into hatred. Our habitual responses, grounded in ignorance, can lead us blindly along, from one poison to the next, continuously.

It is very important that we learn to see our situation as it really is and to become aware of the three poisons; but this alone is not going to make a difference in the way we live our lives. Old habits of greed, anger, and ignorance are hard to change—but they can be changed. There are plenty of examples of people who have transformed themselves through steady and patient effort. We can transform ourselves, too, by working with our habits and reactivity. We can always be more compassionate and less self-centered and angry. We can become more conscious and mindful so that our awareness is expressed more clearly and completely. All of these efforts are practicing the Buddha Way.

I believe that by living our ordinary lives with more wisdom and compassion, we somehow influence the planet as a whole: we counterbalance some of the anger and fear in our world. All around the globe, wars are being fought over territory, politics, and religion; but to think that those are the *real* issues is just another form of ignorance. Most wars are based on greed. Some form of acquisition is going on; one group is trying to take what another group has. So the root of the problem is desire, wanting and craving something more. Then, when there is a threat of losing something, anger and fear are the predictable reactions. Yet there are better ways of responding, and meditation practice is the best training ground. By cooling the poisons of greed and anger within ourselves, we are helping to bring more wisdom and compassion into the world.

We begin, of course, by working with ourselves and our own greed, anger, and ignorance; but at some point we need to move beyond ourselves if we hope to save the planet. Our world is being consumed by greed, and we are running out of resources and time. To become aware of the problem is not enough. We have to *do* something. One of the most important tasks is to fight against our tendency to fall back into denial. We all have strong resistance to staying open and aware. It hurts! We share the pain of the world when we are truly awake and present, so it takes great commitment and effort to continue to expand our awareness. We also need to keep going: we need to draw on the wisdom and compassion that come from awareness and *act*. We are all in this together, and we need to work as a team—as a world—if we want to save ourselves.

Zen practice empowers us with a unique orientation to working with the problems of the world. Buddhism has always been about going to the root of the problem. That doesn't mean we should ignore the branches, but if we really want to solve the problem, we have to go to the root. We Westerners love quick remedies; we like to apply Band-Aids and to hand out aspirin. But quick fixes will never touch the underlying illness: ignorance—the idea of self and other. To see myself as an island, different and completely separate from everyone else, is delusion. There are no islands! What we do affects everything and everybody, and it is our responsibility to stay awake and to do what we can to help others wake up. Global consciousness needs to be our aspiration.

Bodhisattvas are called "heroes" because they accept this task and vow to continue working until all sentient beings have awakened. Bodhisattvas know that nothing less will do the job because we are one body and mind; separateness is only an illusion. The Buddha is also known by another name, the "Great Physician," because after awakening to Oneness, he was driven by compassion to go straight to the root of the disease and to lay out a path to the cure—waking up to our complete interconnectedness. Each one of us has a role to play in bringing about this shift in consciousness on a global scale. As individuals, our practice can always be to deepen our own awareness and to manifest it more clearly in everything we do. Our ordinary life then becomes a vehicle for the Dharma. The Way is created right under our feet!

For the first time in history, we have the ability to destroy life as we know it. This awesome fact means we each have a responsibility to awaken to the absolute Truth, to fully realize this one body, one world, One Mind. We must also remain aware of the relative reality: as individuals, we are completely interconnected. What I do affects you, what you do affects me, and what we do affects the rest of the world. In Buddhism this interconnectedness is depicted by Indra's net, a cosmic net with a multifaceted diamond at every knot so that every diamond reflects all the other diamonds. Our lives are those diamonds. We cannot separate ourselves from one another, and the fate of the planet depends on how conscious we become. By realizing our oneness, we are more able to act with compassion and love for every being, every stone, this whole earth. To save ourselves and this planet, we must see who is responsible. Then we must live it.

37

Practice in Difficult Times

> Give all your merit away as fast as you can offer it. Now is not the time to be sitting with only our own concerns. We can use this tumultuous time to awaken, not just one's self but everyone on the planet. We are one body, One Mind!

DIFFICULT TIMES, whether personal or global, always present the opportunity to test our understanding of the Dharma and to look at how we are living the Buddha's teaching. But global problems also arouse our tendencies to go unconscious, to plug up our ears and not hear the cries of the world. Thus, we ignore our responsibilities to respond with wisdom and compassion. Barraged by daily news of tragedies and horrors around the world, we can find ourselves lulled into a sort of sleepy detachment. Sometimes it takes an especially terrible event, or some crisis close to home, to shake us awake. One way that we can help ourselves stay more conscious and sensitive to the suffering of the world is to really think about the news stories we hear and to put ourselves in the skin of those who are suffering. The awareness and insight that we gain from this practice can be the starting point for investigating how well we are putting our practice into action. Are we really embodying the compassion of Kanzeon Bodhisattva, or are we simply clinging to our ideas about what it means to manifest the awakened life?

The Dharma provides support and guidance for difficult times. We could say that it's a practice for dealing with change. The Buddha taught that nothing is permanent; everything is in constant flux. He went on from there to teach us how to stop resisting change and to instead become one with it. Our practice helps us learn how to let go of the past and open ourselves to the present moment. That doesn't necessarily mean we will feel better, but it does mean that we will see what is really going on; we will notice our reactions to all the change that is happening. Thoughts, emotions, and memories can be stirred up, and they often add to our suffering. The basic teaching of Zen is to "be one with"—no matter what is coming up. So if we are feeling fear, we don't try to hide from or repress it; we simply experience the fear. By being one with our fear, we will see that it, too, is impermanent. We can watch it arise, build, and eventually disappear. Our task is to stay awake and present, to experience all of it. In this way we learn to flow with change.

For the Buddha to have made impermanence his first teaching may seem harsh. Our culture tends to cover up the truths of death and loss, and many of us have been raised to ignore our own impermanence. But sooner or later each one of us is confronted with death and loss in ways that shake us awake. Then we can see the compassion in Buddha's teaching. Compassion, like wisdom, has two aspects—yin and yang, feminine and masculine—and sometimes compassion is quite sharp. For example, I feel terrible when my little dog fights to get free of her leash. I love nothing better than to let her loose in the park and see her run wild—it's such a joy to her. But around busy streets, the compassionate thing is to keep her leashed. And when she gets loose accidentally and runs out on the street, I have to scream at her to stop—it's the only thing she'll listen to. To scream at her is the compassionate thing to do in that moment. At some other time, it will be more compassionate to praise her.

Buddha's teaching of impermanence is like a compassionate wake-up call; it helps us stay present in the moment and aware of how precious life is. When life is going very smoothly, we tend to take things for granted. Crises can actually be useful to our practice because they snap us awake. After even very loud wake-up calls, though, we still have a strong inclination to go unconscious and to return to complacency. Many teachers have likened this situation to war: a war between being awake and conscious on the one hand and being unconscious and unaware on the other. It is really a war between Buddha Mind and ignorance. When we have realized our Buddha nature, it becomes our work and our duty to respond with the compassion of Kanzeon Bodhisattva to those who are suffering. In Zen training centers, we chant the four vows. The first, "Sentient beings are numberless; I vow to save them," is the vow of the bodhisattva. We vow to stay aware of sentient beings throughout the world, to remember that they are not separate or apart from us. I am all sentient beings, and you are all sentient beings. How can we ignore the cries of the world?

To respond as Kanzeon means to respond in a way that is appropriate to the situation. We can do that only when we are fully conscious and aware of what is happening in the moment, so we need to be open and receptive to the details of the particular situation. The best response won't always be what we would typically think or plan. The best response needs to come from a basic intelligence combined with wisdom and compassion. Think of firefighters who run into burning buildings to save others. They are responding in the moment in a very selfless way. They are Kanzeon, acting with the selfless compassion that comes from wisdom.

Kanzeon Bodhisattva is one who chooses to respond selflessly to the suffering of the world. She is able to manifest in whatever shape or form necessary to liberate those who are suffering; therefore, to those who are suffering, she takes the shape of suffering. Our practice is to become one with whatever it is. When we feel fear, our practice is to be the fear. There is nothing ignoble about being frightened; we are living in a scary time. If we stay conscious, we can't deny our own fear or the fear that is pervading our world. By opening to our fear, we can become familiar with its triggers, which are always rooted in dualistic thinking. We fear what appears to be separate and outside of ourselves. So we use practice to chip away at the illusions of separateness. From the enlightened perspective of Heart-Mind, we can see that what appears to be separate is actually like waves on the ocean. The separateness is only the surface reality. Underneath, it is all one ocean. If we want to help relieve the world's suffering, we need the wisdom to see that we are one body-mind. Then our responses can come from true compassion.

Today Kanzeon is manifesting in many new forms, including ways of practicing the Dharma. The ability to know about events on the other side of the globe challenges us to respond in new ways. For the past twenty-five hundred years, monastic life has been the dominant form of practice. In our present time, I believe the whole paradigm for practice is breaking open, especially regarding the forms of practice for laypeople. Traditionally only monks and nuns have been trained in officiating services and in offering and dedicating our practice and its merits to the benefit of all beings. Now is a time, I believe, when we all need to learn how to use those tools. We all need to be empowered to engage with life in a sacred manner. Why shouldn't we teach everyone how to pray for others and to make dedications and offerings using the rituals of our tradition?

In order to act as Kanzeon, we must truly hear and digest the teachings. Every day we witness the first noble truth: Life is suffering. From that awareness comes the desire to understand the cause and the end of suffering. Through our own practice we validate the second noble truth: The cause of suffering is ignorance, delusion. Because we see things dualistically, we cling to our notions of self and other. Always the result is attachment, craving, and clinging. Through zazen we are able to see through the illusion of self to the absolute Truth that we are all One. We are One Mind, one life, and one body, manifesting as the infinite dharmas.

Ignorance causes our own suffering, and we can see this at work in the world, too. Incredible suffering comes from our inability to see that we are all One. As bodhisattvas, our concern can't be limited to ourselves and our personal suffering; we have to take on the suffering of the world. We are One! So when it comes to the third noble truth, that there is liberation and freedom from suffering, we can't settle for some cavalier notion of what that means. To be "free from suffering" doesn't mean that we somehow separate ourselves from suffering; it means we become free and liberated *in* our suffering. Through practice we experience for ourselves that nirvana is not outside this life or our daily experience. Liberation happens in the midst of samsara—our pain, sadness, anger, confusion, and fear—when we are able to be completely one with our experience. Nirvana is being completely free to suffer.

Buddha taught that the way to end suffering is through the Middle Way, the fourth noble truth. We need to remember what that "middle" means. The Middle Way transcends duality. It goes beyond ideas of me and you, us and them, good and evil, this and that. Our life is the Middle Way; we embody all of it. Each one of us is capable of good and evil, and any evil that someone can commit is also within each one of us. We can't simply project the enemy outside; we need to see that the same enemy lies within. Our practice is to bring light into the dark, shadowy places hidden within ourselves and in the world.

We are at war. The entire globe is in a war against time and our tendency to fall back into delusion and unconsciousness. Of course, every one of us will have doubts about our abilities to endeavor and keep going, especially when the world's troubles seem so unsurmountable. But as far as I'm concerned, there is no better time to sit in zazen than right now. Each one of us has a role to play, a job to do. Our job is not only to work toward our own awakening and the deepening of our wisdom and compassion but to help and support this development in one another. Our practice needs to extend beyond us as individuals. This is a time when we should be coming together—as couples and families, as communities and sanghas, as a nation and world—praying together, meditating together, offering our meditation and its merits, offering our recitation of sutras and prayers. By coming together, we can magnify the effects of our efforts to counterbalance the negativity in the world. Life keeps showing us that there really are no boundaries or borders, so why limit our practice?

Sometimes we become discouraged about our ability to make a difference in the world. We may doubt that we have anything relevant to give or any service to offer. But we shouldn't minimize the power of offering our zazen. Bodhidharma went to China because he had a job to do: he was committed to bringing the Dharma to the people there. At the time, he was the sole holder of the Dharma, the only person in the world who was empowered to carry it forward. Even so, he was given only one interview with the emperor before being sent away as an imposter. Did he give up? No way! Bodhidharma found a cave and sat zazen for nine years before someone who could hear the Dharma finally arrived. Sitting in zazen wasn't just a way to kill time. Bodhidharma had complete faith and trust in the power of his meditation. Alone in his cave for nine years Bodhidharma was transmitting the teaching through his zazen! And thanks to the strength of his faith, the teaching still exists sixteen hundred years later.

Since zazen is our practice, we can always offer it to the world and all beings. Every time we sit, we can offer up the merit and positive energy we generate. When we feel ready, we can also include in our meditation sessions a more advanced practice called *tonglen*. The Tibetan Buddhist traditions have developed specific techniques and guidelines for tonglen practice; but briefly, the task is to breathe in the negative energy of the world and to breathe out the positive energy that we build up by sitting in samadhi. So instead of putting up walls of resistance to the pain and suffering in the world, we expand ourselves to embrace and transform it. In this way we offer the world the wisdom and compassion that we have cultivated through our practice.

Give all your merit away as fast as you can offer it. Now is not the time to be sitting with only our personal concerns. We can use this tumultuous time to awaken, not just one's self but everyone on the planet. We are one body, One Mind! Our zazen can be put to work to embrace our own suffering and the suffering of others. And when we offer the merits of our sitting to all sentient beings, we are sharing the light of the Dharma with the world. We become transformers of negative into positive for the sake of all beings.

Practicing in order to deepen our own realization is important, of course, and to have that as a goal doesn't mean we have gone against our bodhisattva vow of selflessness. In fact, dana paramita is the most direct path to realization and to the wisdom and compassion that come with realization. *Dana* means "to give," "to be generous." *Paramita* means "to cross over to the other shore." *Paramita* also implies having already crossed over. It's a paradox. The quickest way to the realization that we are already on the other shore is to give ourselves away—to relinquish our ego-centered self so that our true nature can be revealed. Giving ourselves away to our meditation is the most direct way to have this realization. Buddha nature extends far beyond our ego-centered selves; it is one with the entire cosmos.

When we realize this Heart-Mind for ourselves, we see that we, too, are one with the entire cosmos. This life that appears to each one of us as "my" individual life is a manifestation of Buddha, the Unborn. Our true nature is entirely ungraspable and constantly changing. We are being born and we are dying every instant. There really isn't any self to cling to; to see this is liberation. Finally we can let go of self-clinging, the illusory ideas of a permanent self.

The most turbulent times are often the most fruitful for practice because they make it impossible to deny that tomorrow is truly unknowable. We no longer can live as if each day will be just another day, and we can't take anything for granted, including that others will be there. It is as if our world has been turned upside down. When we live on the edge of the unknown, every moment becomes a wake-up call. We are shaken awake, challenged to be conscious in each moment. Every day we can recommit ourselves to our practice—to deepening our understanding of the teachings and to manifesting compassion in everything we do. Practice is here and now, and it is up to each one of us to live the wisdom we have experienced.

The troubles of the world today are unprecedented. The future of the entire planet is unknown, so this is no time for complacency. Nothing can be counted on as reliable or lasting. This is a terrible truth, but to swallow it is the liberation we seek. In fact, what we call *dai kensho*, the "great death," is simply swallowing this truth completely. Then, when life asks us, "Hey, boss, are you in?" we can answer like Zuigan, "Yes, I am!"

NOTES

CHAPTER 15: THE GREATEST GIFT

1. Genpo Roshi is alluding to Shunryu Suzuki Roshi's now classic book *Zen Mind, Beginner's Mind: Informal Talks on Zen Meditation Practice*, ed. Trudy Dixon (New York: Weatherhill, 1970).

CHAPTER 21: BIG MIND

1. *Big Mind* is also the name of a guided process developed by Genpo Roshi to facilitate individuals in accessing Big Mind awareness. In this chapter the reader is guided through a series of questions that introduce him or her to Big Mind and give a taste of the more extensive Big Mind process. The process itself combines methods of Zen and voice dialogue. It is especially effective in gaining the cooperation of the ego so that the unborn and limitless Mind of the Buddha is awakened and can be engaged in open dialogue for self-exploration. Genpo Roshi leads workshops and trains facilitators in the Big Mind process in several locations in the United States and Europe.

CHAPTER 26: MOUNTAINS AND VALLEYS

1. Zenkei Shibayama, *The Gateless Barrier: Zen Comments on the Mumonkan*, trans. Sumiko Kudo (Boston: Shambhala Publications, 2000), 134.

CHAPTER 27: THE MIDDLE WAY

1. Eihei Dogen, *Shinjin Gakudo—Moon in a Dewdrop: Writings of Zen Master Dogen*, ed. Kazuaki Tanahashi (New York: North Point, 1985), 88.

GLOSSARY

ancestor. Anyone who is a Dharma-successor, having received formal transmission of the Buddha-dharma. *See* patriarch, transmission.

anuttara-samyaksambodhi (Sanskrit). Supreme complete awakening. *See* satori.

Avalokiteshvara. *See* Kanzeon.

awakening. The act of becoming aware of the true nature (emptiness) of all things, including oneself. An alternative term to the Sanskrit *bodhi* (lit. "awakened"). *See* enlightenment, kensho.

Baso (709–788) (Chinese, Ma-tsu Taoi-i). Chinese Zen teacher noted for his use of numerous training methods. He had 139 successors and is famous for many sayings and incidents now incorporated into case koans.

Bassui (1327–1387) (Japanese, Bassui Tokusho). Japanese Zen master of the Rinzai school, known for his insistence on solitary zazen practice and the personal koan "Who Is the Master?"

Big Mind. *Also* Buddha Mind. One's original mind or true mind. Big Mind has neither beginning nor end and is limitless, formless, and colorless, yet manifests as all things. The "Big Mind" process, developed by Genpo Roshi, facilitates a person in accessing Big Mind and using that perspective to consider his or her own life.

Bodhidharma (470–543?). The twenty-eighth Dharma-successor of Shakyamuni Buddha, recognized for bringing Zen to China, where he became known as the first Chinese patriarch. According to tradition, he practiced zazen in a cave for nine years before transmitting the Dharma to Eka.

Bodhi-mind (Sanskrit) (lit. "awakened" mind). *Also* Buddha Mind, unborn Buddha Mind. The mind in which an aspiration to attain enlightenment has been awakened.

bodhisattva (Sanskrit) (lit. "enlightenment being"). One who practices the Buddha Way and compassionately forgoes final enlightenment for the sake of helping others become enlightened.

Buddha (Sanskrit) (lit. "awakened one"). A term that variously indicates the historical Buddha Shakyamuni, enlightened persons who have attained Buddhahood, and the true nature of all beings. *See* Buddha nature, Shakyamuni.

Buddha-dharma. *Also* Dharma. Generally, the teachings of Shakyamuni Buddha and the Way to follow in order to attain enlightenment. In Zen, Buddha-dharma is the realization of one's true nature; it transcends conceptual and intellectual understanding and arises directly out of one's own experience. Buddha-dharma is directly transmitted from Shakyamuni Buddha, from Buddha to Buddha, Heart-Mind to Heart-Mind, outside of words and letters.

Buddha Mind. *See* Bodhi-mind.

Buddha nature. *Also* true nature, true Self, the Unborn. The complete and perfect nature intrinsic to all beings.

Buddha Way. *See* Tao.

dai kensho (Japanese) (lit. "great death"). Great enlightenment or satori, seeing completely into one's true nature beyond all doubt. *See* kensho, satori.

dana paramita (Sanskrit) (roughly "generosity"). *See* paramita.

delusion. The lack of awareness of the true nature of all things, which is emptiness; belief in the separate objective existence of things; the erroneous ascription of inherent existence to the world of appearances, which in turn leads to clinging and suffering. In Buddhism the word *delusion* is used synonymously with *ignorance.*

Dharma (Sanskrit). Central notion of Buddhism, used in various meanings: (1) the cosmic law, Truth, reality; (2) the teachings of Shakyamuni Buddha; Buddhist doctrine; (3) the general state of existence; the manifestation of reality; a thing, phenomenon.

dharmadhatu (Sanskrit) (lit. "realm of Dharma"). The uncaused and immutable totality in which all phenomena arise, dwell, and pass away.

dharmakaya (Sanskrit). First of three aspects of Buddha nature, known as the *trikaya* ("three bodies"). Dharmakaya indicates the absolute reality beyond all discrimination and conceptualization; the unity of Buddha with all beings. The second aspect, *sambhogakaya*, refers to the Buddhas who manifest the powers arising from perfect enlightenment. The third, *nirmanakaya*, is Buddha nature in human form acting for the benefit of sentient beings.

Diamond Sutra (Sanskrit) (*Vajrachchedika-prajna paramita-sutra*, lit. "Sutra of the Diamond-cutter of Supreme Wisdom"). An independent part of the *Prajnaparamita-sutra*, highly regarded in Zen, which sets forth the doctrines of *shunyata*, emptiness, and *prajna*. The sixth patriarch attained enlightenment upon hearing a phrase from this sutra.

Dogen Zenji (1200–1253) (Japanese, Dogen Kigen or Eihei Dogen). Japanese Zen master and Dharma-successor of Tendo Nyojo, who brought the tradition of the Soto school from China to Japan; established Eiheiji, the principal Soto training monastery in Japan; best known for his collection of Dharma essays *Shobogenzo*. *See* Genjokoan.

dualistic thinking. Thinking that is based on duality, the belief in the separate existence of oneself; thinking characterized by the separation of subject and object. *See* delusion.

duhkha (Sanskrit). Suffering; our basic dissatisfaction, suffering, alienation, and loneliness; not being at peace; the first noble truth taught by Shakyamuni Buddha. *See* Eightfold Path, nirvana.

Eightfold Path. The Path leading to release from suffering; the fourth noble truth taught by Shakyamuni Buddha. The Eightfold Path consists of right view, right thought, right speech, right action, right livelihood, right effort, right mindfulness, and right samadhi.

Eka (487–593) (Chinese, Hui-k'o). The second Chinese patriarch, Dharma-successor of Bodhidharma. Eka is famous for his unstoppable determination to become a student of Bodhidharma.

emptiness (Sanskrit *shunyata*). The fundamental nature of all phenomena; the absence of inherent existence.

enlightenment. The experience of emptiness, the true nature of all things, in which duality and separation disappear; the direct experience of one's intrinsic wholeness and complete interconnectedness with all things. Often used synonymously with *dai kensho* and *satori*. *See* awakening, kensho.

Enyadatta (Sanskrit). A character in a story told by Shakyamuni Buddha and recorded in the *Lotus Sutra*. Enyadatta thought she had lost her head and searched frantically to find it, refusing to believe she still had it. Enyadatta's search for her head represents the Zen student's seeking after his or her true nature.

fifth patriarch (601–674) (Chinese, Hun-jen; Japanese, Gunin or Konin). The fifth Chinese ancestor after Bodhidharma; teacher of Hui-neng. *See* sixth patriarch.

Four Noble Truths. The basis of Buddhist teaching. The first noble truth, that life is suffering, refers to our basic dissatisfaction, alienation, and loneliness. The second noble truth specifies the origin of suffering: craving and despising, attachments and aversions, which stem from ignorance (delusion). The third noble truth states that liberation from all clinging brings about complete peace, nirvana. The fourth noble truth delineates the Eightfold Path, which leads to this liberation. *See* delusion, Eightfold Path.

four vows. "Sentient beings are numberless; I vow to save them. Desires are inexhaustible; I vow to put an end to them. The Dharmas are boundless; I vow to master them. The Buddha Way is unsurpassable; I vow to attain it." These vows are chanted by Zen practitioners as an expression of their aspiration.

Ganto (828–887) (Japanese, Ganto Zenkatsu; Chinese, Yen-t'ou Chuan-huo). One of Tokusan's successors and close Dharma-brother of Seppo. Ganto's great shout as he died became an important koan for many who followed.

gatha (Sanskrit). A short chant used in Buddhist ceremonies.

Genjokoan (Japanese) (lit. "The Way of Everyday Life"). Fascicle of Dogen Zenji's *Shobogenzo* that concerns practice and enlightenment in everyday life.

Hakuin Ekaku Zenji (1686–1769). The patriarch of Japanese Rinzai Zen through whom all present-day Rinzai teachers trace their lineage. He systematized koan study as we know it today.

Harada Roshi (1871–1961) (Japanese, Daiun Sogaku Harada). One of the most important Zen teachers of modern Japan, trained in Soto and Rinzai traditions; teacher of Yassutani Roshi.

Heart-Mind (Japanese, *shin*). Also Buddha nature, true nature. Based on the Japanese derivation (*shin*) of the Chinese character *hsin*, which can be translated as "heart, spirit, consciousness, soul, mind, thought," Heart-Mind refers to one's entire consciousness, whole being (body-mind-spirit), or true nature, which transcends the distinction between mind and matter.

Heart Sutra (Sanskrit) (*Mahaprajnaparamita-hridaya-sutra*, roughly "Heart-piece of the *Prajnaparamita Sutra*"). Short section of the *Prajnaparamita Sutra* esteemed in Zen for its concise expression of the experience of emptiness (shunyata).

Hekiganroku. *See* koan.

Hui-neng. *See* sixth patriarch.

ignorance. *See* delusion.

impermanence. The transitoriness of conditioned existence. *See* three marks.

Indra's net. Image from the *Avatamsaka Sutra* that pictures a cosmic net woven with a jewel at every intersection that reflects all the other jewels. Just as one jewel contains all others, every moment of awareness contains the unity, the diversity, and the interrelatedness of all.

jijuyu-zanmai (Japanese) (lit. "joyful, self-fulfilling samadhi"). The hallmark of Zen, which has been transmitted from Buddha to Buddha through zazen. *See* samadhi.

joriki (Japanese) (lit. "samadhi power"). The vital, stabilizing energy arising from strong zazen practice. *See* samadhi.

Joshu (778–897) (Japanese, Joshu Jushin; Chinese, Chao-chuo Ts'ung-shen). One of the greatest Zen masters of ancient China. Many koans originated with Joshu, including the koan "Mu." *See* Mu.

Kanzeon (Japanese, also Kannon; Sanskrit, Avalokiteshvara; Chinese, Kuan-yin) (lit. "One Who Hears the Cries of the World"). One of the principal bodhisattvas in the Zen Buddhist tradition, personifying great compassion. While usually represented in the female form, Kanzeon manifests in whatever form is needed in order to answer the needs of all beings.

Kapleau, Philip Roshi (b. 1912). Author of *The Three Pillars of Zen* (New York: Weatherhill, 1965) and founder of the Zen Meditation Center of Rochester.

karma (Sanskrit). The principle of causality, which holds that for every effect there is a cause. Regarding the human sphere, karma refers to the principle that by our actions we determine the quality of our lives and influence the lives of others.

kensho (Japanese) (lit. "seeing into one's nature"). An experience or a glimpse of enlightenment. Generally *kensho* refers to an early or incomplete experience of enlightenment, whereas *satori* is used synonymously with *dai kensho*, or "great enlightenment."

koan (Japanese) (lit. "public document"). In the Zen tradition, a statement, a question, an anecdote, or a dialogue that cannot be understood or resolved intellectually. Meditation on a koan leads one to transcend the intellect and experience the nondual nature of reality. Koans are given by the Zen teacher to bring students to realization and to help them clarify their understanding. Roughly seventeen hundred koans have been recorded from Chinese and Japanese sources. Many "case koans" recount an exchange between teacher and student or a master's enlightenment experience. They can be found in various collections, most notably the *Mumonkan* ("Gateless Gate"), the *Hekiganroku* ("Blue Cliff Record"), the *Shoyoroku* ("Book of Equanimity"), and the *Denkoroku* ("Book of the Transmission of the Lamp").

Koryu Osaka Roshi (1901–1985). Japanese Rinzai master and lay teacher from whom Maezumi Roshi received confirmation (*inka*) in 1972.

Lotus Sutra (Sanskrit, *Saddharmapundarika-sutra*). One of the most important sutras of Mahayana Buddhism, containing the teaching of the transcendental nature of the Buddha and the possibility for universal liberation.

Maezumi Roshi (1931–1995) (Japanese, Hakuyu Taizan Maezumi). One of a few great Zen masters who brought Zen to the West; the first abbot of the Zen Center of Los Angeles and Zen Mountain Center, and founder of many other Zen centers throughout the United States. He gave Dharma transmission to twelve successors—the first, Bernie Tetsugen Glassman, and the second, Dennis Genpo Merzel. Maezumi Roshi is survived by his wife, Ekyo, and his three children.

Mahakashyapa (Sanskrit). *Also* Kashyapa. An eminent disciple and the successor of the historical Buddha; considered the first ancestor of Zen in India for having received the wordless transmission of the Buddha-dharma when Buddha Shakyamuni twirled a flower.

Maitreya (Sanskrit) (lit. "Loving One"). The Buddha of the future era, the embodiment of all-encompassing love.

mandala (Sanskrit) (lit. "circle"). A symbolic representation of cosmic forces or the universe. The external world; or one's consciousness, whole being, and body may also be thought of as mandalas.

Manjusri (Sanskrit). The bodhisattva of wisdom, often depicted riding a lion and holding a sword of wisdom, which cuts through delusion. Highly regarded in Zen, Manjusri Bodhisattva is the principal figure on the zendo altar.

the Master. The state or condition of being the master (or boss) of one's life rather than at the effect of one's karma. As used by Genpo Roshi in this book and in his "Big Mind" process, *the Master* refers to an aspect of the self that bridges Buddha Mind awareness and conventional awareness, therefore enabling a person to approach situations from a selfless perspective rather than the usual ego-centered view.

Middle Way. Generally, the Way of Shakyamuni Buddha, which teaches avoidance of all extremes. More specifically, living one's daily life with awareness of the true nature of reality (emptiness).

Mind. *Also* Buddha Mind, One Mind. *See* Big Mind.

Mu (Japanese) (lit. "nothing, not, nothingness"). Often used synonymously with *emptiness*. In Zen the word *Mu* is used to point directly at reality and has no discursive content. This use of the word originated with Master Joshu, who, when asked by a monk, "Does a dog have Buddha nature?" answered, "Mu!" This incident is recorded as the first case in the *Mumonkan* and is often the first koan studied by Zen students. *See* koan.

mudra (Sanskrit) (lit. "seal, sign"). A posture or gesture with symbolic meaning, often corresponding to aspects of Buddhist teaching. Sometimes mudras are used in meditation or with chanting to help actualize certain inner states.

Mumon (1183–1260) (Japanese, Mumon Ekai; Chinese, Wu-men

Hui-k'ai). Chinese Zen master who compiled the koan collection best known in the West, the *Mumonkan* ("Gateless Gate"). *See* koan.

Mumonkan. See koan, Mumon.

Nagarjuna. One of the most important philosophers of Buddhism and the founder of the Madhyamika school, which emphasizes the teaching of emptiness and its realization, especially through the use of logical negation.

Nangaku Ejo (677–744) (Chinese, Nan-yueh Huai-jang). Chinese Zen master and Dharma-successor of the sixth patriarch (Hui-neng); teacher of Baso. *See* sixth patriarch, Baso.

Nansen (748–835) (Japanese, Nansen Fugan; Chinese, Nan-ch'uan P'u-yuan). Famous Chinese Zen master of the Tang era known for his vivid expressions and the use of paradoxes in his teaching; Nansen was the Dharma-successor of Baso and teacher of Joshu.

nirvana (Sanskrit). A nondualistic state beyond life and death. The original meaning of *nirvana*, "to extinguish or burn out due to lack of fuel," implies the exhaustion of delusion and craving and the attainment of complete clarity. More specifically *nirvana* is used to refer to the state of complete enlightenment attained by Shakyamuni Buddha. *See* Four Noble Truths.

Obaku school. School of Zen founded by the seventeenth-century Chinese Zen ancestor Yin-yuan Lung-ch'i (Japanese, Ingen Ryuki). The Obaku school is a subsidiary lineage of the Rinzai school and, with the Rinzai and Soto schools, is one of the three remaining schools of Zen in Japan.

oryoki (Japanese) (roughly "containing just the right amount"). In Zen a set of eating bowls used in ceremonial meals eaten in silence; more specifically the largest of these bowls, also known as the "Buddha bowl."

paramita (Sanskrit) (lit. "gone to the other shore"). The six perfections practiced by a bodhisattva, culminating with *prajna paramita* ("perfect wisdom"), which informs and fulfills the other five. The paramitas are a natural expression of the enlightened mind, the mind of meditation. The six paramitas are giving (*dana*), precepts or morality (*sila*), patience (*kshanti*), effort or vigor (*virya*), meditation (*dyhana*), and wisdom (*prajna*). Four more are sometimes added: skillful means (*upaya*), determination (*pranidhana*), strength (*bala*), and knowledge (*jnana*).

the Path. *Also* Buddha Way, the Way. *See* Tao.

patriarch. *Also* ancestor, Dharma-successor. The recipient of formal transmission of the Buddha-dharma. From Shakyamuni Buddha, the lineage of transmission runs through twenty-eight generations of Indian ancestors to Bodhidharma, six generations of Chinese ancestors to Hui-neng, and on to the present day. Since the sixth patriarch in China (Hui-neng), the Dharma transmission has not been limited to just one successor, and anyone who has received the formal transmission is an ancestor. See transmission.

prajna (Sanskrit). Enlightened wisdom; wisdom that transcends duality of subject and object.

realization. Generally an insight into the true nature of all things (emptiness). Realization experiences can vary in clarity and depth, from a glimpse to complete enlightenment. Over the course of Zen practice, a person may have many different realization experiences.

Rinzai Gigen (d. 866–867) (Chinese, Lin-chi I-hsuan). One of the great teachers of the Tang era in China and the founder of the Rinzai school of Zen, noted for its emphasis on enlightenment and its vigorous use of koans in zazen practice. Rinzai was a Dharma-successor of Obaku (Chinese Huang-po Hsi-yun).

roshi (Japanese) (lit. "old teacher"). An honorific title used to refer to a Zen master.

samadhi (Sanskrit) (lit. "establish, make firm"; Japanese *zanmai*). A state of mind characterized by one-pointed attention; a nondualistic state of awareness in which no separation is experienced between subject and object.

samsara (Sanskrit) (lit. "stream of becoming"). The experience of suffering arising from ignorance (delusion), as set forth in Buddha's second noble truth. Samsara is reflected in the condition of our usual daily life in which we perpetuate the illusion of a separate self (ego). *See* delusion, duhkha.

samyak (Sanskrit) (lit. "right, perfect, complete"). Used by Maezumi

Roshi and Genpo Roshi as a prefix to denote a state of wholeness or completeness and the wisdom that comes from the experience of Oneness.

Sandokai (Japanese, "Identity of Relative and Absolute"; Chinese, "Ts'an-t'ung-chi"). Poem of the Chinese Zen master Shih-t'ou Hsi-ch'ien (Japanese, Sekito Kisen) on the enlightened state of mind that transcends all duality. This profound poem, highly esteemed in Zen, is chanted daily in Soto Zen services.

sangha (Sanskrit). Originally referring to the community of Buddhist monks and nuns, *sangha* later came to include laypersons as well. In Zen, *Sangha* also connotes the harmonious interrelationship of all beings, phenomena, and events, the inseparability and harmonious working of Buddha-dharma.

satori (Japanese). The experience of great enlightenment. *See* enlightenment, kensho.

sentient being. Generally, a person or being possessing consciousness. More broadly, all things, existence. In Buddhism a sentient being is one who has not yet awakened to his or her true nature. *See* delusion.

Seppo (822–908) (Japanese, Seppo Gison; Chinese, Hsueh-feng I-ts'un). One of the most important Zen masters of ancient China; Dharma-successor of Tokusan and Dharma-brother of Ganto.

sesshin (Japanese) (lit. "collecting the Heart-Mind"). An intensive Zen meditation retreat focusing on zazen and conventionally lasting seven days.

Shakyamuni (Sanskrit) (lit. "Sage of the Shakya Clan"). Title that refers to Siddhartha Gautama, the historical Buddha, after his enlightenment.

shikan (Japanese) (lit. "just"). Used by Genpo Roshi as a prefix to denote doing something completely, with one's whole being.

shikantaza (Japanese) (lit. "just sitting"). Zazen; the practice of zazen without supportive devices such as breath counting or koan study. According to Dogen Zenji, shikantaza is the purest form of zazen; he described it as resting in a state of alert, nondiscursive awareness.

Shobogenzo (Japanese, "Treasury of the True Dharma Eye"). Masterwork of Dogen Zenji and one of the most subtle and profound works in Buddhist literature, the *Shobogenzo* is a collection of his teisho and writings dealing with a wide variety of Buddhist topics.

Siddhartha Gautama (Sanskrit). The name of the historical Buddha prior to his enlightenment. *See* Shakyamuni.

sixth patriarch (638–713) (Chinese, Hui-neng; Japanese, Eno). The sixth Chinese patriarch after Bodhidharma. Traditionally said to have been illiterate, Hui-neng was enlightened while still a layman upon hearing a recitation of the *Diamond Sutra*. All existing Zen lineages can be traced back to Hui-neng. His teaching, recorded in the *Platform Sutra*, stresses "sudden enlightenment" (as opposed to "gradual enlightenment," taught by the Northern school of Zen) and the identity of meditation (dhyana) and wisdom (prajna). Hui-neng was largely responsible for the widespread flourishing of Zen in the Tang dynasty.

Soto school. With the Rinzai school, one of the two most important schools of Zen in Japan. The Soto school was founded in the ninth century by the Chinese Zen masters Tung-shan Liang-chieh (Japanese, Tozan Ryokai) and Ts'ao-shan Pen-chi (Japanese, Sozen Honjaku). The Japanese branch was founded by Dogen Zenji and Keizan Jokin, the compiler of the koan collection *Denkoroku*.

sutra (Sanskrit) (lit. "a thread on which jewels are strung"). A Buddhist scripture. Sutras are the purported dialogues and sermons of Shakyamuni Buddha and of certain other Buddhist teachers.

Suzuki, D. T. (1870–1966) (Japanese, Daisetz Teitaro Suzuki). One of the best-known scholars and most widely read interpreters of Zen in the West. D. T. Suzuki trained in Zen as a layman and was primarily interested in the intellectual interpretation of Zen teaching.

Suzuki, Shogaku Shunryu (1905–1971). Author of *Zen Mind, Beginner's Mind* (New York: Weatherhill, 1970) and founder of San Francisco Zen Center, Zen Mountain Center, and Tassajara monastery.

Tao (Chinese) (lit. "way, path"). *Also* Buddha Way, the Way, the Path. In Zen the word *Tao* is used to indicate the way to, or of, enlightenment, and also Buddha nature. Because Zen is a marriage between Indian Buddhism and Chinese Taoism, the word *Tao* has historic significance.

Tathagata (Sanskrit) (lit. "thus coming, thus going"). A title used to refer to the Buddha; more generally, the state of complete enlightenment (also "suchness").

teisho (Japanese). A direct expression or presentation by a Zen teacher of his or her realization, sometimes presented as a formal commentary on a koan or other Zen text. In the strictest sense, teisho are nondualistic presentations rather than discursive teachings or lectures.

Ten Ox-Herding Pictures. An ancient set of pictures representing the stages of realization in Zen practice. There are many versions of these pictures. The best known are based on those of the twelfth-century Chinese Zen master K'uo-an Chih-yuan.

Tendo Nyojo (1163–1228) (Chinese, T'ien-t'ung Ju-ching). Chinese Zen master and teacher of Dogen Zenji.

Theravada (Pali) (lit. "teaching of the elders"). A school of Buddhism based on the early teaching of the Buddha and widely practiced in Southeast Asia.

three marks (Sanskrit *trilakshana*). The three aspects of conditioned existence: impermanence, suffering, and the absence of an independently existent self; also commonly accepted as the three hallmarks of Buddhist doctrine.

three poisons. Greed, anger, and ignorance. In Zen, ignorance (delusion) is viewed as the basis of the other two. When a person is ignorant of his or her true nature and intrinsic wholeness, clinging (the root of greed) and aversion (the root of anger) arise as ways to perpetuate the illusion of a separate self. See delusion.

Three Treasures. Also Three Jewels. The three essential components of Buddhism—Buddha, Dharma, and Sangha—which can each be understood from different levels. See each one for a more complete description.

Tokusan (781?–867) (Japanese, Tokusan Senkan; Chinese, Te-shan Hsuan-chien). An influential Zen master from whom several important teachers received Dharma transmission, including Ganto and Seppo. After living in seclusion for many years, Tokusan finally accepted the position of abbot of a monastery, where he established a reputation for compassionately severe training, later known as "Tokusan's thirty blows."

Tozan (910–990) (Japanese, Tosan Shusho; Chinese, Tung-shan Shou-chu). Chinese Zen ancestor famous for his "one-word limits" or koans. Dharma-successor of Ummon.

transmission. Also Dharma transmission. The "seal of approval" handed down from Buddha to Mahakashyapa and through each successive generation of ancestors to the present. In transmission, Buddha Mind is given from Buddha to Buddha. People who have received Dharma transmission from an authentic lineage holder are called by various titles, including ancestor, patriarch, and Dharma-successor.

Ummon (864–949) (Japanese, Ummon Bun'en; Chinese, Yun-men Wen-yen). One of the most important Chinese Zen ancestors and among the first to use the teachings of preceding teachers in a systematic way as part of Zen training. Many of his own teachings are recorded in the major koan collections.

upaya (Sanskrit). Skillful means or methods used by a bodhisattva to guide beings to liberation; skill in expounding the teaching, especially in accordance with the needs of the student.

vipashyana (Sanskrit, "insight, clear seeing"). A form of meditation that emphasizes the analytical examination of the nature of things, leading to insight into emptiness as their true nature.

the Way. Also the Path, Tao. *See* Tao.

Yamada Roshi (1911–1989) (Japanese, Koun Yamada). Dharma-successor to Yassutani Roshi.

Yasutani Roshi (1885–1973) (Japanese, Hakuun Ryoko Yasutani). One of the first authentic Zen masters to teach in the West. He was trained in both Rinzai and Soto Zen traditions.

zazen (Japanese) (lit. *za*, "sitting," and *zen*, "absorption, samadhi"). Zazen, the traditional form of Zen meditation, contains both sitting and concentration, yet neither method encompasses the whole of zazen. In its purest form, shikantaza, zazen is dwelling in an alert state free from conceptual thought. According to the Zen tradition, zazen is the most direct way to enlightenment. In the words of Dogen Zenji, "The Way of the Buddhas and patriarchs is nothing but zazen!"

Zen (Japanese). A school of Buddhism whose hallmark is zazen, or "sitting meditation." The word *Zen* is the Japanese rendering of the Chinese *ch'an*, which comes from the Sanskrit *dhyana*, meaning "meditation" or "concentration." Generally *Zen* is used to indicate meditation in all its aspects rather than simply concentration or samadhi.

zendo (Japanese) (lit. "Zen hall"). A place set aside for the practice of zazen.

zenji (Japanese) (lit. "Zen master"). An honorific title used to refer to the head of a school of Zen.

Zuigan (Japanese, Zuigan Shigen; Chinese, Jui-yen Shih-yen). Chinese Zen ancestor of the ninth century about whom very little is known. Dharma-successor of Ganto. "Case 12" of the *Mumonkan* tells about Zuigan's personal meditation practice in which he would ask himself, "Master, are you in?" and then reply, "Yes, I am!"